THE CRISIS OF THE UNIVERSITY

The Crisis of the University

Peter Scott

CROOM HELM
London & Sydney

© 1984 Peter Scott
Croom Helm Ltd, Provident House,
Burrell Row, Beckenham,
Kent, BR3 1AT

Croom Helm Australia Pty Ltd,
G.P.O. Box 5097
Sydney, NSW 2001
Australia

British Library Cataloguing in Publication Data

Scott, Peter, 1946-
    The crisis of the university.
    1. Education, Higher—Great Britain
    I. Title
    378.41   LA636.8

    ISBN 0-7099-3303-7
    ISBN 0-7099-3310-X Pbk

Printed in Great Britain by
Biddles Ltd, Guildford, Surrey

CONTENTS

INTRODUCTION

This book is divided into two parts. In Chapters 1 to 4 an attempt is made to describe in general terms the evolution of the modern university, and in particular to examine the development of the university as an institution within the broader context of the changing construction of intellectual life. Perhaps it is naïvely done, but the attempt can be justified nevertheless because so few attempts have been made in the past to relate the administrative and intellectual aspects of higher education in a common framework. Yet the connection is clearly crucial. For too long studies of higher education have been studies of institutions with little attention being paid to the ideas and values which these institutions represented.

The second part, Chapters 5 to 7, is a more detailed study of British higher education, but in the context established in the first part. The achievement of the Robbins expansion of the universities is assessed, and the successes and shortcomings of the binary policy which established the polytechnics and other non-university colleges are examined. Finally, there is an attempt to bring the two parts of the book together in Chapters 8 to 9 in a speculation about the future of higher education, and more broadly of modern secular society.

The ideas developed in this book were first expressed in a speech for a conference organised by the Edinburgh University Students' Association on a very snowy day in 1979. They were revised and refined in a paper for a Rockefeller Foundation conference held at Bellagio in the summer of 1980. An earlier version of Chapter 6 on the binary policy was written for the seminar on the structure and governance of higher education in the Leverhulme programme of study into the future of higher education, which was held at Warwick University in 1982.

However, my main acknowledgement must be to *The Times Higher Education Supplement*, and especially to my colleagues. Most of the ideas developed in this book grew out of the weekly task of reporting and reflecting on higher education. The last four years

have been a period of exceptional turmoil in British higher education. But this has made it more rather than less important to stand
back, not in a spirit of resignation or disinterest, but to make sense
of what is happening to universities, polytechnics, and colleges. This
is deliberately not a book about cuts in higher education, although
the cuts are a part of the story. It is a book about the condition of
higher education towards the end of the twentieth century.

Peter Scott

Chapter One

GOODBYE TO ROBBINS

Britain's traditionally benign public culture, even the British character itself, seems to be passing through a period of strain and crisis on a scale not experienced since the years surrounding the First World War — or even, some would argue, since the successful consolidation of industrial society in the mid-nineteenth century. So it is hardly surprising that British universities, polytechnics, and other colleges of higher education seem to be passing through a period of similar strain. Some of the symptoms of this strain are simply functional, like the cuts in public expenditure on higher education imposed since the general election of May 1979, but foreshadowed in the low growth rates of the middle 1970s; the University Grants Committee's (UGC) selectivity strategy of July 1981 when the cuts passed on to individual universities by the Committee were highly discriminatory, ranging from almost nothing to 40 per cent; the clumsy and crude capping of the advanced further education pool (the element in the annually negotiated rate support grant earmarked for polytechnics and other colleges); the arrival of the new National Advisory Body with a brief to put the non-university sector's house in order; 'full cost' tuition fees for overseas students again imposed since 1979, but foreshadowed by the introduction of differential fees for home and overseas students as long ago as 1965, and so on.

Other symptoms take the form of increasingly disturbing questions. Doubts about the future of higher education cluster like crows. How can higher education in the austere 1980s sustain the more liberal role it acquired during the Robbins expansion of the 1960s and 70s in a fit half of absentmindedness, half of acquisitive imperialism? 'Should it even try?' whisper the more conservatively inclined. Liberals wonder whether that momentum can be maintained if doubting conservatives can no longer be bribed by ever increasing resources. Will higher education face a stark choice between students (= jobs and money?) and standards (= academic

1

integrity?) when and if demographic decline bites in the late 1980s? What is the future of the polytechnic alternative in a steady-state or even shrinking system? And so the questions go on.

But even these questions, important as they are, are out-ranked by questions of greater significance. After all, the functional difficulties faced by higher education, however much they may dominate immediate policy-making, are concerned essentially with the political dimensions of the system, the turbulent and quickly changing surface layer of the whole enterprise. Even this second set of disturbing questions penetrates only one layer deeper, to a sub-surface where the relationship is shaped between higher education and our society and economy through the market, politics, and culture. Beneath both is a third layer moved by a quite different rhythm, the *longue durée* of the university. It is in this academic layer where truth is searched for, and if never found at any rate approached, that the heart of higher education is to be found. Is is here that the remarkable intellectual creativity of British higher education since at least the 1930s, in pure science initially and more recently in the social sciences and humanities, is at work. It is a creativity that does not appear to be diminishing. In physics, biology, history these are years of exceptional excitement. So the most important question of all is whether this creativity will continue with the same vigour into the future or whether it will be slowly eroded by the storms above, by the troubles with which higher education will have to live during the next few years. Only if the latter is true will it be fair to talk of a crisis in British higher education that matches in intensity the crisis in British society.

This is the broad issue with which this book will be concerned. Does higher education face a really fundamental crisis, one that affects its academic values, or does it simply have to come to terms with a period of difficulty and uncertainty brought on by external accidents and threats? Or to put it another way, how deep into higher education's longue durée will the present and obvious crisis of resources cut? Nor can the issue be contained there. For if higher education's crisis is one of purposes as much, or more than, of resources then it is difficult to segregate the future prospects for universities and colleges from those for the wider intellectual system, of which they are the most prominent instruments, and by extension those for modern secular society as a whole, which has become critically dependent on intellectual advance for both its material growth and its social organisation.

These close and even incestuous links between higher education, the intellectual system and modern society are comparatively recent. The university in an institutional form that would be approximately recognisable today is not especially ancient (despite Bologna, Paris, Oxford and the rest). Three centuries of neglect, decay and even obscurantism separate the medieval universities from the reformed institutions of the nineteenth century which are the true ancestors of today's universities. The renaissance, the scientific revolution, the enlightenment largely bypassed the universities. Indeed, the liberal university — an ideal and arbitrary type that could be said to have flourished from the mid-nineteenth to mid-twentieth centuries particularly in non-science disciplines and in institutions in non-industrial towns — never really overcame its marginality in the intellectual market. Certainly it never achieved or even aspired to the 'market leader' or occasionally monopoly position captured by the modern, post-1945, institution. It saw its job as to teach students rather than to discover new knowledge. Cardinal Newman, the household god of the traditional university it should be remembered, believed that formal research was best undertaken in institutions other than universities. Half a century later the PhD was a new-fangled idea reluctantly introduced to wean wealthy Americans off the universities of Germany.

At this stage in its development the university had three main roles: First was the custodianship of an intellectual tradition derived more from the culture of a social elite than the codification of scientific principles by a *corps* of academic experts. This emphasis on 'cultural' knowledge' rather than 'scientific knowledge' had mixed results; it encouraged philistinism by undervaluing scientific rigour and enthusiasm for new discoveries, but it displayed liberalism, even humanism, by placing people rather than ideas at the centre of higher education. Secondly, was the reproduction of traditional professions which were defined more perhaps by customary than technological requirements — with malignant results, among which were alienation from the new industrial spirit, reciprocal philistinism in industry, and the exclusion from higher education's first division of those emergent professions with insufficient social clout. Thirdly, was the transmission of cultural capital in its broadest and possibly most allegorical sense by the formation and, more important, the legitimation of political and administrative elites. These qualities of the traditional, or better liberal, university will be explored in Chapter 2.

Of course, these twin attempts first to define an ideal type and then to describe its essential characteristics are open immediately to detailed refutation. But both can perhaps be defended by emphasising the charismatic power of myths — the continued primacy of Oxford and Cambridge shows this power at work — and by arguing that even hidden layers of values, unacknowledged and perhaps forgotten, may retain an active and powerful presence. At least this characterisation of the traditional university helps to explain strange features of Britain's intellectual and university culture such as:

*Anti-intellectualism even among intellectuals and the suspicion/absence of an intelligentsia

*An enthusiasm for pragmatism and suspicion of over-abstraction

*A continued commitment to the close and careful teaching of students

*An obscure but evocative distinction between scholarship and research

*An apparently almost unbridgeable cultural gap between science and non-science

*An unnatural separation between 'human' and 'social' sciences

*A high degree of independence from the state combined anomalously with an equally high degree of solidarity with established political society

All of these, of course, have come under increasing challenge in recent years. The growth of an intelligentsia, most prominently located within higher education, has been pronounced. Pragmatism as an intellectual style is very much on the defensive. The traditional commitment to the careful teaching of students has been modified partly in response to the larger scale of the operation which has been a direct result of the expansion of higher education, and partly because of shifting priorities within the academic profession. Scholarship as opposed to research is stigmatised by more than a whiff of amateurism. The growth of the social sciences and the 'scientification' of the humanities have bridged the gap between science and non-science, or at any rate made it much narrower. The independence of the universities has been very much compromised by both recent cuts in public expenditure, and less obviously but perhaps more influentially by the more active role and engaged style which higher education has adopted in its relationship with lay society. Yet there is enough left of all these features of British intellectual and university culture for them still to be recognised, and on many crucial occasions to continue to be influential.

Yet for 30 years following the end of the Second World War the story seemed to be of the rise and rise of the modern university (again a somewhat arbitrary and simplified category). Although it had its origins in the nineteenth century and especially in the rise of the natural sciences, the modern university achieved its apotheosis between 1955 and 1975 with the Robbins expansion in Britain, the even more impressive expansions and diversifications of university systems in Europe, and, of course, the growth of the 'multiversity' in the United States. If Newman was the household god of the liberal university, Clark Kerr occupied the same icon-like position for the modern university. Yet it is wrong to imagine that there was as sharp a break in the quality, the values, of higher education, as that which occurred in its quantity. The modern university is the result of a process of accretion as much as of evolution or reform. But it can be argued that there was a significant change in the university's conception, even ideology, of knowledge. This started in the nineteenth century with the rise of the natural sciences, which became as central to the modern university as classics, philosophy and history had been to the liberal university. But so rapid and so destabilising have been advances in the theoretical foundations of the natural sciences that they can never be restrained within an essentially cultural definition of the intellectual tradition. Their links with technology and so with industrial society also threaten the subtle links between the traditional university's ideology of knowledge and a privileged social order. Finally, they have as their priority the discovery and codification of theoretical knowledge rather than the satisfaction of the culturally defined intellectual needs of students.

The revolutionary impact of the natural sciences spread in time to all disciplines, with the humanities last to be captured. Disciplines came to be organised on the basis of the degree of association between theoretical preoccupations rather than of the coherence of undergraduate teaching. Disciplines divided and subdivided. The growing prominence of new disciplines derived from the expanding 'service' role eagerly taken up by the modern university accelerated this process. Scholars also became more professional in their work as teachers and above all as researchers, which again increased the distance between disciplines. The modern university valued academicism more highly as an approach to intellectual questions than did the liberal university which had clung to a form of humanism, however tainted by social privilege. Two important results flowed from this change. First, the intellectual culture was splintered into many not easily reassemblable fragments. Secondly, the university became less and less a community of academics with similar values which they could share, and more simply a shared bureaucratic environment. This essentially internal process was accelerated by external events. The utilitarian values of industrial society which had been slowly seeping into the university for more than a century rushed in after 1945, partly because of the expansion of student numbers (which meant it was no longer realistic to base the character of the university on the assumption that most graduates would occupy elite positions in administration and the professions) partly because of the incorporation of technological higher education (the colleges of advanced technology (CATs) and the polytechnics) within the broad university tradition. In the 1960s the university's traditions also had to be stretched to give more prominence to the 'service' values of the post-war Welfare State and their intellectual and vocational preoccupations.

But it is wrong to place too much emphasis on these external pressures and the ways in which the post-war university has accommodated them. It is a mistake to assume that they are the whole story and so explain the great differences between the liberal and the modern modes of the university. At least as revolutionary in its impact on the university has been the internal momentum, even dynamism, of disciplines. If the modern university has become a confusing, and possibly disintegrating, institution, it is not solely or even mainly because it has tried to do too many jobs for people outside. The confusion is as much the result of changes in the construction of intellectual life. It is probably wrong to imagine that academicism, in the sense of the discovery and codification of (mainly theoretical) knowledge, has the strongest claim to be regarded as the core preoccupation of the university. If it has, it is a recently established claim. But even if the first claim is allowed it is not much help in sorting out the core purposes of the university from those which are more peripheral. The fracturing and re-fracturing of disciplines have been accompanied by the cultivation of mini-cultures within disciplines which those outside find difficult to penetrate and by the professionalisation and so bureaucratisation of scholarship. These characteristics, and dilemmas, of the modern university are discussed in Chapter 3.

The dilemma for higher education in the 1980s is clear. At no time since 1945 has there been a more urgent need to establish priorities, within the system, within sectors, within institutions, within departments, and within disciplines; but at no time since 1945, because of the developments within the modern university which have been described, has it been more difficult to find the basis for a consensus about how to establish priorities. It goes much much deeper than an immediate shortage of resources. Indeed, this dilemma would exist and even intensify whatever the level of the university grant or of the advanced further education pool. This ambiguity and confusion are endemic qualities of the modern university. But there is also a further dimension. In certain important respects the development of the modern university has offended the submerged values inherited from the liberal university. First, we have acquired, absentmindedly perhaps, an intelligentsia especially and most intensely in some social science disciplines. Secondly, there is a growing tension between teaching and research, especially in the natural sciences, which has not only created a host of practical and expensive difficulties, but offended some strongly held assumptions about university education. Thirdly, the establishment of academicism at the heart of the modern university and the displacement of elitist humanism have begun to undermine the British fashion for pragmatism. Ideology and theorising have reared their ugly heads, even in the once pure humanities. Historians look longingly at the *Annales* school across the Channel. English dons dabble in structuralism and even semiology. There is a growing interest in Marxism. All very un-English. All very disturbing.

Of course, some will claim that this amounts to a caricature of modern university life and the exaggeration is admitted. Yet it is interesting to reflect that the Robbins expanion of the universities which was seen at the start and still by Lord Robbins himself as an experiment in enlightened pedagogy (broader and more general first degrees) was actually a period of creeping academicism and of a burgeoning intelligentsia. A similar point could be made about the contrast between the intentions and results of Anthony Crosland's binary policy for the polytechnics and colleges although here there is more room for optimistic dissent. None of this, of course, is conclusive evidence of a deep crisis in British intellectual and university life to match the crisis of resources. But it is perhaps slight evidence of a *prima facie* case for believing that the drift of higher education's longue durée over the past 25 years may be at least as interesting (and exciting or alarming, depending on one's viewpoint) as marginal shifts in funding patterns and policies. The extent of this crisis is explored in Chapter 4.

Of course, it is important to keep such speculation under tight rein. Old values and traditional commitments are still strong in Britain's 45 universities. Indeed, what is perhaps most remarkable is how resilient these values and commitments have proved to be in the face of the great and potentially destabilising expansion of the number of students that has taken place over the past generation. Unlike universities in the United States and most of Europe, British universities still place a surprisingly high value on the teaching of undergraduates, usually one of the first things to go to the wall in the movement to a mass system. Research in British universities, even in the more sensitive areas of inquiry, is not politicised on the foreign pattern, either in the sense that disciplinary networks have been irreparably torn apart by academic sectarianism or in the equally important sense that our universities have not yet become the foci of an oppositional intelligentsia at silent war with political society (although Mrs Thatcher is doing her best to bring this about). So in considering the universities' longue durée what will probably be remembered about the Robbins period is not how much was lost and squandered but how much of the peculiar quality of British universities was preserved. The achievements of the Robbins expansion are discussed in Chapter 5.

Another temptation is to seize on a slogan metaphor — the menopausal university, perhaps? After all, a case can be made for the advancing middle age of the British university. The Robbins expansion is now well in the past. The 1960s were the decade of university expansion: in the 1970s the main thrust of expanding student numbers was in the polytechnics and colleges. No new universities have been created either by foundation or promotion for 18 years. The latest cuts are simply the culmination of reductions in public expenditure on universities that have been made with depressing regularity since the first crisis of 1973. Any empires that were built in British universities in the 1950s and 60s have seen their foundations crumbling for half a decade or more. Projected forwards, the metaphor of middle age looks equally accurate. After all, with only a trickle of new appointments (if that) the academic community will quite literally age. The prospects for the revival of large-scale public investment in the expansion of the universities on the Robbins pattern appear almost hopelessly remote over the next decade (any revival is much more likely to boost the polytechnics and colleges). So it can be argued that the most likely pattern is one of increasing intellectual conservatism and detachment from wider social and educational goals as the arteries of the academic profession harden, to be followed by a new outburst of radicalism towards the end of the century as the retirement of the Robbins generation opens the way to substantial numbers of new recruits.

But just as the thesis of creeping academicism and a burgeoning intelligentsia has to be severely qualified by attention to the contrary evidence that the peculiar quality of the British university has been surprisingly well preserved, so this second thesis of a cycle of radicalism/growth followed by conservatism/steady state has to be equally critically examined. There *is* firm evidence of an ageing academic profession, of slackening public investment in universities (to put it as civilly as possible), and that morale among university teachers is lower than it has been for a generation or more, probably two. But there is no real evidence that academic creativity will be blunted by these factors, or that academic standards are about to slip into some kind of somnolence. To suggest that these malignant results might flow from such political factors is to enter the territory of speculation. For it can equally be argued that the public, political life of higher education may be troubled, while its private, academic life remains serene. In fact, even the most superficial attempt to penetrate the mentality of the modern British university throws up a whole series of paradoxes and inconsistencies which make it difficult to believe that any single thesis can hope to be an adequate description. The first paradox is that while many might have expected there to be a revulsion against the more 'social' ambitions of Robbins, a growing conviction that the universities had been the victims in the 1970s and 80s of their own over-ambition in the 1960s, there seems to be remarkably little evidence that any such revulsion has in fact taken place. Professor R.V. Jones up in Aberdeen is as much a prophet crying in the wilderness in 1981 as he was 20 years before, when he was one of the most distinguished critics of the Robbins blueprint for expansion.

At the most there is a feeling that the universities would benefit from a period of calm (although not, of course, of cuts) after two decades of expansion. But even among the more conservatively inclined the emphasis is on consolidation of what are almost universally accepted as gains and successes in the 1950s and 60s, not on some reactionary return to some pre-Robbins golden age. Much more common, indeed, is a sense of regret that the Robbins

✓ experiment was not carried through with sufficient vigour. The reasons for this unbroken faith in Robbins are probably many. Of course, some are practical and selfish. The Robbins wave created new institutions, departments, careers. But perhaps more interesting is the light this faith sheds on the stubborn streak of altruism that runs through British universities despite frequent (and often accurate) assertions about their commitment to traditionalism and elitism. Perhaps at times it shades into a form of paternalism. But whatever it is called, this commitment to the expansion of university education founded on a firm belief in the high quality of such education seems to have survived both the disdain of the anti-Robbins *ultras* and the depredations of recent government policy. The social conscience of the universities is not as vestigial as its naïve critics and real enemies imagine.

The reason for this is probably that the hopes for a better and broader future embodied by Robbins seem natural and right to majority opinion within the universities. They seem to fit so exactly the humanist (although elitist) preoccupations of the liberal university which have already been mentioned. Perhaps it is because the expansion of opportunity encouraged by Robbins had such traditional roots that the commitment to such an expansion has remained so strong. Robbins was not offering mass higher education on the American pattern, let alone that of Nanterre, but something much more in tune with British ideas of what a university is for. Another, barely noticed, factor is the way in which the greater democracy in universities today allows younger (and more liberal?) academics a stronger voice in their affairs. Perhaps this helps to explain the second interesting aspect of the mentality of the modern British university, that is, the rather surprising way in which the commitment to the student and to good undergraduate teaching has held up in a time first of rapid expansion and then of growing strain. Indeed, contrary to what might have been expected there seems to be a widespread conviction that both teachers and students are better than they were ten years ago. The teachers themselves perhaps because the shock of student revolt in the late 1960s and 70s underlined the fact that the needs of students could never safely be relegated to second place in the priorities of the university (in this sense the popular parodies of this period represented by Malcolm Bradbury's *The History Man* probably get it wrong. Student revolt encouraged a return to more traditional pedagogy as much as it opened the flood gates to politicised mediocrity.) The students have to be more serious today than they had to be in the 1960s. One fairly obvious reason is jobs. Another is that meeting the tough entry standards for British universities is perhaps more difficult for the new ranks of students who benefited from the Robbins expansion and may have come from a less differentiated secondary school system, than it was for the gilded (and brilliant?) youth of the 1950s and early 60s before the expansion of opportunity got under way. The fact that today there are many more women students may also have contributed to a more serious and more mature mood among students generally.

The third paradox is perhaps the most interesting of all. It is that while depression among university teachers seems to be widespread, it also seems to be only skin-deep. A lecturer at a London college may try to avoid telling people her profession because she feels the social esteem of university teachers has fallen so low. A northern professor may say that at a recent departmental evaluation meeting they sat round the table gloomily contemplating how much further they would slide down before falling off the end. But put against this the belief of the physics lecturer that there has not yet been a time when there has been a shortage of money for truly good research, and the bubbly enthusiasm of the new (and therefore very rare) chemistry lecturer who simply says: 'Really, it's my hobby. I had a lab at home at a very early age and now my hobby's my job.' Of course, the severity of present problems is admitted even by such enthusiasts. Everywhere there is concern about the malignant effect of the freeze on recruitment into the profession. The scientists in particular fret about the way in which a whole generation of scientific talent has almost been sacrificed, although even here some are sanguine and point out that this infusion of redirected talent will do industry good. There are already many departments that have not made a new appointment since the mid-1970s. Fears increase about how it will feel in 1990 when the faces along the corridor have been the same ones for 15 or 20 years.

But everywhere also there seems a strong determination not to allow this problem (and related less serious problems arising from the cuts) to become the occasion for academic ossification. Indeed, in certain circumstances the very absence of new blood has underlined the need for serving academics to maintain their creativity and energy in ways which were not perhaps demanded so intensely in the past, because the burden of scholarly progress could more easily be taken up by the next generation. Indeed, there is a reluctance to accept that the cuts and the virtual end of expansion will inevitably damage academic standards. Even when such damage is admitted, it is talked of in almost deliberately low-key terms, the shortage of laboratory technicians, the difficulty of keeping up with administration, and other marginal distractions from academic work. This is perhaps to underestimate the problem of academic creativity that the universities will have to face over the next ten years. Too easy advancement in the academic profession may not have been an incentive to good scholarship; but neither is no advancement at all. After all, what practical incentive is there to publish when the career rewards are likely to be so meagre. It would not therefore be altogether surprising if there were to be a fall-off in the productivity of the profession in its scholarly work (especially as the demand from good, hard-working, but perhaps passive students is bound to increase as teaching loads get heavier and demographic decline allows competition for students to rear its ugly head). This in turn might, to adopt the categories used earlier in this chapter, erode the academicism of the modern university and restimulate the humanism intrinsic in a more liberal model for the university. Fewer scholars, more teachers, or at any rate a readjustment of the balance between scholarship and teaching — it is an intriguing prospect for the universities, disturbing in its academic aspect but exhilarating even in its implications for a liberal higher education.

To move from the universities to the polytechnics and other colleges, to cross the binary chasm, is to move from a world of (comparative) orthodoxy to one of absolute heterodoxy. Although there are substantial differences of emphasis between the natural sciences with their austerely theoretical, and so perhaps neutral, preoccupations and the social and human sciences, which are inevitably more culture-bound in their definition of knowledge, there is general agreement that universities are about the life of the mind. Of course, attempts to tease out that rather clunkish phrase immediately run into trouble — what room is there for active and engaged intellectual activity alongside the more traditional reflective academic variety? There are many similarly difficult questions of definition which in turn provoke even more searching questions about the relationship between any intellectual activity and the society and individuals which are its context. From these latter questions, of course, eventually flow all the practical policy issues that face higher education, science policy, the UGC's selectivity strategy, manpower planning, and so on. But at least for the purpose of this preliminary discussion these questions can be ducked by saying simply that the overwhelming majority of university teachers feel, believe, and behave as if they are engaged in a shared and harmonious activity with deeply common values and self-evident goals. From this conviction of the value of disengaged, or at any rate autonomous, intellectual activity grow practical assumptions about the autonomy of the universities, within them a non-corporatist academic community, and the academic freedom of the individual — in short the whole environment of the university.

With the polytechnics and colleges the same easy assumption about common purposes cannot be made. Of course, a substantial number of those who teach in these institutions see their intellectual responsibilities in terms that are analogous to those of their colleagues in universities (although in a more modern and down-to-earth context, they would tend to argue). But there are many others who are engaged in tasks with no academic or even intellectual pretensions. They make no claim, and express no desire, to be involved in a process of critical inquiry, not one at any rate which requires the 'distance' between themselves and society provided by traditional barriers of academic freedom. They have an entrepreneurial, not a fiduciary relationship with the world beyond the campus. There are various intermediate groups which are perhaps in a process of shifting from the latter to the former style of higher education, a shift that is often shallowly described as 'academic drift'. There are even people in polytechnics, pre-eminently perhaps in some fine-art departments, who see their role not just in intellectual terms but also and more intensely in aesthetic and so moral terms, as the core of conscience in a mechanistic world. Not many people in universities today go as far as that. The rise of academicism has encouraged an often amoral approach to intellectual responsibility.

There have, of course, been attempts to produce some overarching philosophy of polytechnic education which tries to capture all this heterodoxy in a common gravity and to apply to it a common principle, attempts that go back far beyond Crosland through Lunacharsky to Owen. These attempts have tended to emphasise the aspect of 'doing', of application, of capability. To suggest that they have largely failed is not to say that they have not been, and do not remain, a valuable element in the necessary discourse about the future purposes of higher education. But it has always been difficult to make a sensible distinction between the creation and the application of knowledge, or between the capacity for creative reflection and the practical capability of the individual. Too often at both a conceptual and concrete level the processes of creation and application are so closely entwined that they cannot be safely separated. Perhaps in the end the only adequate 'polytechnic' philosophy for higher education is no philosophy at all, to come to terms with the inevitable and perhaps enriching heterodoxy of intellectual activity once it has escaped from the gravity of the university.

Instead, the preoccupations of the polytechnics are necessarily more diverse, reflecting their more fissiparous quality. Many people within them, and more still in the colleges with their often more liberal traditions, are prey to the same gloomy preoccupations as their colleagues in the more harassed disciplines in universities. But as many see themselves as engaged, not in an organic academic enterprise in which they are joined by all their colleagues, but in a functional and mutual relationship with their clients beyond the campus. So the quality of such relationships is the key stone of their well-being — and so their morale. It would be going too far to suggest that while universities have a single overarching mission, the polytechnics do a multitude of marginally connected jobs. But it is not altogether wrong to say that the polytechnics have a greater diversity of purposes and practices, with important and surprising implications for their resilience. Of course, the problem of maintaining intellectual creativity is as acute, or perhaps more acute, in the polytechnics as in the universities. In many ways the margin for creativity — the tradition of the freedom and the time to do research, for example — is much tighter. The problem also takes different forms. In the universities the overwhelming difficulty is how to introduce new blood; in the polytechnics, where comparatively there is much more new blood, the problem is how to stop it becoming sluggish. In the context of the more active and more externally directed intellectual patterns of work that prevail in the polytechnics this means above all opportunity for promotion, to course leaderships, headships of departments and so on. The poor passive scholar is not a model that works well in a polytechnic environment.

The polytechnics have to put up with a lot of disdain from the universities, little of it deserved. The colleges of higher education as is the way of the world have to put up with double disdain. Both will have to put up with hostility and cuts from government which bear even less relation to any assessment of their value or achievement than the parallel hostility which the universities are having to endure. But to write off the influence of the polytechnic experiment on the future shape of all higher education would be mistaken. At a deeper level the process of up-rating forms of intellectual and educational activity once dismissed as quite outside the scope of higher education has broadened and diluted not only our view of what higher education is and is for, but also perhaps our very definition of academic knowledge. The pluralism of the polytechnic may even in time undermine the catholicism of the university. The successes, and short comings, of the binary policy are discussed in Chapter 6.

The 1980s are unknown territory for higher education — and unknown territory is too easily peopled by the imagination with fearful prospects. Robbins looked forward only 20 years and those 20 years are now up. No map equally magisterial (and reliable) is available to guide universities, colleges, and polytechnics through the next 20. As a result higher education has lost a horizon many times more important to its well-being and healthy development than the planning horizon which the universities lost when the quinquennial system of university funding collapsed in the mid-1970s. Perhaps it could be called the horizon of aspiration. Anyway it is for the moment lost. Instead, higher education against its will concentrates myopically on the next few years of senseless austerity and is overwhelmed by the immediate prospect of the cuts. But beyond that brief period — nothing. All perspective in which the deeper development of higher education can be continued has been lost. All this is undenied and probably undeniable. But the appropriate interpretation to place on these events, and the context in which higher education should be placed in 1981 and which flows from this interpretation, are open to question. Many, perhaps a majority, argue that the impetus provided by Robbins and accelerated by Crosland is now exhausted, that Britain's enthusiasm and willingness to pay for great liberal reforms is also exhausted, and that the only sensible course is to accept these iron realities and plan for a narrower and austerer future. 'Snibborism' (Robbins in reverse) sums up this baleful approach.

There is another possible approach, although in such difficult times it is inevitably one that has fewer supporters. It can be argued that far from being over, Robbins is just about to begin. For although the quantitative message of Robbins, that there should be three-fold expansion of the number of students in higher education, was received and obeyed during the 1960s and 70s, it is only now that the qualitative message, that a more liberal as well as a larger higher education system should be built in Britain, is starting to be received. After all, great changes in the character of any social institutions, let alone of educational systems so pregnant with human and intellectual values, do not take place quickly. It can be argued that it took at least a generation, from the Butler Education Act of 1944 to the comprehensive reforms of the 1960s, to establish both the principle and practice of secondary education for all (rather than elementary education with a bit added on for most). Why should we expect changes in higher education at least as great to take place in less time? So two contrasting interpretations of the present state of Britain's universities and polytechnics are possible. On the one hand, a 'steady-state' or shrinking system accompanied by growing disengagement from the more generous ambitions characteristic of the recent past and by an intellectual thrombosis as the academic arteries harden. On the other, a state of incomplete liberalisation with higher education on the brink of new expansion (more qualitative perhaps than quantitative) accompanied by an intensification of intellectual creativity and invention.

In such confusion how can we hope to recreate the horizon of aspiration? Believers in 'snibborism' may feel that such an attempt is hardly worth while: it would only get in the way of their reality. The rest of us have to be a little more hopeful and even a little more courageous. A good starting point, of course, is the Robbins Report itself. There is a strong case for saying that Robbins's prescription for a more liberal system of higher education — more general first degrees, greater diversity of postgraduate study, more emphasis on the higher education of adults and so on — still holds good and that Robbin's description of the aims and principles of higher education in paragraphs 13–40 has still not lost its power and its freshness. There was really almost nothing in Model E, the radical, continuing education, option, of the 1978 discussion document, *Higher Education into the 1990s*, that was not better said by Robbins, which is remarkable considering Robbins's brief was confined to *full-time* higher education. The experience of the polytechnics, their practical expansion of the scope of higher education and their up-rating of academic standards across a wide range of new subjects and para-professions, has also demonstrated the potential for progressive reform, although perhaps as too strictly controlled an experiment mainly within the vocational tradition of British higher education. What we have not seen, or seen very little of, is a similarly liberal movement within the more academic university tradition. That is what we should look forward to and encourage during the 1980s and 90s. There are five reasons why moderate optimism is not entirely out of place despite contradictory indications on the troubled surface layer of higher education. These will be discussed in greater detail in Chapter 8.

The first is that there may be a reaction against the academicism of the modern post-war university and a return to the humanism of the liberal university (or, to adopt the scheme of Robbins, a restoration of the balance between the committee's third aim: the advancement of knowledge, and its second: the promotion of the general powers of the mind, and possibly its fourth: the transmission of a common culture and common standards of citizenship). If this does happen the prospects for the Robbins prescription for broader first degree courses actually being fulfilled would be much improved. Of course, it can be argued that the momentum of academicism is unstoppable, that the organisation of knowledge round principles other than the association of theoretical preoccupations has become impossible given its contemporary sophistication, and that there are strong and interesting parallels between the fracturing of the university's knowledge base and the formation through credentialisation of a new intellectual/professional division of labour. But it is just as possible things will turn out differently. The conservatively-inclined who committed themselves to the academicism of the modern university as a defence against the inroads of mass society and culture, may come to regard the professionalisation, even bureaucratisation, of scholarship and the fracturing and refracturing of knowledge as deadly enemies of the liberal university tradition. At the other end of the spectrum radicals who committed themselves confusingly to the 'service' and/or autonomist values of the modern university because these challenged what they saw as a reactionary academic tradition and/or repressive 'relevance', may also have growing doubts now that society is no longer represented by the benign social democratic state of the 1960s but by the neo-conservative state or some vast 'technostructure', a modern tower of Babel piled up with microchips.

The second reason is that the accelerating pace of scientific and technological advance will undermine the value of specialised initial higher education. In Daniel Bell's post-industrial society the information technology revolution will radically alter our perception of expertise. Although a new corps of ultra-experts will be required, the majority of the technological intelligentsia will find its detailed expertise undermined by the rapid turnover of theoretical knowledge and its applications. It can be argued that this will only make explicit what has always been implicit. After all, a majority of science and technology graduates work on the periphery of their disciplines, in sales, management, and so on, rather than at their cores in research and development. Nevertheless, the accelerating pace of knowledge will deeply influence not only the content of higher education (towards more general or more abstract courses?) but also its structure (more continuing education?). This tendency towards more liberal forms will be supported by a third factor. It is becoming increasingly clear in the advanced societies of the world, and especially in those with stubbornly rooted democratic cultures like Britain, that the main blockages occur in the human 'software' not the technological 'hardware'. The key issue for the next century, therefore, will not necessarily be the advance of science, or the improvement of engineering technology, but the improvement of human technology. This will not be easy because the revolutionary character of some new technologies (and in particular their impact on employment) will provoke stubborn resistance and because the spreading tide of participatory democracy, in particular industrial democracy, will increase the strain on the executors of policy. But both may shift the whole balance of professional and technological higher education away from the authority of the expert towards the sponsorship of collaborative human skills.

The fourth reason is that the relationship between higher education and society is also likely to be modified — and in a similar direction to that taken by the much tighter relationship between higher education, technology and the economy. The value of a higher education may be perceived quite differently as the social or economic advantage it brings declines (either because of slower economic growth generating fewer graduate jobs, or because of expansion of opportunity increasing the supply of graduates). It may be seen less in instrumental terms, less as a few essential rungs on the ladder of social or occupational advancement, and more in humanist terms, more as a personal right without which individuals will feel deprived and unsatisfied. In the former capacity higher education is almost entirely a positional good; in the latter it is potentially at any rate an absolute one.

The fifth reason is more speculative but still persuasive. In the next 20 years, even without much further absolute expansion, higher education will recruit students from more diverse backgrounds than in the past. More will be older than today's average, and their motives may therefore be rather different from the severely practical ambitions of an adolescent on the brink of a career. More will be women, and whatever progress is made towards employment equality, the presence of a larger proportion of women will have an important influence on the aspirations of students generally. More will come from the working class with whatever is left of its more collectivist and even fraternal values which are probably different from the highly individualist and competitive culture of the entre- ✓ preneurial and professional middle classes. In these and other ways the whole character of higher education could undergo a sea change.

Here are five clear reasons for believing that 'snibborism' is unlikely to become the guiding principle for higher education (except perhaps, briefly and superficially, at the level of the allocation of scarcer resources), and for believing that far from being exhausted the liberal momentum of Robbins is actually likely to increase. It will take much, much more than a little tinkering with public expenditure plans to frustrate such a powerful movement for social and cultural progress. Austerity may encourage this flow and inhibit that one, but it can make little difference to the total direction. There are two further considerations which support this interpretation. The first is the widespread feeling of regret that the modern university has by and large followed a path of ethical neutrality, even amorality, and that this amorality has been justified by its ideology of knowledge which is so different in its balance from that adopted by the liberal university. The true, it could be said, has sometimes become the pharisee enemy of the good and the beautiful. It is almost embarrassing to recall those phrases in Robbins about education ministering 'intimately to ultimate ends' and about the 'good society', let alone Matthew Arnold's phrase about man's need to relate knowledge to his sense of conduct and his sense of beauty. Yet at a time when the university often seems to have become a prisoner of amoral technocratic or cognitive values, the ethical — and so ultimately and logically the intellectual — adequacy of such values is being called into question. Of course, it is possible to dismiss all the evidence, from student and now 'green' revolt and youth culture in the west to the revival of religious fundamentalism or other divergences from 'modern' patterns of development in the Third World, and to regard universities as islands of rationality in an irrational world. But this merely underlines the intellectual limitations of a rationality which provided such an imcomplete description of the world, and would also run contrary to the submerged but still powerful cultural values of the liberal university.

The second consideration also arises from the construction of intellectual life, higher education's longest of longue durées but also its most revolutionary. Earlier in this chapter it was argued that the transition from liberal to modern modes of the university owed as much to the internal momentum, even dynamism, of disciplinary change as to any attempts to satisfy new social and pedagogical pressures from outside. If the modern university has become a confusing, and possibly disintegrating, institution, it is not solely or even mainly because it has tried to do too many jobs for people outside. It is also because of the disintegration of the cohesive cultural definition of knowledge it has inherited from the liberal university. Yet today there are powerful centripetal forces in intellectual life as well as centrifugal ones. In more than one discipline the exciting areas are not to be found in its cooling core but at the periphery, in the borderland with other disciplines. In the end, perhaps, such nuclear attraction will glue disciplines together (and so reintegrate the university?) with greater force than the electrical repulsion of fracturing disciplines will force them apart. If this does happen, then in an intellectual, as well as a moral and social dimension, the prospect for a liberal university will appear far brighter than the obscuring gloom of cuts and crisis immediately suggests.

Chapter Two

THE LIBERAL UNIVERSITY

The university is the key knowledge institution of modern society. It is the producer of much of the theoretical knowledge which our society increasingly uses as an organising technology. It is the home territory of the most influential component of the new intelligentsia. Because of its long tradition it is a formidable instrument of cultural preservation and renewal. Finally, of course, it is the commanding institution of the educational system, educating directly society's political, administrative, and scientific elites and influencing substantially the values of schools in which the entire population is educated.

'University', of course, can be used in two senses; as in the preceding paragraph when it is simply a shorthand to describe the whole system of higher education and scientific research, or in a more precise and limited sense as meaning the tradition of a liberal university. The possibility of clarity is not increased by the confusion of actual titles possessed by institutions of higher education in the same and different countries. Some universities are distinctly illiberal institutions, while many institutions that do not enjoy the title of university should be placed firmly within the tradition of a liberal university. In this narrower sense, of course, the university has never enjoyed a monopoly of higher education let alone of the advance of knowledge. In the Middle Ages universities had to compete initially with court and monastic schools. In the early modern period the universities then very much in decline saw their intellectual leadership usurped by the scientific academies, like the Royal Society, established all over Europe in the seventeenth and eighteenth centuries. In the industrial revolutions they had to cope with the irruption of technological higher education, sometimes as in England containing it within an adapted university tradition, sometimes standing powerlessly aside while formidable rivals like the French *grandes écoles* were established. In France today the universities form the second division of higher education having become in effect institutions of mass learning. Above them come the grandes écoles, products of the centralist and technocratic values of nineteenth-century France, which place less emphasis on the traditional university qualities of tradition, rationality, cultivation, and autonomy, and the more recently established research institutes like the Centre des Recherches Nationales Scientifiques (CRNS) and the Ecole des hautes Études with its many sections. The French universities have lost both their elite and 'knowledge' functions to other institutions.

Nor is the French experience untypical. In West Germany there may be no grandes écoles, but the separation of research into extra-university institutes in quite common. In the Soviet Union and Eastern Europe the key institutions of intellectual power are the academies of science and the research institutes they maintain. A modernising and authoritarian state, it seems, has similar instruments whether in the eighteenth or the twentieth century. The universities, with their potentially liberal and autonomist ambitions, occupy a clearly subordinate position within these higher education systems. In the quieter parts of Europe like Scandinavia the liberal university has been accepted as a more useful model. But in large parts of Asia, Africa, and Latin America (taking the example from Southern Europe) the étatiste model of France is more closely followed, partly for reasons of economic efficiency, partly no doubt because a liberal university tradition may appear a dangerously subversive political experiment. Finally, in North America and Britain (and the countries within their cultural universe) the model of the liberal university has maintained its position as the dominant and most influential form but it has never achieved a total monopoly. Although the role of the university as the educator of the elite has been widely accepted, its parallel role as the leading knowledge institution has been more frequently challenged. So the creation of the polytechnics in England and Wales can be seen as a reinforcement rather than a challenge to the university tradition in Britain, precisely because becoming part of higher education means accepting the most important ingredients of the university tradition. But the growing importance of the research councils is clearly a more substantial challenge to the integrity of the liberal university.

Yet when all the qualifications have been entered the university remains an extraordinarily successful institution. The particularist universities of the European Middle Ages with their apparently arid

Aristotelian scholasticism have grown into global institutions, the carriers of a modernist culture throughout the world and the producers of the scientific knowledge on which technological and material progress seem to depend. The stages of this metamorphosis are of great importance: first in understanding the role of ideology and science in modern culture and, more particularly, in understanding the place of a liberal university tradition within the explosion of this 'knowledge industry'. There have been three main stages: the medieval university which represents the prehistory of higher education yet is not entirely without significance to a modern understanding of the university tradition; the humanist, or traditional, or perhaps best of all, the liberal university which grew up essentially in the nineteenth and early twentieth centuries with the revival of a proper university tradition after the decay of three centuries; and the multiversity, the technocratic, or perhaps most simply, the modern university of our own age.

The universities were the product of Europe's high Middle Ages, the twelfth and thirteenth centuries. The cultural renaissance of the early Middle Ages, the ages of Northumbria and of the Carolingians, had certainly produced important court and monastic schools that were formidable centres of learning and education, but only in the more sophisticated society of four centuries later did the university develop as a separate institution.[1] Marc Bloch summed up perhaps the most important difference between these two great ages of medieval society in this way:

> In the second there was no longer a divorce between the means of expression and the thought to be expressed. It is a significant fact in the history of the relation of thought and practice — still so obscure a subject — that towards the end of the twelfth century men of action had at their disposal a more efficient instrument of mental analysis than that which had been available to their predecessors.[2]

Many factors played their part in this process: the growing knowledge, mainly through Arab sources, of the intellectual achievements of the Hellenistic world provided a more direct link with ancient philosophy and science than the late Roman and debased models on which the age of Bede and Charlemagne had had to rely; the revival of Roman law and Aristotelian scholasticism supplied more effective analytical instruments; the consolidation of the feudal state, which placed a new emphasis on the legal and bureaucratic organisation of society rather than customary and personal relationships provided the material context for the creation of the universities. Yet the creation of the medieval universities remains a surprising outcome. Islamic, Indian, and Chinese civilisations of the Middle Ages, of course, possessed powerful intellectual institutions but they never achieved the separate and autonomous form of the medieval universities of Europe. They remained either direct agencies of the state in the form of 'court schools' or of the religious bureaucracy like the Madrassahs of Iran. In other words they remained at the stage of institutional development reached by the Northumbrian and Carolingian schools. In Europe this form was transcended by the development of the university. The most plausible general explanation is that it was probably the weakness of political authority in a feudal society where effective power had been parcellised for economic and social reasons and the historical memory of an universal empire, now represented by an universal church, which gave the medieval universities their peculiar form. For they superimposed an intellectual order on political disorder. Both the contemporary reality of political parcellisation and the historical memory of the ancient world were of crucial importance. The first meant that the weak political authority of the feudal state did not rest on its own intellectual authority. It was not self-sufficient in ideology. This latter authority came from the church and religion, with their faint memories of empire and philosophy. As Bloch described the situation:

> We find a powerful and wealthy Church, capable of creating novel legal institutions, and a host of problems raised by the delicate task of relating this religious 'city' to the temporal 'city'; problems ardently debated and destined to influence profoundly the general evolution of the West.[3]

The interesting and important result was that the idea that knowledge could be distinct from power (if only because it belonged to a rival and not entirely secular power) was made conceivable in medieval Europe half a millenium before the same idea became conceivable in the traditional civilisations of Asia. The memory of the ancient world had a similar effect. Medieval man knew that there had previously existed in Europe a quite different form of political organisation that had produced intellectual achievements equal or superior to his own. In Bernard of Chartres's memorable phrase: 'We are dwarfs perched on the shoulders of giants.' This memory also discouraged too absolute an identification of intellectual authority with political power. In one of the most famous passages in Bede's *History of the English Church and People* one of King Edwin's 'chief-men' supports the conversion of the Northumbrian people and their king to Christianity in the following terms:

> When we compare the present life of man on earth with that time of which we have no knowledge, it seems to me like swift flight of a single sparrow through the banqueting-hall where you are sitting at dinner on a winter's day with your thanes and counsellors. In the midst there is a comforting fire to warm the hall, outside, the storms of winter rain or snow are raging. This sparrow flies swiftly in through one door of the hall and out through another. While he is inside, he is safe from the winter storms; but after a few moments of comfort, he vanishes from sight into the wintry world from which he came. Even so, man appears on earth for a little while; but of what went before this life or of what follows after, we know nothing. Therefore, if this new teaching has brought any more certain knowledge, it seems only right that we should follow it.[4]

This speech by a Northumbrian chief-man 1350 years ago, offering an essentially intellectual rather than spiritual justification for conversion to Christianity, can perhaps be counted as an early demonstration of the scientific method. It also demonstrates the lack of intellectual self-sufficiency that was the result of the influence of Christianity, and of the memory of ancient philosophy, and which was perhaps an unique feature of the European Middle Ages. In other contemporary civilisations the complete identification of religion with the state, as in China, or of the state with religion, as in Islam, provided that self-sufficiency that left no room for the emergence of distinct intellectual institutions such as universities.

For this separation of intellectual and political authority, however slight and conditional, is the germ from which grew both the idea of a university as a separate institution and the possibility of scientific knowledge. Both the liberal university tradition and the scientific tradition had this common origin in the prehistory of the medieval university, because science is only possible when knowledge has been freed from the constraints of political expediency. Of course, it would be entirely wrong to exaggerate the intellectual independence of the medieval university. Its relative autonomy was the outcome of the parcellisation of authority in the feudal state, not of any commitment to independent knowledge in a sense understood today. This autonomy was simply a reflection of the superior intellectual and spiritual authority of the Church, although the very existence of universities marked the first step towards a secular definition of knowledge. The southern European universities were remarkably secular institutions and the compatibility of faith and reason was the transcendent intellectual issue of the Middle Ages. In two indirect ways the medieval university did establish characteristics that are still present today in the liberal university tradition. First, it was a strongly pedagogical institution which, often at a remarkably early age, transmitted to the next generation of 'intellectuals' (priests) and administrators (again almost, without exception priests, although of a more worldly inclination) the established authority of theology which, of course, in an entirely Christian society covered a wide range of political, intellectual, and even proto-scientific speculation. Secondly, it did so by means of rigorous analytical tools of logic, rhetoric and so on derived from the intellectual practices of the ancient world and refined to Christian purposes by the medieval 'school-men'. Pedagogy, an intellectual tradition, scholarship (or the intellectual tools of criticism), therefore, are all concepts first generated and institutionalised in the medieval university.

But the most important product of the medieval university was clearly the idea itself of a university, and the separation of intellectual authority from the political power on which this depended. The importance of this semi-separation of knowledge from power for the future intellectual history of Europe was recognised by Antonio Gramsci, the Italian communist and philosopher. In his discussion of the role of intellectuals in Italy he separated them into two groups, the 'traditional' (priests, scholars, artists) and the 'organic' (the more immediate intellectual servants of the prevailing political order). Characteristic of the first group, he suggested, was their sense that they represented an 'historical continuity uninterrupted by even the most radical and complicated changes in social and political systems', and that they saw themselves as 'autonomous, independent of the dominant social group.'[5] Although a Marxist, Gramsci accepted that the relationship of traditional intellectuals with the social forces of production was not immediate, but expressed through the parts of society's superstructure. He was even prepared to concede that some important categories of traditional intellectuals might openly reject the world-view of the dominant group in society and yet be permitted to fulfil important ideological roles, for example in teaching. He clearly had in mind the position of the Church in the secular Italian state, but his view can be applied much more generally to traditional intellectual institutions in the pluralist societies in which the idea of a liberal university has become established. It may not be flattering to suggest that the institutional autonomy of universities, their most important attribute, is of feudal origin rather than liberal inspiration, but it may nevertheless be true. For it was the parcellisation of the feudal state which created the institutions that provided a (relatively) secure social base for intellectual independence, and so for the emergence of a proper tradition of science.

In very broad terms such was the inheritance of the medieval European university. But the status of the medieval university, of course, was simply a reflection of the relationships between the religious 'city' and of the 'temporal' 'city,' and of the superior ideological authority of the former. As this balance was challenged by the rise of the secular state, its own intellectual framework very much strengthened by the development of law and bureaucracy in the later Middle Ages, and the authority of the church was undermined by its corruption, the intellectual independence of the university was slowly eroded. From mid-sixteenth to mid-seventeenth century this relative loss of independence did not affect the material fortunes of the universities. Indeed, the century from 1560 to 1660 marked a high point in the development of higher education that was not really surpassed until almost the twentieth century. The rise of humanism, the growing assertiveness of royal bureaucracies (and gentry oppositions), above all the extreme volatility of ideas in the wake of the Reformation, stimulated the popularity of higher education. But when religious passions waned and stable political conditions returned, whether on the basis of absolutism or the gentry state, the enthusiasm for university education declined. The number of students fell sharply and the elites abandoned the universities for their own *salons*, the Grand Tour, or the court.

With the growth of national erastian churches in much of Protestant Europe and the intellectual retrenchment that accompanied the Counter Reformation in much of Catholic Europe, the university entered a period of obsolescence even of somnolence. In both parts of Europe the need for universities that transcended political authority in the name of a universal intellectual authority disappeared. The clerical connexion, once a source of intellectual independence, now became a cause of obscurantism. Three centuries of neglect, decay and dogma separated the universities of medieval Europe from the restored and greatly extended universities of the late eighteenth, nineteenth, and early twentieth centuries. Three great intellectual movements, the Renaissance of the sixteenth century, the scientific revolution of the seventeenth, and the philosophical 'Enlightenment' of the eighteenth, seemed to pass the universities by. Sir Isaac Newton may have been a Cambridge University professor but the most powerful intellectual institution of his day was the newly formed Royal Society. Similar academies of scholars and scientists were established all over Europe during the seventeenth and eighteenth centuries from France to Russia, demonstrating quite clearly the intellectual frailty of the university. Furthermore, it can be argued that a fourth great movement, the industrial revolution, that reshaped the intellectual contours of society as decisively as the first three, also took place far away from the world of the university. The distance at which Cambridge University insisted the new railway station must be built from the town was an eloquent, and permanent, comment on how one mid-nineteenth-century university at any rate regarded the invasion of the values in industrial society!

Yet it was the rise of science, in political economy as much as physics, and the new industrial society which provided both the intellectual and the material bases for the restoration of the university. The revolution in the physical sciences provided both an example of more rigorous scientific method and a metaphor for a new kind of objective knowledge that could be applied to all branches of intellectual life. By these means intellectual authority, which since the Reformation and the Renaissance had come dangerously close to being interpreted in terms of *raison d'état*, regained a necessary social independence. Science replaced religion as a potentially universal intellectual authority which transcended more partial political authorities, and so re-established the ideological basis for the revival of an independent university tradition. At the time the much more elaborate division of highly skilled labour in the modern bureaucratic and industrial State intensified the need for the enlightened, elitist pedagogy practised by the medieval university. The decline of religion made it necessary to construct more secular interpretations of tradition that would act as a form of stability in a rapidly changing society, again a role for which the university seemed well designed.

Finally, the growing sophistication of knowledge made it necessary to construct powerful, and professional, intellectual institutions. *Salons* of intellectuals, literary and philosophical societies, mechanics institutes, and all the other apparatus of academic amateurism were no longer sufficient. The elaboration of higher education systems was a necessary consequence of the advance of science, the sophistication of all knowledge, and the demands of an industrialising society. In the *Edinburgh Review* of April 1832 Macaulay published an acerbic review of a new history of William Cecil by the Rev. Edward Nares, at that time Regius Professor of Modern History at Oxford, which brings out very well the decay of scholarship in the unreformed universities and also the growing demands for the professionalisation of knowledge. He wrote:

His [Nares'] book is swelled to its vast dimensions [more than 2,000 pages] by endless repetitions, by episodes which have nothing to do with the main action, by quotations from books that are in every circulating library, and by reflections that when they happen to be just, are so obvious that they must necessarily occur to the mind of every reader. He employs more words in expounding and defending a truism than any other writer would employ in supporting a paradox. Of the rule of historical perspective, he has not the faintest notion. . .It would be not unfair to deny that Dr. Nares is a man of great industry and research; but he is so utterly incompetent to arrange the materials which he has collected that he might as well have left them in their original repositories.[6]

Macaulay himself, of course, was an eventual victim of the professionalisation of scholarship. His attack on the amateurism of Dr Nares led finally not to some enlightened, rigorous and didactic 'public' history constructed to Whig designs but to the creation of history as a scientific discipline, a detailed branch of academic knowledge. As Sheldon Rothblatt has recently commented:

Whig historiography was not and could not be truly academic in the nineteenth century, although it was inclining that way. In the long run, the reform of the ancient universities of England and Scotland, the establishment of a metropolitan university and civic universities with a research mission and the example of the Germans in basic knowledge, joined to the expansion of the British economy's service sector, created specialised audiences for the various disciplines and broke the Whig historian's monopoly of the readership.[7]

But this did not happen overnight. It was not until the 1920s and 30s that Whig history ceased to dominate academic history (only to be replaced by conservative statist or radical popular history as rival myths, some would argue) and its grip over popular perceptions of history is not yet entirely broken. Long before this the liberal university had become established as the dominant institutional form in higher education and in the 'knowledge industry'. It was a form full of paradoxes — the product of industrialising society, yet full of distrust for industrial values; committed to a restoration of scholarly standards yet believing strongly in the integrative and didactic possibilities of scholarship; freed by the 'objectivity' of science from the constraints of political authority, yet suspicious of the natural sciences and even more suspicious of technology. However, it is perhaps possible to identify two main clusters of values that help to describe the characteristics of the liberal university. The first is the university's commitment to the custodianship of an intellectual tradition that was derived as much from the culture of an elite as the codification of scientific principles by a corps of academic experts. Contained in this cluster of values were two important beliefs, that knowledge is as much about preserving and refining existing culture as it is about 'inventing the future', and that a major responsibility of universities is to initiate into this intellectual culture those members of the succeeding generations whose academic aptitude (and social origins?) suggest they can be trusted with the responsibility of this knowledge. These twin emphases on tradition and pedagogy are important characteristics of the liberal university.

The second cluster of values confirms and reinforces these preoccupations. The liberal university saw its responsibility as to reproduce professions, but professions defined as much by social custom as by technological requirements, and to transmit cultural capital in its broadest and perhaps most metaphorical sense by the formation of elites. As a result the liberal university distrusted vocationalism and technology and often appeared alienated from the values of industrial society. Of course, the liberal university is being used here as an ideal type, the description of a broad category, in an attempt to emphasise the most typical qualities of universities from their revival in the late eighteenth to the first half of the twentieth century. These qualities inevitably must be described in broad and general terms because they span institutions and values from the Scottish universities of the 1780s to the 1820s with their Augustan style and intellectual preoccupations with philosophy and political economy, to contemporary universities, particularly elite universities and especially in certain branches of the humanities, which are still very much influenced by the model of a liberal university. For although this model may have been superseded or more accurately overlaid by the technocratic values of the modern university, it is still of considerable contemporary significance.

The first important characteristic of the liberal university was and is this custodianship of an intellectual tradition that has been derived from the culture of an elite rather than the codification of scientific principles by a corps of experts. Of course, these are not mutually contradictory sources; an important part of that culture may be the codification of scientific principles and experts may be an important component of that elite. It is mainly a question of balance. Yet tradition is clearly a key word and science is to some extent its opposite. In the liberal university as it revived from its long somnolence alternately attracted and repelled by the dynamism of industrial society, the key discipline was philosophy, to which mathematics was a junior partner rather than a later rival and an eventual conqueror. It is interesting to note that physics in most Scottish universities still retains the old fashioned title 'natural philosophy', an echo of an obsolete organisation of knowledge. The liberal university was a pluralist intellectual institution but not a fissiparous institution like the modern university; it felt the need for disciplines that struggled to integrate and incorporate knowledge rather than simply to advance knowledge on a narrow front. It was in this urge to transcend specialisation and expertise that the importance of philosophy consisted.

Towards the end of the nineteenth century philosophy lost its leading place to history, partly because the pedagogic discipline rooted very much in ancient philosophy was being left behind by the 'knowledge' discipline with its increasingly mathematical and logical preoccupations. As a result philosophy as a field of study lost its former coherence. In any case, history seemed better suited to act as the key discipline in the liberal university on the brink of a mass society. The abstractions of philosophy could never have appealed to the broader intellectual constituency which the universities had begun to serve by the beginning of the twentieth century. History in contrast was concrete, accessible and before the arrival of the social sciences the most didactic or 'political' of all disciplines. Yet it remained firmly a component in a tradition of intellectual cultivation. If this tradition could no longer be so effectively transmitted to a small elite through the abstract principles of philosophy, it could still be transmitted to a much broader elite by the managed memory of the past through history. Finally, and most obviously after the First World War, English literature replaced history as the key liberal discipline within the university. Part of the reason, of course, was that history had started to go down the same path as philosophy towards a more scientific and more professionalised model of knowledge. It abandoned its mission of cultivation. English, it seemed, would be unable to follow this path because of its commitment to sensibility and subjectivity (semiologists and structuralists may prove this wrong). Moreover, few disciplines seemed better designed to articulate the liberal conscience, that borderland between intellectual and aesthetic life. As the horrors of the twentieth century drowned the complacent memories of the nineteenth this appeared a vital task for the liberal university. So the reign of English as the key integrative discipline of the university after history and philosophy had the quality of a rearguard struggle against the invasion of the barbarians from the sciences (social, natural and even human) and from outside the university. This final phase was marked by a powerful element of cultural pessimism. Leavis's Cambridge (which was really Rutherford's anyway) was a desperate enterprise compared with Stubbs's Oxford or Hume's Glasgow. Briefly, it seemed in the early 1960s that the social sciences, and especially sociology, might aspire to the vacant throne of the key liberal discipline, the discipline that makes sense of all knowledge. But the moment passed.

Yet the liberal university's determination to define knowledge in terms of tradition rather than of science was not entirely wasted. Indeed the contrast between 'cultural knowledge' and 'scientific knowledge' is not so easily dismissed by concluding that the latter is superior. Of course, in its cruder forms a cultural definition of knowledge can lead to an insipid, static and ultimately degenerative intellectual tradition. It can give little encouragement to the discovery of new knowledge. This was certainly the condition of the universities in the early modern period. Cardinal Newman, in many ways the household god of the liberal university, it should be remembered, believed that research should be undertaken in institutions other than universities. Yet to describe cultural knowledge as a tradition of intellectual dogma is as much a caricature as to suggest that scientific knowledge is absolute truth untainted by its cultural context. In fact the contrast between these two ideologies of knowledge, between tradition and science, may really be quite slight. Tradition is not impervious to reason; nor does science promise to offer a completely satisfactory version of reality. As Bertrand Russell wrote:

> The authority of science, which is recognised by most philosophers, is a very different thing from the authority of the Church, since it is intellectual not governmental. No penalties fall upon those who reject it; no prudential arguments influence those who accept it. It prevails solely by its intrinsic appeal to reason. It is moreover, a piecemeal and partial authority; it does not, like a body of Catholic dogma, lay down a complete system. . .It pronounces only on whatever, at the time, appears to have been scientifically ascertained, which is a small island in an ocean of nescience.[8]

A point made, perhaps more pessimistically by Pascal: 'Reason's last step is the recognition that there is an infinite number of things that are beyond it. It is merely feeble if it does not go as far as to realise this.'[9]

This essential modesty is in fact one of the most outstanding characteristics of scientific knowledge in its proper form. Science is not a key to all knowledge, only to the next step. Tradition in its turn is not a total and satisfactory description, merely the context in which that step is related to all previous steps. They therefore appear complementary rather than competitive intellectual techniques. The contrast can be sharpened by those who make exaggerated claims for science. In the same book Russell warns:

> I have been speaking of *theoretical* science, which is an attempt to *understand* the world. *Practical* science, which is an attempt to *change* the world, has been important from the first, and has continually increased in importance, until it has almost ousted theoretical science from men's thoughts. . .The triumph of science has been mainly due to its practical utility, and there

has been an attempt to divorce this aspect from that of theory, thus making science more and more a technique and less and less a doctrine as to the nature of the world.[10]

The true danger in scientific knowledge as opposed to cultural knowledge, its potential illiberality, lies precisely in this exaggerated and not always explicit claim of science, or more properly technology, to change the world. The proper process of scientific inquiry is in contrast much more modest. It is really at the arrogance of science/technology and its alleged intellectual absolutism that most criticism has been directed. For example in his book *The Poverty of Theory*, essentially an attack on the casuistical Stalinism of Althusser, E.P. Thompson, author of *The Making of the English Working Class* and an old-fashioned radical liberal in his intellectual preferences as much as his political style, argues that to regard history as science has always been unhelpful and confusing because historical knowledge is inevitably provisional and incomplete. 'The older, "amateurish", notion of history as a disciplined "humanity" was always more exact.'[11] He therefore appeals for a restoration of history to its former preeminence in the liberal university in terms that appear to be an endorsement of a cultural ideology of knowledge rather than a scientific or 'modern' ideology.

History must be put back upon her throne as the Queen of the humanities, even if she has sometimes proved to be rather deaf to some of her subjects (notably anthropology) and gullible towards favourite courtiers (such as econometrics). But, second and to curb her imperialist pretensions, we should also observe that 'History', in so far as it is the most unitary and general of all human disciplines, must always be the least *precise*. Her knowledge will never be, in however many thousand years, anything more than approximate.[12]

In fact there is nothing here that separates history from physics in the principles of intellectual inquiry. Marc Bloch in *Le Métier d'Historien* defended history's status as a science because it offers 'un classement rational et une progressive intelligibilité', and defended its need for abstraction: 'No science can do without abstraction and is the chlorophylic function more "old" than the economic function?'[13] Even the most apparently precise scientific knowledge is relative, in the important sense that it is incomplete.

Even the best tested scientific law may have exceptions to its operation yet to be discovered. Also, even in the natural sciences the same facts may suggest several different theoretical explanations. One may appear much more plausible than others which in time may be proved by further inquiry or experiment to be false. But the choice of explanations never disappears entirely. Again, although a law of nature discovered by science has a more solid intellectual existence than an hypothesis in history or sociology (because causal connexions can be proved by experiment), even the more solid scientific generalisation can never be complete because of the infinity of observable facts. As Lezek Kolakowski writes:

> Truly absolute knowledge, either in the sense of mentally reproducing the whole universe or of formulating a law of unalterable and final validity, is an unattainable goal to which we can only approximate indefinitely. In so doing, however, we come to possess an increasingly full and accurate picture of reality as a whole.[14]

If this point of view is accepted, and except among the more rigid Marxists there is little apparent inclination to disagree, then the philosophical differences between culturally based knowledge and scientifically determined knowledge are slight indeed. Both the most 'amateurish' of the humanities and 'professional' of the natural sciences advance knowledge by essentially the same intellectual method. Physics in this sense in no more holistic than history.

Yet there are important differences still between the intellectual style, if not methods, of those integrative disciplines like philosophy, history, English and of those disintegrative, or at any rate exclusivist, disciplines in the natural sciences. First, the former rely more on intuition and imagination, while the latter are experimentally based. Secondly, progress in scientific knowledge although not entirely linear is largely progressive. Very occasionally an Einstein will come along and overturn a Newtonian system, but the normal advance of knowledge is more orderly and less destructive. One theory is refined into another. Yet in the humanities and social sciences the advance of knowledge is much more anarchic. Frequent counter-revolutions occur which entirely overturn the theoretical knowledge painfully accumulated in the past, and scholars have to build a new intellectual construction almost entirely from first principles. The number of available hypotheses is so large that although they can be ranked in terms of intellectual rigour or pragmatic plausibility there is little hope of any solidifying into an orthodoxy. There is clearly a difference in terms of scientific solidity between the laws generated in the natural sciences and the hypotheses that are all that can be produced by the humanities. The social sciences seem to occupy an intermediate and ambiguous position, but in the last resort they must be bracketed with the humanities rather than the natural sciences, because although their pragmatic hypotheses can be tested with greater rigour and success than those in the humanities, the intellectual hypotheses that underpin them can be no more testable than a hypothesis in history or English literature. There is no way that a social theory can be tested or falsified as a 'law' in the natural sciences can. So, although the application of scientific method as a tool of intellectual inquiry is general across all disciplines and applies as much to the 'cultural knowledge' of the liberal university as to the 'scientific knowledge' of the modern university, it is a more effective tool in the case of the natural sciences than of the humanities and more arguably the social sciences. This is because the knowledge that can be tested or falsified in the former case is both important and extends to the fundamental processes of intellectual advance within these disciplines, while that which can be tested or falsified in the latter case is confined to the mundane.

The process of intellectual advance in the human and social sciences is not so dependent on the accumulation of testable facts, although this clearly must inform and constrain any theories and hypotheses that are constructed. It depends also on an intellectual creativity that is closer to artistic creativity than with the experimentally based sciences, and also on the absorption of tradition and culture in its widest sense. Of course, there are dangers in pursuing this argument too far or the conclusion can be reached that such intellectual disciplines are essentially metaphysical. Metaphysics can degenerate into dogmatics, and eventually the whole process of rationality is at risk. The example of Marxism reveals the ambiguity of this conclusion. Marxism is clearly untestable as a social theory (its component predictions can, of course, be tested so suggestive conclusions about its theoretical plausibility can be reached). So in this sense it is a metaphysical speculation. As such it can degenerate into the arid dogma of state power as has happened in most communist-ruled countries. But it can also continue to be a very important source of intellectual creativity at the same time (although not in the same countries). It is possible to regard Freudianism in a similar light, and of course all truly metaphysical systems like the world's great religions must be included in this ambiguous intellectual category.

What this suggests is that scientific method in its austere and therefore modest sense may be a necessary, even indispensable, condition of intellectual progress, but it can never be an entirely sufficient one. The existence of God, for example, is a question not only of entirely legitimate intellectual interest but of transcendent practical significance. A philosophy of knowledge, therefore, that turned its back on such questions would not only be inadequate within its own terms but of limited social application. Many of the most important ideas in the humanities and even social sciences have a semi-metaphysical quality: yet to rule them out of intellectual order would be to diminish these branches of knowledge substantially. Of course, it is possible to regard such ideas as provisional theories or metaphors for more satisfactory scientific theories that will eventually replace them. But in many cases the possibility of replacement by a proper scientific theory does not exist. Either as in literature the ideas themselves are aesthetic as much as intellectual, or as in history the empirical evidence is incomplete, or as in many of the social science permanently unavailable. The problem remains of how to reconcile such intuitively based knowledge, as opposed to experimentally based knowledge, to properly rigorous scientific standards of inquiry — how to retain the value of Marxism, to take a concrete example, as a source of creative ideas, but to prevent it becoming an anti-intellectual dogma. The key element surely must be to the role tradition can play in disciplining new ideas that are not immediately or ever testable by strictly scientific criteria. Used in this sense tradition is not simply an intellectual form — indeed as a purely intellectual form it might even place too much emphasis on conformity and conservatism — but also a social form. The liberal tradition of the autonomy of the university, academic freedom, intellectual integrity and other general principles of conduct has as important a part to play in maintaining tradition as the more detailed intellectual values within individual disciplines. In its relationship with the intuitively based disciplines, with 'cultural knowledge', tradition must not be a policeman licensing new ideas, but a guardian of properly rigorous standards of inquiry. In other words it must be concerned with the process not the product of knowledge.

So far 'cultural knowledge' or intuitively based disciplines have been identified with the humanities, and more doubtfully with the social sciences, while 'scientific knowledge' or the experimentally based disciplines have been identified with the natural sciences and technology. In fact this is too simple; all disciplines contain elements of both. History has a large scientific component, while physics has a small but perhaps crucial component of intuition. Of course, strict scientific method only permits speculation that is subject to (fairly) immediate investigation as to its truth or falsehood. In its modesty it must learn to live patiently with the great sea of nescience. Not all scientists show this modesty and patience, fortunately, and the greatest of all are often the least modest and patient. There was simply no way in which Charles Darwin could have had the means to prove or disprove his theory of evolution in the middle of the nineteenth century. Nor is the quality of his intellectual contribution to science really diminished by the fact that more recently doubts have been cast on some quite important elements of this theory in the light of more recent knowledge. Evolution was clearly a much more satisfactory explanation of the origins of life than biblical creationism, its main ideological rival, but this cannot conceal the fact that it was devised by a process of imagination or intuition informed by practical observation. It was a grand, holistic, intellectual system of the sort disapproved of by Sir Karl Popper. In *The Poverty of Historicism* he writes:

> The difficulty of combining holistic planning with scientific methods is still more fundamental than has so far been indicated. The holistic planner overlooks the fact that it is easy to centralise power but impossible to centralise all knowledge which is distributed over many individual minds, and whose centralization would be necessary for the wise wielding of centralized power. But this fact has far-reaching consequences. Unable to ascertain what is in the minds of many individuals, he must try to simplify his problems by eliminating individual differences: he must try to control and stereotype interests and beliefs by education and propaganda. But this attempt to exercise power over minds must destroy the last possibility of finding out what people really think, for it is clearly incompatible with the free expression of thought, especially of critical thought. Ultimately, it must destroy knowledge; and the greater the gain in power, the greater will be the loss of knowledge.[15]

Here, of course, Popper is talking about political power. But the creation of grand, holistic, theories has a similar effect in the intellectual world as that of the totalitarian planner in the social world. Such theories, like all theories, are intellectual attempts to gain greater control over physical or social reality through a process of generalisation which is also necessarily simplification. If it is a successful theory like Darwin's, it destroys less successful theories. A successful scientific theory can be as imperialist within its own field as great metaphysical systems like Christianity or Marxism. Nor is this field simply intellectual, because the intellectual world also consists of very concrete social institutions, in the case of modern systems of higher education very substantial and influential institutions. Yet such a process creates knowledge, not destroys it. The bolder the theory, the more intellectual victims it claims, the more knowledge it often creates. In a later collection of essays Popper positively encourages such intellectual boldness. He writes:

> If the progress of science is to continue, and its rationality not to decline, we need this kind of success; it is not for nothing that the great theories of science have all meant a new conquest of the unknown, a new success in predicting what had never been thought of before.[16]

Later he is even more direct:

> For our aim as scientists is to discover the truth about our problems; and we must look at our theories as serious attempts to find the truth. If they are not true, they may be, admittedly important stepping stones towards the truth, instruments for further discoveries. But this does not mean that we can ever be content to look at them as being *nothing but* stepping stones, *nothing but* instruments; for this would involve giving up even the view that they are instruments of theoretical *discoveries*; it would commit us to looking on them as mere instruments for some observational or pragmatic purpose. And this approach would not, I suspect, be very successful, even from a pragmatic point of view: if we are content to look at our theories as mere stepping stones, then most of them will not even be good stepping stones. Thus we ought not to aim at theories which are mere instruments for the exploration of facts, but we ought to try to find genuine explanatory theories: we should make genuine guesses about the structure of the world.[17]

Guesses, of course, are the product of intuition not of experiment. This is not inconsistent with Popper's definition of scientific knowledge which depends on the ability of hypotheses, or guesses, to be falsified by empirical evidence. Successes, on the other hand, present more difficulty partly because according to this definition of scientific knowledge the best that can be said about a theory is that it is not yet a failure. Success after all must depend on some process of verification. Yet these are philosophical questions that cannot be pursued here, and in any case are discussed at length by Popper in the same essay. However, this requirement to make 'genuine guesses about the structure of the world', to construct successful theories, is very relevant to the distinction between the liberal university's 'cultural knowledge' and the modern university's 'scientific knowledge'. For if this requirement is accepted as valid — and most anecdotal and common-sense evidence suggests that it is an accurate description of how successful scientists see the advance of knowledge — it suggests that historians, sociologists, physicists, make hypotheses in very much the same way through a process of intuition informed by empirical information and theoretical tradition. So it seems evident that advances in knowledge in both the humanities and the natural sciences are made by an identical intellectual method (although in the case of the former theoretical tradition may play a more substantial informing role and in the case of the latter empirical information). The difference occurs at the second stage when advances in knowledge are confirmed and consolidated. With the 'scientific knowledge' of the natural sciences this is a comparatively straightforward process, so helping to explain the linear quality of scientific advance. With the 'cultural knowledge' of the humanities and social sciences the process is much more ambiguous, so helping to explain the frequency of destructive revolutions and counter-revolutions in these disciplines. Yet this is essentially a difference between how knowledge is consolidated not of how it is created.

Marxists, of course, would doubt whether 'scientific knowledge' is capable of achieving such objectivity. Marx himself was dogmatically simple-minded on this question. In *The German Ideology* he wrote:

> The class that has the means of material production at its disposal has control at the same time over the means of mental production, so that thereby, generally speaking, the ideas of those who lack the means of mental production are subject to it.[18]

The function of intellectuals is to perfect the illusion that the interest of the ruling class expressed in an ideal form is the only rationally valid one. It has to be remembered that for Marx, although not for Engels, capitalism was still as much a mercantile as an industrial capitalism. He had only a limited sense of the power of science and the revolutionary importance of technology. The ideas he had in mind were political and social rather than scientific. He also, to be fair, used the rather tentative qualification 'generally speaking'. Later Marxists, pre-eminent among them Gramsci, have tried to elaborate the crude and simple view of the relationship between society and ideas held by Marx and his more orthodox successors. But his separation of society into political society where the ruling class got its way by repressive violence; and civil society where the ruling class usually got its way by a mixture of ideological domination and therefore consent (echoed later by Althusser in his distinction between the repressive state apparatus and the ideological state apparatus, i.e. the education and cultural system) is really subversive of basic Marxist ideas about materialism, and comes close to accepting that ideas have a substance that Marx and other realists would deny them. The fact that contemporary followers of Marxism have been very much attracted to this idea of ideology as a commanding metaphor for society cannot conceal that it is the opposite of the traditional Marxist view.

However, the Marxist perspective is not entirely without relevance to a discussion of the differences between the liberal university's 'cultural knowledge' and the modern university's 'scientific knowledge'. No sensible Marxist would attempt to argue that the ruling class could 'fix' the results of scientific experiments. Control of the means of production does not confer the power to prevent the false from being falsified by empirical evidence. But the objectivity of the scientific method appears to be an essentially secondary process, to confirm or disprove advances in knowledge. The initiative for such advances has other sources than the observation of empirical evidence or experimental investigation. It is a much more subjective process, 'genuine guesses about the structure of the world' was Popper's phrase. After all, only those hypotheses that have actually been made can be tested by scientific inquiry. It is logically possible that there are other hypotheses that would be more satisfactory scientifically but are never made in the first place. So the Marxist critique concentrates on the production of hypotheses or more generally of sets of assumptions which social scientists insist on calling paradigms. Such a critique is consistent with Thomas Kuhn's view of how and why scientific revolutions occur.[19] Briefly, he argues that most scientific advance is 'normal' science, Popper's stepping stones, and that only when there is an accumulation of evidence that the basic context and assumptions, within which these step-by-step advances are being made (the paradigm) is becoming less and less satisfactory as an over-arching intellectual structure, does a revolution occur that creates a new paradigm (Einstein's physics instead of Newton's, or Darwin instead of *Genesis*) within which the process of 'normal' science is resumed. Such a view is quite consistent with Popper's description of scientific method. In large theories as in little experiments a better hypothesis replaces a worse, a kind of Gresham's law in reverse. The Marxist, however, would inquire more closely into the reasons for the breakdown of one paradigm and in particular for the choice of the successor paradigm. He would doubt whether internal intellectual superiority was the only criterion, and suspect that the fall and rise of successful paradigms owed a great deal to their relevance to social reality and so to those social groups which have the largest influence over the definition of social reality — in other words 'tradition' or the 'ruling class' depending on taste. The relevance of this to the contrast between the intuitively based disciplines and the experimentally based disciplines is clear and startling. For it may be that the latter too are subject to a process of revolution and counter-revolution that is as much the product of culture ('tradition', 'the ruling class', or whatever particular description is chosen) as of science, and that this process is only less visible because it is linear or at any rate progressive.

This point is emphasised by David Harvey in *Social Justice and the City*.[20] He points out that although it is normally believed that the humanities and the social sciences are 'pre-scientific', the same process as that described by Kuhn in the natural sciences can be observed. In economics, for example, two revolutions at least can be clearly seen: the Adam Smith/David Ricardo revolution that overthrew the former orthodoxy of mercantilists (and physiocrats?), and the Keynesian revolution that overthrew the orthodoxy of the classical economists themselves, or so it seemed until Keynesianism itself came under pressure in the late 1970s.[21] In both cases, Harvey suggests, the causes of these revolutions were political rather than intellectual. What tipped the balance in both cases was that the great changes in social and economic reality in the eighteenth and later in the twentieth centuries had made previously adequate intellectual explanations clearly inadequate and so they were replaced. Harvey adds:

Revolution and counter-revolution in thought are therefore characteristic of the social sciences in a manner apparently not characteristic of the natural sciences. Revolutions in thought cannot
ultimately be divorced from revolutions in practice. This may
point to the conclusion that the social sciences are indeed in a
pre-scientific state. The conclusion is ill founded, however, since
the natural sciences have never been wrested for any length of
time out of the control of restricted interest groups. It is this fact,
rather than anything inherent in the nature of the natural science
itself, that accounts for the lack of counter-revolutions in the
natural sciences. In other words, those revolutions in thought
which are accomplished in the natural sciences pose no threat to
the existing order since they are constructed with the requirements of that existing order in mind.[22]

So he concludes that far from the social sciences being in a 'pre-
scientific' state, the natural sciences are in a 'pre-social' state. While
many people would not be prepared to go as far as this, they would
probably concede that the superior objectivity of 'scientific knowledge' to 'cultural knowledge' is not as great as is commonly supposed. Even in the most apparently pure of 'scientific knowledge',
there is an important cultural element which is no less important
because it is inadequately recognised.

So a reasonable conclusion might appear to be that the liberal
university and the modern university which has incompletely
usurped its position, do not, in fact, have different philosophies of
knowledge. The contrast between tradition and science is too sharp.
Historians and philosophers do not operate by different intellectual
rules from physicists and biologists. Both accumulate knowledge in
a piecemeal way that is entirely consistent with the empirical traditions of science. Both also advance knowledge by intuition and
imagination, the construction of semi-holistic theories which either
thrive because they are sustained by a suggestive accumulation of
evidence or decay because they are gradually worn down by an
accumulation of falsifications. These new theories are in both cases
rooted in the intellectual traditions of their disciplines and the surrounding social reality. Of course, there are important differences
of emphasis between the 'cultural' and the 'scientific' disciplines.
The latter are progressive; they are more easily and obviously
falsified by empirical evidence. The former suffer from frequent
and devastating counter-revolutions in thought; and they must rely

on verification by cultural tradition as much as falsification by empirical evidence.

Yet there are perhaps two even more important differences between 'cultural knowledge' and 'scientific knowledge' which justify placing this contrast at the heart of the difference between the liberal university and its modern successor. The first is that philosophy, history, English and other leading humanities, the most typical of the 'cultural', intuitively led disciplines, were integrative disciplines. Their ambition in their various heydays was to provide an overarching intellectual context for human existence. Indeed, they had ambitions that went beyond the intellectual in a narrow sense. Their mission was to cultivate and to educate. Physics, the most important of the 'scientific' disciplines and in many ways the key discipline in the modern university, has lesser ambitions. Although it seeks to provide a complete semi-mathematic account of the physical world, the modesty inherent in the scientific method makes it unwilling to adopt the broader civilising role of the key disciplines it has replaced. Through the rigour of its methods, it may educate the intellect but not the sensibility. So it is not an exaggeration to say that for the 'cultural' disciplines it is knowledge-as-process which counts, while for 'scientific' disciplines it is knowledge-as-product. Of course, most philosophers would regard all knowledge as process, and there is nothing inherent in the nature of these disciplines which means that they must adopt these different priorities. But neither of these qualifications affects the validity of this contrast and its practical significance for the intellectual and pedagogical style of the university.

The second difference is an extension of the first. It is that the intellectual characters of different disciplines come not so much from their philosophies of knowledge — these, as has been shown, are less in conflict than is usually believed — but from their social functions. In a sense the ideologies of disciplines matter a lot less than their sociologies. It is how particular types of knowledge are used that explains their different intellectual styles, and the contrast between the liberal and modern universities which is really functional not philosophical. In this human and social context the knowledge-as-process of the 'cultural' disciplines led to an emphasis on education, while the knowledge-as-product of the 'scientific' disciplines led to an emphasis on technology. This, therefore, is the key difference between the liberal and modern university, not that the former had an essentially cultural definition of knowledge which was superseded in the latter by a superior scientific definition, but that the former was led to emphasise the process of education while the latter emphasised the production of technology.

In this context the second characteristic of the liberal university, its emphasis on the initiation of young people into the prevailing intellectual (or professional) culture, is easier to understand. It can be argued that this commitment to pedagogy was humanist, although in an extremely narrow social sense, because it placed students rather than the codification of theoretical knowledge at the centre of the liberal university's mission, much less the development of specialised academic disciplines into which this totality had been arbitrarily divided. But it can also be argued that this priority for people-through-knowledge rather than knowledge-through-people carried with it the danger, if not of philistinism, at least of a passive attitude to the expansion of knowledge. It sometimes seemed that the true intellectual mission of the liberal university was to bring together powerful people and traditional ideas, to initiate those young people destined to live privileged and possibly powerful lives into the best of existing intellectual culture. If in the process that culture was expanded, or more likely refined, so much the better — but the emphasis was on preservation and initiation.

In fact this argument is possibly overdrawn. Under the intellectual conditions that prevailed between, say, 1800 and 1930, there was much less conflict than might be supposed today between the liberal university's emphasis on undergraduate education and its contribution to scholarship. The pursuit of knowledge was essentially a personal, artisanal occupation, as it has remained in many humanities disciplines with the partial exception of history. The intellectual character of these disciplines made, and make, them unsuitable for conversion to 'factory' research. These reflective, non-linear characteristics make the development of a more 'professional' and more organised approach to research inappropriate. The resources scholarship in these disciplines require are essentially libraries and the time of teachers. The first requirement is simply an elaboration of the resources required for high-quality undergraduate education in these disciplines, while the second conflicts much less in practice with the demands of teaching students than would be supposed in theory. Anecdotal evidence suggests that one stimulates the other, that good teachers are also productive scholars. This is not doubt because whatever temporal competition may exist, the mentality, the intellectual habits and qualities required to teach (good) undergraduates in the humanities are also required to produce good scholarship. So to the extent that the key disciplines within the liberal university were the great integrative, didactic humanities, a commitment to good undergraduate teaching and the drive to exhibit scholarship were complementary activities. Even in the natural sciences, until the successive revolutions in physics in the 1920s and 30s, research remained a small-scale affair involving individual scientists surrounded by, very small, groups of assistants. Their requirements in terms of laboratories and other equipment were still comparatively modest. Although at the level of intellectual values the potential already existed for a serious divergence between the demands of the general scientific education of undergraduates and those of research, until the 1930s this had not become actual. So it would be quite unfair to stigmatise the liberal university as a form of intellectual institution that favoured teaching at the expense of research. Such a conflict was simply not seen as existing until comparatively recently, perhaps as late as the 1940s in the natural sciences or even the 1960s in the social sciences. Such a conflict still does not exist in most of the humanities or, of course, in large areas of professional and technological higher education. The idea that students and knowledge are competitors is very much a symptom of the modern post-war university.

A more substantial criticism of the liberal university's commitment to undergraduate students is that it was a commitment to the preservation of social privilege, not to the spread of enlightened pedagogy, and therefore should be seen as part of the university's role in the reproduction of cultural capital through the formation of elites. The argument, briefly, is that education systems with universities as their pinnacle are the carriers of cultural capital which they transmit to successive generations through teaching and, at the highest levels, research. The various stages of this argument need to be separated to assess their respective plausibility. First, and most easily accepted, is the argument that only a minority of the population is provided with the intellectual tools to enjoy reasonable social autonomy or to exercise social control over his fellow citizens. As Basil Bernstein has written,

> historically and now, only a tiny percentage of the population has been socialised into knowledge at the level of the meta-languages of control and innovation, whereas the mass of the population has been socialised into knowledge at the level of context-tied operations.[23]

The next stage in the argument is that access to these superior forms of education is very unevenly and unfairly distributed through the general population. This too cannot be sensibly disputed. The third stage is the argument that only those already to some extent familiar with this elite intellectual culture through the micro-cultures of family and class will be able to succeed in gaining access to superior forms of education. As Pierre Bourdieu has put it,

> an educational system which puts into practice an implicit pedagogic action, requiring initial familiarity with the dominant culture, and which proceeds by imperceptible familiarization, offers information and training which can be received and acquired only by subjects endowed with the system of predispositions that is the condition for the success of the transmission and of the inculcation of the culture.[24]

This final stage is more difficult. In one sense it is a truism, because clearly middle-class children will take more easily to an education suffused with middle-class values, but in another sense it seeks to establish a causal connexion because this is an essential part of the theory of cultural capital.

Although this is not the place to examine this theory in detail, it is possible to explain both the character of education and the inequality of access to it without recourse to a theory of cultural capital. Certainly in the case of the liberal university a simpler and more pragmatic explanation is perhaps better. If the style of education was designed for those who would later form a political and administrative elite or become scholars, it was because only such people could be conceived of as students in a university. It would be wrong to conclude that the university itself had played any active role in defining the elite that was to be reproduced, except in so far as its intellectual qualities included Bernstein's 'metalanguage of control and innovation' and it was part of the superstructure of an unequal society. Indeed it could be said that the liberal university played less part in the selection and reproduction of elites than its modern successor. Under the *ancien régime* in Europe birth bestowed rank which bestowed power. Education, except in the forms of relatively superficial intellectual cultivation, hardly came into the picture at all. In the nineteenth and early twentieth century the development of the liberal university made much less difference in this respect than might be supposed. So few people went to university anyway that the reproduction of elites through the educational system took place at a lower level, through the public schools and grammar schools. In terms of social advancement going to university was rather like buying a country estate, something to be done when one had already 'arrived' not as a prelude to such arrival. Nor was this always necessary. Going to public school was always more significant than going to university. Indeed, in the nineteenth century it could be argued that the university was even a marginal institution in the process of reproducing elites. Memories of impoverished clergymen hung round Oxford, while round the newly founded civic universities of the north and midlands hung the ambiguous values of industrialism. The poor scholar competed with the cultivated gentleman in the popular image of the liberal university. Later, towards the end of the century and in the early half of the twentieth century the image was modified. The end of clerical dominance at Oxford and Cambridge in the 1850s and 60s made both universities considerably more exclusive in terms of the social-class backgrounds of their students. Between 1850 and 1899 four-fifths of students at Oxford came from the newly expanded public schools.

But even in Oxbridge's most aristocratic period between, say, 1890 and 1930, it would be hard to describe the liberal university as a central instrument of class power. Indeed, the social eccentricity which was one result was itself a form of marginality. It is difficult to regard Beerbohm's or Waugh's Oxford as a powerful institution of intellectual hegemony for the British professional and commercial middle class only then just escaping from the grip of Nonconformity, teetotalism and Samuel Smiles. Of course, such eccentricity was not typical of either Oxford or of the liberal university generally, but it is nevertheless interesting that the connexion between the more socially privileged student intakes that followed the end of clerical domination and the university's ideological importance does not seem to support a rigorous theory of cultural capital. Indeed, so few people went to university in Britain up to 1945 that it can be argued that within the narrow constraints of an educational elite determined elsewhere a career open to the talents could be said to apply within the liberal university. It is the modern university that must answer the charges of cultural capitalism.

Yet there are two clear characteristics of the liberal university that are the result of its restricted social character. The first is its commitment to general or liberal education. It saw its role as the education of generalist-administrators or teacher-scholars, not of expert technocrats. Cardinal Newman in a famous phrase described the university as

> the high protecting power of all knowledge and science, of fact and of principle, of inquiry and discovery, of experiment and speculation; it maps out the territory of the intellect, and sees that there is neither encroachment nor surrender on any side.

He dismissed useful knowledge as a 'deal of trash', and then in a panegyric for the liberal university said that a university education

> aims at raising the intellectual tone of society, at cultivating the public mind, at purifying the national taste, at supplying true principles to popular enthusiasm and fixed aim to popular aspirations, at giving enlargement and sobriety to the idea of the age, at facilitating the exercise of political powers, and refining the intercourse of private life.

It prepared a man 'to fill any post with credit, and to master any subject with facility'.[25] It is sometimes suggested that Newman spoke for the past, and then even in the 1850s the science-based universities of Germany were already beginning to serve as a rival model to the liberal university. But this is probably to misunderstand both Newman and the liberal university.

When Newman criticised 'useful' knowledge, the point he was making was not really so different from that made today by those who question the distinction between 'pure' and 'applied' research. Newman certainly did not regard a university education as useless. He clearly regarded a liberal education as the intellectual means by which the political and administrative elite should be educated to fill the commanding positions in society. Scholarly contemplation was almost the opposite of what he had in mind. It is sometimes assumed that the liberal university was very much concerned with the life of the mind, while its modern successor is a much more practical and utilitarian institution. In fact it can be argued, that, when a suitable allowance has been made for the fact that the former existed in a more hierarchical society in which opportunities for education were much less dispersed, the liberal university was a thoroughly practical institution, while the modern university which sees knowledge rather than students as its primary product is a more theoretical, if not always reflective, institution.

The truth behind the liberal university's commitment to general education (however well disguised as Oxford 'Greats' or the Harvard Law School) is perhaps two-fold. First, and probably more important, this commitment fitted in with the liberal university's conception of knowledge as a cultural process rather than as a scientific product, which has been discussed earlier. Not only did this push knowledge towards a pedagogical expression, but by the clear desire to integrate new knowledge in one discipline with new knowledge in other disciplines and into the existing intellectual tradition, it encouraged general or liberal education. According to this definition of knowledge general education was regarded as superior and more rigorous rather than diluted as might be the view today. The intention, therefore, became to mould the general intellectual, even aesthetic and moral, character of students rather than to train them in specific academic skills. Secondly, this commitment reflected the social role of the liberal university as the educator of a political, administrative and professional elite. Such people in a society not yet as differentiated as our own in its market for highly skilled manpower of this nature had to be generalists. Even today many of the most influential positions in society need to be filled by people with the intellectual confidence to relate detailed and technical information and concepts to a broad picture. The kind of intellectual synthesiser at which the liberal university aimed is by no means obsolete. Indeed, democracy being in the last resort government by the amateur this need is perhaps greater than in the nineteenth century. In other ways, of course, time has moved against the intellectual generalist. As Norman Birnbaum has put it,

> In the nineteenth and early twentieth-century market societies of Britain and the United States and in the bureaucratic societies of France and Germany, the university could form (or contribute to the function of) persons who had reasonable expectations of the work awaiting them in adulthood. In a relatively fixed social framework, socialization by means of a single set of intellectual or spiritual assumptions was possible.[26]

Today general education at university level runs not only into social difficulties such as the lack of a fixed 'public' intellectual culture to which a stable majority is prepared to give its consent, but also into difficulties of an ideological or philosophical nature. What should be the content of a liberal education towards the end of the twentieth century? To whom should it be directed? and so on. But it would be erroneous to mistake growing difficulties of the means for the declining value of the goal.

The second characteristic of the liberal university that flowed from its restricted social character was its independence from the values of industrial society. This is an issue that must be handled with some care because most of the universities established in the nineteenth century owed their origins or their expansion to the industrial revolution. This is perhaps a necessary corrective to the impression created by such statistics as that only about 7 per cent of Cambridge University graduates between 1800 and 1899 entered industry or commerce — and this during the century of Britain's most dynamic industrial and technological development. Yet the liberal university, although by no means an unworldly institution, saw itself as an independent institution that stood slightly aside from detailed social and industrial demands. Indeed, its intellectual independence was seen as the most important contribution it could make to society. Again, it is a view easy to criticise from the perspective of the late twentieth century. But administrative arrangements that have institutionalised this view of the relationship between universities and society are still the basis for the financing and control of Britain's universities. The creation of the University Grants Committee in 1919 and the formalisation of adequate grants from the state marked not the beginning of direct social control through the state, but the ending, or at any rate curbing, of direct social control through industrial sponsorship and student fees.

Of course, this independence can be cast in a negative light as the exclusiveness of the academic caste or else as the universities' own special contribution to the sustenance of an anti-entrepreneurial culture such as has been described in Martin Wiener's recent study of the decline of the 'industrial spirit' in Britain.[27] Neither of these factors can be ignored, but both are probably of secondary importance. The liberal university, in its roles as the institutional memory of an intellectual culture and as the conscience-critic of contemporary intellectual values, could never have seen itself as subservient to industrial values any more than it could have a agreed to submit to political demands. Like the medieval university, although for very different reasons and in different forms, it saw intellectual authority as distinct from political, social or industrial power. This, indeed, was seen as the essence of the liberal university.

So it is clear that the liberal university is far from being an obsolete type. Many of the features of the modern university, and many of the most enduring, are simple borrowings; the institutional autonomy of universities; their custodianship of an intellectual culture, including the stricter scientific method; their commitment to pedagogy (even if it does have to be of the brightest and the best); an independence from industrial values and a resistance to political demands; a defence of liberal or at any rate broad, education for undergraduates and a scepticism about the professionalisation or bureaucratisation of scholarship; all are still very live values in the modern university even if they are occasionally at war with newer values. Perhaps the aims of higher education emphasised by the Robbins Committee 20 years ago and 111 years after Newman spoke in Dublin, underline this essential continuity. They were instruction in skills suitable to play a part in the general division of labour, the promotion of the general power of the mind, the advancement of learning, and the transmission of a common culture and common standards of citizenship. Newman would almost have approved.

Notes

1. H. Rashdall, *The Universities of Europe in the Middle Ages*, London, 1936.
2. M. Bloch, *Feudal Society*, London, 1965, p. 108.
3. Ibid., p. 86.
4. Bede, *A History of the English Church and People*, Harmondsworth, 1968, p. 127.
5. A. Gramsci, *Collected Works, volume III: Intellectuals and the Organization of Culture*, Turin, 1947, pp. 4–7.
6. T. B. Macaulay, *Critical and Historical Essays*, London, 1961 p. 78.
7. S. Rothblatt in *London Review of Books*, 21 January — 3 February 1982, reviewing *A Liberal Descent: Victorian Historians and the English Past*, Cambridge, 1981.
8. B. Russell, *A History of Western Philosophy*, London, 1946, p. 480.
9. Pascal, *Pensées*, Harmondsworth, 1966, p. 170.
10. Russell, *Western Philosophy*, p. 492.
11. E. P. Thompson, *The Poverty of Theory*, London, 1978, p. 387.
12. Ibid., p. 262.
13. M. Bloch, *Le Métier de l' historien*, Paris, 1948 p. 74.
14. L. Kolakowski, *Main Currents of Marxism, volume I: The Founders*, London, 1981, p. 396.
15. K. Popper, *The Poverty of Historicism*, London, 1957, pp. 89–90.
16. K. Popper, *Conjectures and Refutations: The Growth of Scientific Knowledge*, London, 1969, p. 243.
17. Ibid., p. 245.
18. K. Marx, *The German Ideology*, London, 1965, p. 39.
19. T. Kuhn, *The Structure of Scientific Revolutions*, Chicago, 1962.

20. D. Harvey, *Social Justice and the City*, London, 1973.
21. Ibid., p. 122.
22. Ibid., p. 127.
23. B. Bernstein, *Class, Codes and Control*, London, 1971, p. 239.
24. P. Bourdieu, and J. C. Passeron, *Reproduction in Education, Society, and Culture*, London, 1977.
25. J. H. Newman, *The Idea of a University*, London, 1852.
26. N. Birnbaum, 'Students, Professors and Philosopher Kings' in Carl Kaysen (ed.), *Content and Context*, New York, 1973, p. 466.
27. M. J. Wiener, *English Culture and the Decline of the Industrial Spirit 1850-1980*, London, 1981.

Chapter Three

THE MODERN UNIVERSITY

In 1930 Abraham Flexner in his influential book *Universities: American English German* called the university 'an expression of the age.'[1] Certainly, it is as the product of the successive scientific, technological, and social revolutions of the twentieth century that the modern university is naturally regarded. It belonged in the here and now. That quality of standing slightly apart from society, of transcendence in both time and place of parochial intellectualoid preoccupations in the cause of a universal intellectual tradition, which had been an important feature of the liberal university, was very much eroded in the 30 years of explosive university growth after 1945. Universities became almost entirely instrumental institutions losing their semi-spiritual quality. More and more they were seen as institutions that could make a direct and powerful contribution to the acceleration of economic growth or the promotion of social justice, not simply through the students they educated or the academic knowledge they discovered and elaborated but in quite immediate and specific ways. Knowledge itself was seen as the primary product of higher education, not students. Everyone and everything was in a hurry; so it seemed natural to try to make advances in science (social and human as well as natural) immediately and directly useful to society through the route of technology, rather than to allow them to feed slowly and indirectly into society through the medium of pedagogy.

This, of course, led to an important shift away from teaching and towards research — as knowledge-production rather than as reflection — within the university, which will be discussed later. But it also substantially modified the relationship between the universities and society in two main ways. First, the preoccupations of the university were more directly and intensely influenced by the interests of the state, of the economy and of civil society. Knowledge became more subservient to power. The distinction between intellectual authority and political power, which in the case of the medieval

54

university had been sustained by the superior authority of religion and in the case of the liberal university, more weakly by the authority of science and the intellectual tradition, was very much weakened in the case of the modern university. So the basis for the intellectual independence of the university was undermined as much because of the eagerness of the universities to regard knowledge as a powerful and immediately useful product as because of the imperialism of the state. Secondly, this new emphasis in the modern university on knowledge as product or commodity (rather than as process) led to a revolution in how the university saw its critical role in society. Previously this had been seen as an intellectual process, in terms of both the rigorous example of the scientific method itself and the detailed subversion of established knowledge within individual disciplines, and as a pedagogical process, because students were educated to observe these standards of criticism. But in the modern university it became also a political process. After all, if theoretical knowledge through technology could become directly and immediately useful, then through a similar process it could become directly and immediately critical or even subversive. From this conclusion flowed the view that the modern university, far from acting like the liberal university as an important element in the internal self-critical function of society, should see itself as an external critic enjoying a precarious and qualified independence on the fringes of a monolithic technocratic society. In this context the modern university was seen as an oppositional rather than critical institution, so preparing a comfortable base for an intelligentsia of a similar character. A superficial assessment would suggest that this development had been provoked by the growing identification of the modern university with the prevailing political and economic order through the confusion of science with technology. In fact these two developments are twins, not rivals. Both arise from the identification of knowledge itself as a product and the consequent confusion of intellectual authority and political power. The technocratic enthusiasm for a 'knowledge society' and the belief in ideology as a commanding metaphor for society have a close similarity and a common origin.

Of course, these subtle and largely unintended changes in the character of the university were largely hidden by the spectacular achievements in science that were their ultimate cause. In a period that saw the Einsteinian revolution in physics, the splitting of the atom, the discovery of DNA, and many other discoveries of theoretical science almost as great, it is hardly surprising that science should have mesmerised society. Nor were these intellectual achievements confined to the natural sciences. It can be argued that the Keynesian revolution in economics provided the conceptual basis for the Bretton Woods settlement of the post-war economic order, and that the generation of rapid economic growth which followed provided the material basis for the new social state (and, incidentally, the great expansion of the universities). Similarly, although more arguably, the work of political scientists and sociologists helped to establish the intellectual legitimacy of the policies of social reform, whether of Roosevelt's 'New Deal' or of the 1945–51 Labour Government in Britain, which have made such an important contribution to political stability in the West since 1945. Academic knowledge seemed not only immensely more powerful than in the past but much more relevant. Keynes himself made this claim for the influence of ideas at the end of his *General Theory*:

> The ideas of economists and political philosophers, both when they are right and when they are wrong, are more powerful than is commonly understood. Indeed, the world is ruled by little else. Practical men, who believe themselves to be quite exempt from any intellectual influence, are usually the slaves of some defunct economist. Madmen in authority, who hear voices in the air, are distilling their frenzy from some academic scribbler of a few years back. I am sure the power of vested interests is vastly exaggerated compared with the gradual encroachment of ideas.[2]

After the war the rapid development of high-technology industry increased this sense of the power of science, which came to be seen not simply in terms of spectacular individual intellectual achievements but in terms of the large-scale organisation of the production of new knowledge. The metaphor of the factory seemed more and more appropriate. To the extent that scientific and technological progress came to be seen as a collective enterprise, the randomness of such progress was apparently removed. Breakthroughs could no longer simply be hoped for by providing the right conditions for creative individuals, but organised for by the establishment of teams of scientists, none perhaps a brilliantly creative individual, but whose cumulative efforts could achieve as good results. In fundamental scientific inquiry that seeks to question Kuhn's paradigms such an approach might be in vain, but for Kuhn's 'normal' science and especially in technology it often worked well. E.F. Schumacher in his polemic *Small is Beautiful* describes a visit to an oil refinery in these terms:

> As we walk around in its vastness, through all its fantastic complexity, we might well wonder how it was possible for the human mind to conceive such a thing. What an immensity of knowledge, ingenuity, and experience is incarnated in equipment! How is it possible? The answer is that it did not spring ready-made out of any person's mind — it came by a process of evolution. . .What we cannot see on our visit is far greater than what we can see: the immensity and complexity of the (technological) arrangements . . .the intellectual achievements. . .Least of all can we see the great educational background which is the precondition of all, extending from primary schools to universities and specialized research establishments.[3]

The modern university, it seemed, could mobilise and organise the intellectual resources of society and so manufacture progress, in the same way that a modern economy could mobilise and organise the physical and human resources of society to create wealth. Compared with the liberal university it was a mass institution, mass in the sense of the greatly increased numbers of students and also, perhaps more important, mass in the sense of the mass as opposed to artisanal production of knowledge.

The result has been a very substantial increase in the relative size of the higher education system. After a period of a stable or even declining number of students in the 1920s and 30s, the size of the system more than quadrupled between 1945 and 1980. First Keele was founded and then the new universities were planned. The colleges of advanced technology were established in the late 1950s after the 1956 White Paper on technical education.[4] During the 1960s the new universities opened, their ambition very much increased by the expansive forecasts of the Robbins Committee[5] which also recommended a further promotion of the CATs to become technological universities. Partly in their place the 30 new polytechnics were established in the late 1960s.[6] Finally during the 1970s more than 60 colleges of higher education were created out of the debris of a contracting system of independent teaching education and from some leading further education colleges. In all these various institutions the number of students increased from 179,000 in 1960/1 to

520,000 in 1980/1. The proportion of the age group receiving higher education rose from 6.9 to 12.5 per cent (this had been higher, at 14.9 per cent, in 1976).[7] Nor was this phenomenon of rapid expansion confined to Britain. Indeed, expansion in Britain was modest by international standards. In the United States the number of students in higher education increased from 5,967,000 in 1965/6 to 11,415,000 in 1977/8, although the growth in students in university institutions was more gradual from 4,791,000 (80 per cent of the total) to 7,336,000 (just over 60 per cent). In France the rise over the same period was 525,000 to 1,047,000; in Germany 345,000 to 906,000; in Italy 425,000 to 1,020,000; and in Japan 1,080,000 to 2,196,000.[8] Significantly, perhaps, growth rates in Eastern Europe were much more modest. The increase in the USSR over this period was from, 3,860,000 to 4,950,000; in Hungary from 94,000 to 110,500; in East Germany from 11,600 to 130,200; and in Czechoslovakia from 145,000 to 168,000.[9]

Looking at the subjects students chose to study, we find there has been, perhaps surprisingly, little change in the overall balance. The modern university is not becoming more science-based, at any rate in terms of the subjects students choose to study. Nor has it rushed into the embrace of the social sciences. Indeed, during the 1960s the most obvious growth area was in the humanities.[10] More recently in most countries the only pattern that can be observed is a slight decline in the proportion of students studying humanities compensated for at first by a slight rise in the proportion studying social science, a gain that has subsequently been lost. Only in Sweden and the United States do the social sciences appear to have made spectacular and permanent gains in student preferences. A similar pattern can be observed in relation to pure and applied science.[11] In Eastern Europe a similar pattern of stability emerges, although traditionally a much higher proportion of students study technology subjects and rather fewer the social sciences. At first sight this stability is surprising.[12] It would not have been unreasonable to expect that the balance of subjects studied in the much expanded modern university would be significantly different from that which prevailed in the much more restricted liberal university. In fact this does not appear to be so, although such broad categories can conceal important shifts in intellectual values within disciplines.

A final measure of the scale of the expansion is the growing share of the gross national product devoted to expenditure on higher education, because clearly the expansion in higher education has been much greater than the growth in national wealth. In 1975 higher education's share of the Gross National Product (GNP) was 1.2 per cent, almost three times as great as in 1960.[13] In the last 20 years the higher education system has expanded by more than 200 per cent, while GNP has increased by just over a third.[14] Some economies of scale of course have been achieved, and in the last few years some actual cuts made, but expenditure on higher education (together with further education) now amounts to £3,296 million, more than a quarter of all expenditure on education and 5 per cent of all public expenditure.[15] The growth of higher education expenditure in other countries is even more dramatic. In Belgium it has increased its share of GNP by four times, and in the Netherlands from 0.3 per cent in 1961 to 2.2 per cent in 1975. In France and Germany the share increased more slowly but mainly because of superior economic growth.[16]

Why did this spectacular growth occur? It is perhaps significant that this growth was most marked in those countries with the highest rates of economic growth and the most open societies. The expansion of higher education that took place during the same period in Asia and Africa, although equally rapid, had a different character and different consequences. The need for cultural liberation, the creation of substitute elites, and urgent tasks of national development were important considerations in the Third World, but hardly applied to the conditions of North America and Western Europe. In Eastern Europe, as we have seen, the expansion of higher education was much more modest. So the conclusion must be that the modern university is very much an institutional phenomenon of countries that are both advanced in their economies and open in their societies. Which of these two qualities is more influential remains a sharply contested issue. Twenty years ago the emphasis would almost certainly have been placed on the economic dimension of the modern university. Educate or perish would have been regarded as the stark alternatives, rather as A.N. Whitehead had written in the middle of the First World War:

> In the conditions of modern life, the rule is absolute: the race that does not value trained intelligence is doomed. Not all your heroism, not all your social charm, not all your wit, not all your victories on land and sea, can move back the finger of fate. Today we maintain ourselves. Tomorrow science will have moved forward yet one more step, and there will be no appeal from the judgment which will be pronounced on the uneducated.[17]

Despite their melodramatic phrasing, these words seemed very true to a generation of Americans on the brink of the space race or a generation in Britain mildly enthusiastic about the prospect of 'the white-hot heat of the technological revolution'.[18]

Technological innovation and the necessary social adaptation, both seen as the direct products of the application of theoretical knowledge generated within the university, were, perhaps are, widely regarded as the preconditions of national success and even survival. Even those still attached to the older purposes of the liberal university recast their justifications of a university education in this more utilitarian mould. In 1930 the Cambridge economist Alfred Marshall argued that greatly increased expenditure on universities could be justified because

> the economic value of one great industrial genius is sufficient to cover the expenses of the education of a whole town; one new idea, such as Bessemer's chief invention, adds as much to England's productive power as the labour of a hundred thousand men.

He adds that advances in medicine, or biology, or mathematics can similarly be productive even though their benefits may not be so immediately apparent, and concludes: 'All that is spent during many years in opening the means of higher education to the masses would be well paid for if it called out one more Newton or Darwin, Shakespeare or Beethoven.'[19] It is an interesting and revealing justification for the popular expansion of higher education in the name of village Hampdens and mute Miltons, a justification repeated 40 years later by Eric Ashby when he wrote:

> All civilised countries depend upon a thin clear stream of excellence to provide new ideas, new techniques, and the statesmanlike treatment of complex social and political problems. Without the renewal of this excellence, a nation can drop into mediocrity in a generation. The renewal of excellence is expensive: the highly gifted student needs informal instruction, intimate contact with other first-class minds, opportunities to learn the discipline of dissent from men who have themselves changed patterns of thought: in a word (if it is one that has become a five-letter word of reproach) this sort of student needs to be treated as *élite*.[20]

The means suggested are certainly those of the liberal university, but the end, to avoid a nation's drop into mediocrity, is typical of the modern university in its most self-confident mood. Today in less confident mood a greater emphasis might be placed on the cultural dimension of the modern university as an explanation for the great quantitative expansion of the post-war period. Cynics might even suggest that rich countries possess sophisticated systems of higher education not because these make countries rich, but because only rich countries can afford them. Even when such cynicism is repudiated and a more balanced view of the economic costs and benefits of the modern university is insisted upon, this new emphasis on the modern university's cultural dimension should be retained. The relationship between an open and democratic society and the development of the modern university is at least as important as higher education's more ambiguous relationship with economic growth.

However, it would be wrong to suppose that the modern university developed out of the liberal university only in response to external pressures. At least as radical in its impact on the university has been the internal momentum, even dynamism, of knowledge and its constituent academic disciplines. If the modern university has become a more confusing and fissiparous institution than its liberal predecessor, it is not solely or even mainly because it has tried to do too many jobs for external groups like the state, industry, or the community. The confusion arises as much from changes in the construction of intellectual life. These can be summed up as the displacement of humanism by academicism. Of course, such a statement raises new questions rather than answering old ones. For instance it is clearly not possible to suggest that the liberal university institutionalised an essentially cultural definition of knowledge, which has been superseded in the case of the modern university by a superior scientific definition. This distinction was discussed in the last chapter, and the conclusion reached that the fundamental method by which knowledge is advanced is essentially the same across all disciplines. The differences are really secondary and concern questions like the progressive character of the advance of knowledge in certain disciplines, the ease with which hypotheses can be falsified, the distinction between 'laws' and hypotheses, and so on. There are, of course, important sociological differences as well beween the integrative, reflective disciplines like philosophy, history, and English, successively the key disciplines in the liberal university, and the isolationist, experimental disciplines like physics, which established a similar primacy in the modern university. Finally, of course, the uses to which these contrasting disciplines were put, pedagogy in the case of the former, technology in the case of the latter, led to quite different balances of intellectual preoccupations in the liberal and modern universities.

There is, however, another difference between the styles of knowledge preferred by these two distinct forms of the university which may help to justify and explain this contrast between the liberal university's 'humanism' and the modern university's 'academicism'. No forms of knowledge or sets of intellectual values, however abstract, can ever be composed entirely of cognitive values. As Talcott Parsons and Gerald Platt have put it, such values 'must somehow be integrated with those of non-cognitive significance. These other values, for example, in effective attainment to predominantly non-cognitive goals like wealth or economic production, or in effective socialisation into the role of educated citizen, should be as fully cognitively grounded as possible, but should not neglect non-cognitive concerns. Non-cognitive concerns are at cultural levels more expressive, more moral-evaluative, or more constitutive and can be combined with the cognitive in complex value structures.'[21] Clearly history or, to an even greater extent, English contain a larger element of such non-cognitive values, goals and concerns than physics or chemistry. So as the natural sciences have replaced the humanities as the hegemonic disciplines within the modern university, the latter's emphasis on cognitive values at the expense of others, moral-evaluative and expressive, has increased. There is perhaps a further aspect of this difference between the less cognitive humanities and the cognitive sciences that should be mentioned. In the case of the latter, although non-cognitive values may influence what people want to know and what knowledge they want to use, the cognitive validity or invalidity of any hypotheses is not determined by such non-cognitive values (or barely so); in the case of the former the two sets of values are often more entwined so it is more difficult to be sure that non-cognitive values have not influenced the validity or invalidity of any hypotheses. The result is that for most of the natural sciences non-cognitive values make up smaller components of total disciplines than with most of the humanities subjects, and such values are seen as peripheral and clearly separate from the core cognitive values of the discipline. This second aspect is important because in the nineteenth and early twentieth centuries the natural sciences were very much subject to industrial influence and so by extension to non-cognitive values. Indeed, the theoretical sciences grew out of the practical sciences, not the other way round. Pure science developed to answer the questions asked by applied science. Yet these non-cognitive values, however intrusive in a practical sense, remained peripheral in an intellectual sense.

The result is that in modern universities the rise of the natural sciences and their dependent technologies and the relative decline of the older liberal disciplines have made the university an institution more completely devoted to cognitive values, or to academicism. The organic and didactic view of knowledge treasured by the liberal university has been undermined, but no satisfying alternative view with the same holistic ambitions has been found. The advances in the theoretical foundations of the natural sciences were so rapid, subversive, and even destabilising that such an alternative seemed impossible to construct, and that an essentially cultural definition of the intellectual tradition appeared to be an anachronism. This dynamism of the natural sciences focused all attention on the discovery and incorporation of theoretical knowledge, cognitive values, often at the expense of the liberal university's traditional emphasis on the intellectual formation of the student and his/her socialisation into the role of educated citizen, which were essentially non-cognitive or perhaps better semi-cognitive concerns. This new emphasis was hardly surprising. After all, that was where the action was, where the identifiable progress was being made. The modern university was not a superior pedagogical institution to the liberal university. Indeed, because it had to teach a mass, heterogeneous student body, it might actually be inferior, and anyway progress in pedagogy was almost impossible to measure except by crude and insensitive quantitative criteria. But as a 'knowledge' institution the modern university was clearly superior. Moreover, its progress was apparent within and without the university.

In the modern university, therefore, the product was knowledge as much as students. Parsons and Platt had no doubt that the true obligation on the university was a fiduciary duty to protect and advance cognitive values.[22] So they had no hesitation in their analysis of the modern American university in describing research and graduate training as its 'core sector', although they conceded that claims for this honour could be made on behalf of the undergraduate college and the professional school. Interestingly the Robbins Committee only ten years earlier had placed the advancement of learning third in its list of the purposes of higher education after instruction in useful skills and the promotion of the general powers of the mind, no doubt demonstrating both the preoccupations of the members of the

Committee with liberal (and non-cognitive?) values and perhaps the 'pre-modern' condition of British higher education as recently as 1963. Although this new emphasis on knowledge rather than students arose first and most naturally in the pure sciences, it spread gradually to non-science disciplines, first to the social sciences and finally and least definitively to the humanities. In the case of these last two to refuse to accept this new priority was to run the very substantial risk of being (mis)labelled 'pre-scientific' and consequently to see one's discipline lose status and resources within the university. So discipline after discipline underwent an intellectual revolution in the modern university. Increasingly each was organised on the basis of the degree of association between theoretical preoccupations rather than of the coherence of undergraduate curricula, either for the benefit of under-graduates or their eventual employers, or of society at large. As a result it became less and less reasonable to believe in an intellectual tradition, except at the mundane level of common methodologies and techniques, or in an organic, holistic intellectual culture.

The organic knowledge of the liberal university was replaced by the fissiparous knowledge of the modern university. With the association of theories as their guide, disciplines divided into sub-disciplines which were divided into specialties which were dividual into 'schools'. Occasionally, very occasionally, an intellectual merger might take place, but specialisation and yet more specialisation was the general rule. By this means knowledge could be most effectively advanced, however damaging an effect it might have on the effective teaching of students, or however much over-specialisation might encourage an intellectual chaos in the university at large. Neil Smelser accepts that

> the institutionalization of cognitive rationality is also closely associated with the potential for conflict *within* educational institutions. Parsons and Platt note the centrifugal trend in the development of intellectual disciplines — the trend towards specialization in subject matter which also involves differential achievement in reputation and renown. This tendency would split academic organizations and persons apart from one another in terms of common interest and ranking. Such appears to be one of the inevitable consequences of the institutionalization of the values of universalistic achievement.[23]

Here Smelser is considering the influence of centrifugal specialisation on the integrity of the academic profession, but it clearly has an enormous impact also on the character of the university itself.

It is important to emphasise that the production of knowledge or the advancement of learning has been given a higher priority in the modern university than it enjoyed in the liberal university, because there is a common assumption that it was the other way round. In an important sense the modern university is a more 'cognitive' institution than its predecessor. As Clark Kerr has put it,

> this evolution has brought departments into universities, and still new departments; institutes and ever more institutes; created vast research libraries; turned the philosopher on his log into a researcher in his laboratory or the library stacks; taken medicine out of the hands of the profession and put it into the hands of the scientists; and much more. Instead of the individual student, there are the needs of society; instead of Newman's trend 'truths of the natural order', there was discovery of the new; instead of the generalist, there was the specialist.[24]

At a more anecdotal level the conspicuously late introduction of the PhD into British universities (and then mainly to offer a counter-attraction to the German universities) shows how recent has been the incorporation of a 'research culture' into the university tradition. This requires emphasis because it is often assumed that in its commitment to cognitive values the modern university is less rigorous than its liberal predecessor.

Especially in America and during the student revolt of the 1960s it was feared that the university was about to be take over by entirely non-cognitive values. Hence the warning of an almost Spenglerian future delivered by Parsons and Platt:

> The academic system as the culminating focus of the educational revolution is grounded in its status, both at the cultural and societal levels, as a sector of the modern system, a sector differentiated from others with respect to the relative primacy of cognitive interests and functions. The balances between cognitive and other interests leave room for considerable adjustments in the course of developing processes of social and cultural change, but in the radical subordination of these cognitive interests to others would subvert the system. If continued sufficiently long so that other interests became strongly consolidated in the academic system, it

would work towards the repeal of the educational revolution, with incalculable consequences for the future of both society and culture.[25]

That particular danger seems less substantial today. The end of mass student growth in higher education, and the discriminatory effects of reductions in public expenditure on higher education make it more likely that the predominance of cognitive values in the modern university will be intensified rather than eroded. In any case in proper historical perspective the modern university appears more intensely and specifically an academic institution than the liberal university which it has replaced. Not only does it see its role more as a 'knowledge' and less as a pedagogical institution, but it enjoys a more certain hegemony than its liberal predecessor as the main producer of theoretical knowledge in society. So it seems reasonable to emphasise its academicism and to contrast this with the (very elitist) humanism of the liberal university.

This academicism has had important consequences for the environment of the modern university. First, it has encouraged the development of an intelligentsia, pre-eminently, of course, in the social sciences, but to some extent based in all academic disciplines. It has done this by emphasising knowledge as product, in the forms of theory and more loosely ideology, at the expense of knowledge as process, in the form of pedagogy; and through the specialisation and so sophistication of detailed knowledge within disciplines that are themselves theoretical paradigms, by again stimulating theoretical and occasionally ideological formulations of reality. Although this can only be speculation, it may be that the prominence of pragmatism within the British intellectual tradition may be a reflection, now fading, of the status and uses of knowledge within the liberal university. With academicism now established at the heart of the modern university and the elitist humanism of the liberal university plainly in decline, this intellectual tradition may be in the process of modification. Certainly there is anecdotal evidence to support this view. Historians look longingly across the channel to the *Annales* school with its more striking orientation to the social sciences, leaving both the G.R. Eltons and the E.P Thompsons semi-stranded by the shifting intellectual tide. English dons dabble in structuralism and even semiology. The British seem to be 'discovering' Marxism just when many of our European neighbours seem to have increasing doubts about its continuing intellectual value.

The second consequence is that undergraduate teaching and research have drifted further and further apart. What were once seen as entirely complementary activities in the age of artisanal research are now increasingly regarded as competitive, especially in the natural sciences. In an intellectual system that practises, or tries to practise, the mass-production of new knowledge on a series of narrow scientific fronts, it is hardly surprising that the distance is often considerable between the type of comprehensive, integrative knowledge required for the teaching of undergraduates, even in the natural sciences, and this ragged frontier of research. In the more reflective humanities disciplines and the more accessible social sciences the dilemma is not normally so acute, but it is still there. In all its branches the professionalisation of academic knowledge has made it increasingly difficult to regard teaching and research as harmonious activities in an intellectual form (in a personal or institutional form a stronger case can be made for their continued association). The extent to which their association is still valued in British higher education is a considerable measure of the anachronism of the system, for this was an important quality of the liberal university not of its modern successor. But it is difficult to escape the impression that the near-unanimous enthusiasm for keeping teaching and research in close association is a traditional view rather than a contemporary need, at any rate in the natural sciences. Nor is it easy to deny that the 'professorial' tradition (with its emphasis on research and at the best large-scale impersonal lecturing which is exemplified in London and the larger civic universities) has become the model for British higher education as a whole rather than the 'collegiate' tradition exemplified by Oxford and Cambridge with its emphasis on careful undergraduate teaching and close pastoral care. This is not simply a question of the higher cost of the latter or of its almost incestuous relationship with a privileged social order. It is the result of an important shift in the intellectual preoccupations of the modern university away from teaching and towards research.

The third consequence is that the modern university is a bureaucratic institution constructed of rules and procedures. The liberal university at its best was a collegial institution constructed of common intellectual and other values. The modern university no longer possessed a common intellectual language. Instead each specialised academic discipline has its own language that is intelligible in a substantial sense only to its own practitioners. The 'visible college' of the university has been largely abandoned as a focus of loyalty, and certainly as a source of intellectual values, in favour of the 'invisible college' of the subject. Senates of generalists cannot sit in judgement over academic departments made up of specialists. The university has ceased to be an academic community, except in vacuous rhetoric, and has instead become a shared bureaucratic environment. As decisions that involve institutional and intellectual questions can no longer be made by consensus or by judgement of peers (for in what sense is the historian the peer of the physicist?), then they must be made by academic politicians or administrators who still attempt to use a bureaucratic dialect of the almost-dead common language of the university, or by politicians. Conflict is therefore common. As Neil Smelser has written,

> the educational system stands continually in a state of precarious balance and potential conflict over different priorities: to what extent should it be permitted to maximise its own values of cognitive rationality (generating knowledge, searching for truths, teaching and learning in the broadest sense), and to what extent should it be required to 'service' the values and needs of other sectors of society? This question is a subject of continuous uncertainty and conflict. . .Since higher education serves many masters, including itself, it is to be expected that it stands on the precipice of value conflicts at all times.[26]

For the modern university has moved away from a collegial to become a bureaucratic institution, not simply because of the Babel of competing cognitive values generated by increasingly specialist individual disciplines, or the growing emphasis on 'knowledge' rather than pedagogy, but also the new conflict between cognitive and non-cognitive values. The academicism of the modern university is only half of the story.

The intellectual culture of the liberal university has splintered in its modern successor not just because of the development of academicism, but also because of a growing commitment to vocationalism, often of a highly specific kind that would have been almost inconceivable a century ago. Of course, the liberal university too had been a vocational institution. This was especially clear in the case of the early liberal university when clerical influence remained strong. It has been estimated that of the 25,000 who matriculated at Oxford between 1800 and 1850, 10,000 were subsequently ordained.[27] Medicine and, in its higher levels, law remained university monopolies. Yet it would be wrong to exaggerate the liberal university's commitment to vocationalism on their account. The education of lawyers continued to be conducted largely on apprenticeship lines. Even today there is nothing in Britain to compare with the powerful professional law schools in the United States. Legal education was, and essentially still is, under the control not of the university but of the profession which was dominated by those in practice rather than in academic life. The training of doctors was, and is, conducted in medical schools and hospitals as decisively dominated by the profession (although medical educators and scientists play a more influential part in their profession than academic lawyers do in the legal profession). In both cases it is possible to see the role of the liberal university in the formation of these professions as one of initiation rather than one of highly specific vocational training.

The liberal university significantly found it very difficult to meet the more specific needs of the newer professions created by industrialism, professions with a lower social status than law and medicine and a correspondingly higher technological content. The most obvious example is the various branches of engineering. In some countries entirely new institutions of advanced technical education arose unaffected by the cultural constraints felt so strongly by the liberal university, like the grandes écoles in France and, a rather more ambiguous example, Imperial College in Britain. This route through technological universities was most typically followed in Europe where responsibility for the formation and registration of engineers was assumed directly by the state. In those countries with a stronger tradition of free professions, and which therefore left such matters to be decided by engineers themselves, two patterns emerged. Either as in the United States the education of engineers and similar specialists was undertaken within the university but in professional schools normally quite distinct from undergraduate colleges; or as in Britain universities were reduced to acting as the service agents of the profession which retained a surprisingly detailed control over the education that new practitioners received. In both cases the education and training of engineers and technologists were marginal and badly incorporated activities within the liberal university. The one vocation for which the liberal university did train its students openly and with pride was the vocation of government, both generally in the sense of their future membership of the political class and quite specifically as potential members of an administrative elite. For the development of the liberal university was closely influenced by the growth of the state during the nineteenth and early twentieth centuries. As important a change for its intellectual and pedagogical orientation as the ending of clerical domination in the 1850s was the opening up of the Civil Service to competitive examination at the same time.

The commitment of the modern university to vocationalism has been much more intense. In the last 50 years the university has accumulated a substantial 'service' role to complement (or conflict with) its roles as a 'knowledge' and pedagogical institution. This accumulation has been least marked in the elite layers of the higher education system and most marked in the newer and more popular layers, but not even the most famous and ancient universities have avoided being substantially modified by this new 'service' role. It is perhaps possible to distinguish two stages in this process of modification. First, the utilitarian values of industrial society which had been slowly seeping into the liberal university for more than a century, rushed in on the modern university after 1945. This was entirely predictable, as Margaret Archer has pointed out,

> the support of business had been a precondition for the establishment of the civic universities from 1850 onwards, whether this had taken the form of sponsorship by local industry (e.g. Sheffield, Birmingham and Manchester), funding by a particular firm (e.g. Bristol and Wills's tobacco, Reading and Palmer's biscuits), or industrial support for a national concern (e.g. Newcastle and mining).[28]

Of course, it is not always easy to distinguish philanthropy from self-interest, or to disentangle civil pride from industrial advantage. Nevertheless, until the state itself became involved in scientific research, which can be conventionally dated from the creation of the Department of Scientific and Industrial Research (DSIR) in 1916, and before industrial firms had grown sufficiently large to generate their own research function, the universities occupied a crucial position as perhaps the only reliable source of scientific expertise. As a result their product was very much in demand in industry. Equally, of course, until the establishment of a reliable system of state grants to universities in 1919 with the creation of the University Grants Committee, universities were chronically short of money. The only source of money in the face of an indifferent state was industry. So universities needed the financial support of industry as much as industry needed their scientific expertise. It can be argued that between 1919 and 1945 the relationship between the universities and industry became less tight. Research laboratories outside the universities were developed either by government or industry itself. The universities became less dependent on industrial charity, so allowing the academic profession more freedom to assert its preference for the values of a liberal university. The development of further education offered alternative sources of expertise, especially in training. Indeed it is possible to trace this process of disengagement between universities and industry through to the 1960s. The Percy and Barlow Reports, the 1956 White Paper and the CATs, even the binary policy and the polytechnics are all evidence of this disengagement. One has only to compare the origins of the new universities of the 1960s with those of the civic universities a century earlier to measure the apparently declining influence of industry.

However, it would be wrong to conclude from this apparent decline that the modern university, at least in Britain, is a less vocational institution than its liberal or at any rate pre-modern predecessor. By any measure this is a nonsense, one which no doubt arises from the confusion of the direct influence of industry in the shape of leading businessmen, with the indirect and much more substantial influence of industrial values. The Robbins Committee, normally a very accurate barometer of the institutional values of the higher education system in the middle of the post-war expansion, placed at the top of its list of the purposes of higher education 'instruction in skills suitable to play a part in the general division of labour'. The committee then added half-apologetically, 'we put this first, not because we regard it as the most important, but because we think that it is sometimes ignored or undervalued' — although not apparently by students because the report continues:

> We deceive ourselves if we claim that more than a small fraction of students in institutions of higher education would be where they are if there were no significance for their future careers in what they hear and read; and it is a mistake to suppose that there is anything discreditable in this.

The paragraph concludes:

> And it must be recognized that in our own times, progress — and particularly the maintenance of a competitive position — depends to a much greater extent than ever before on skills demanding

special training. A good general education, valuable though it may be, is frequently less than we need to solve many of our most pressing problems.[29]

This rather ambiguous acceptance of vocational values by the Robbins Committee is perhaps typical of the modern university as a whole. The modern university is not especially convinced of the intellectual validity of such values for a university education — indeed it may have even greater doubts on this point than at the beginning of the century when the university was a more peripheral social, and certainly less prosperous, institution, and the possibilities of industrial capitalism seemed without limit. But it has accepted industrial values as a by-product of the very substantial expansion of higher education. As higher education in Britain has moved from being an unambiguously elite to an at any rate semi-mass system, it has become impossible to maintain an intellectual character that depends on the assumption that most graduates would go on to occupy elite jobs in the professions and administration. It now has to be accepted, with whatever reluctance, that most students will become the future middle managers and technologists of the industrial state or even the lumpen intelligentsia of the Welfare State. The result is that vocational values that were discreetly veiled and seemed closely allied to the pedagogical ambitions of the liberal university have been replaced by much more explicit vocational values that are highly specific and seem to have little in common often with the 'knowledge' ambitions of the modern university.

This conflict has been exacerbated by the invasion of the university of the 'service' values of the post-war Welfare State and the accompanying demands to meet its vocational requirements. Again, it can be argued that this is not a new obligation. Even the liberal university had served the state in this way by initiating the leading administrative cadres of the future into the dominant intellectual culture. But the modern university faces difficulties in this respect never encountered by its predecessor. First, the scale is quite different; where the liberal university had to deal with hundreds, the modern university must cope with tens of thousands. Secondly, there is no longer a dominant intellectual culture. It has been replaced by a series of micro-cultures centred on individual disciplines, and this confusion has been confounded by the development of the new 'service' disciplines generated by the intellectual and vocational demands of the Welfare State. Some of these subjects with strong if not always explicit commitments to social action jar with the modern university's commitment to value-free scientific knowledge (which, of course, is more pronounced than in the case of the liberal university). Other 'service' disciplines are objected to on the grounds that their intellectual content is too slight to justify a place in a university. Again, the modern university's emphasis on 'knowledge' at the expense of pedagogy makes it unhappy to accept new disciplines that do not seem to have a reasonable potential for research. Of course, it is wrong to see the arrival of the new 'service' disciplines as a negative process. The modern university, in fact, was much more open to the 'new' professions of the twentieth century than the liberal university had been to the older professions of the nineteenth century. Perhaps town planners and social workers appeared less threatening than engineers. Certainly their civic and low-technology values represented less of a challenge than the industrial and high-technology values of the engineer. Their presence within the university was more acceptable both because of the residual but still strong values of the liberal university and of the growth between the 1950s and 1970s of an intellectual estate. Perhaps the influence of the state, often the employer directly or indirectly of these 'new' professionals, was decisive. Now almost entirely dependent on the state for its income, the university probably had little choice in this matter. Having been brought in during the first half of the twentieth century to protect the liberal university from tutelage to industry, the state in the second half of the century has made more active vocational demands on the modern university. In any case this new and substantial commitment to vocationalism, whether traditional industrial values or newer 'service' ones, reflected to some extent the disintegration of a traditional intellectual culture in the realm of academic values. But to a larger extent it was a response to external pressures and in particular to the imperatives of expansion.

For the modern university 'is not outside, but inside the general social fabric of a given era', to borrow a phrase of Flexner. Especially after 1945 the university had thrust upon it growing obligations to promote the expansion of educational, and wider social, opportunities and to contribute to economic growth and the creation of wealth. Leaving to one side the conflict between cognitive and non-cognitive values that these new obligations bring in their wake, their practical consequences are enormous. As early as 1930s Flexner was complaining that universities were becoming 'secondary schools, vocational schools, teacher-training schools, research centres, "uplift" agencies, businesses — these and other things simultaneously'. They were becoming ' "service stations" for the general public'.[30] Or as Martin Trow has written more recently, 'mass higher education continues to be influenced by. . .elite groups, but is increasingly shaped by more "democratic" political processes and influenced by "attentive" audiences'.[31] It can be argued that the university's assumption, under external pressure, of non-cognitive values and goals marks a discontinuity in its development, a move away from its central academic purpose. In fact it is more complicated. The liberal university, as has been seen, was far from exclusively directed to the advancement of theoretical knowledge. Instead, its elitist humanism allowed it to contain both cognitive and non-cognitive values within an organic intellectual tradition. In contrast the very academicism of the modern university has sharpened the contrast, and therefore the potential conflict, between cognitive and other concerns. At the same time external circumstances obliged the university to find more room for these other non-cognitive concerns. These two apparently conflicting trends were contemporaneous rather than consecutive.

This two-sided conflict has perhaps given an exaggerated sense of discontinuity. The modern university's role in the promotion of educational opportunity is not really so different from the liberal university's role in the reproduction of elites. The intention has been to make access to these elites more equitable and broader, not to repudiate the university's traditional role in the formation of elites. As Martin Trow has put it,

> In mass higher education, the institutions are still preparing elites, but a much broader range of élites that includes the leading strata of all the technical and economic organisations of the society. And the emphasis shifts from the shaping of character to the transmission of skills for more specific technical élite roles.[32]

But although the substance of the social purpose of the university has not really changed in the transition from liberal to modern modes, the scale of the operation is so vastly different that the appearance of revolutionary new purposes has been created. Again, it is the expansion of the system that has given the impression, half-bogus and half-true, of a significant change in the orientation of the university in the years since 1945. In its response to the educational revolution the university has followed events rather than being in their vanguard. The Robbins principle, although in its implementation a policy with radical consequences, had the modest intention of ensuring that entry into higher education should not be allowed to become more difficult. This objective in fact has barely been achieved. In 1963/4 there were 56,600 'qualified' school leavers (those with two or more A-levels, or three or more Scottish 'Highers') and the number of home entrants into higher education was 54,000. Not all these home entrants, of course, came to higher education with formal academic qualifications, but the great majority did. In 1976/7 122,200 school leavers were qualified, while the number of home entrants in that year was 107,200.[33] In other words higher education growth has merely been a response to the revolution in schools that has taken place as a result of the 1944 Education Act and the comprehensive reorganisation of secondary schools during the 1960s and 70s. This British experience is in marked contrast to that of the United States, where higher education itself was at the centre of the post-war educational revolution.

If the two most consistent features of the modern university that distinguish it from its liberal predecessor are greater academicism in its intellectual values and greater instrumentalism in its social relationships, then it is not unfair to say that in Britain higher education has been considerably more enthusiastic about the former than about the latter. The response to the educational revolution in the schools has been cautious and barely sufficient, and occasionally grudging. The common assumption made among many others by the Robbins Committee was that the appropriate university response was to keep pace with the increasing number of well-qualified school leavers by a carefully planned and executed policy of expansion. Although in the new universities of the 1960s there has been talk, and even a little action, about redrawing the map of knowledge and recreating an integrative undergraduate curriculum through interdisciplinary courses, and although the Robbins Committee itself was anxious that most of the new students that would come into the system as a result of the recommended expansion should study for general rather than specialist academic degrees, there has been little serious attempt to modify the academicism of the modern university. Part of the reason no doubt was that under the rather modest expansion envisaged in Britain in which the supply would barely keep pace with the demand from school leavers, it was not adequately recognised that these new students, although as well qualified in formal terms as their predecessors, might have different expectations of higher education for social, economic, and cultural reasons. The Robbins expansion appeared an almost conservative enterprise and as a result provoked little protest from conservatives. Conclusions such as that of Sir James Mountford, 'if truth and the advancement of learning are the stars by which the universities set their course, a sense of public duty must be their helmsman',[34] seemed quite adequate statements of the conventional wisdom. Another and certainly more important reason was that the academicist trajectory of the modern university was much too powerful to be modified by recalling the anachronistic values of the liberal university, by reciting contemporary pieties, or by appealing to a mass future that made little sense and had even less appeal in the strictly contained British system of higher education. What had been intended by Robbins as an experiment in enlightened pedagogy turned out to be a period of creeping academicism and of a burgeoning intelligentsia. In Britain, unlike the United States, the internal values of the modern university proved to be stronger than the external pressures. Academicism triumphed over instrumentalism.

If a few more enlightened people in universities dimly perceived that quantitative expansion on the scale of the years from 1955 to 1975 was bound to lead to qualitative change and that students, despite their superficial similarity in the future, might have radically different intellectual needs, this was recognised more clearly outside the academic system. One way to satisfy these more diverse intellectual needs, it seemed, might be not to rely on the internal flexibility and adaptability of the university tradition, but to create instead a diversity of institutions, university and non-university. This was the genesis of the binary policy, although other less salubrious motives were attached to it along the road to implementation. This policy will be discussed in detail in Chapter 6. Of course, higher education had always been more than simply the universities, so in a sense a binary policy had always existed. What was different about Anthony Crosland's policy in the mid-1960s and the establishment of the 30 polytechnics that flowed from it was that it was a deliberate attempt to promote institutions that would embody intellectual and educational values distinct from those embodied in the universities. As Mr Crosland put it in a speech at Lancaster University in 1967, 'At a time of rapid expansion and changing ideas we want not a monopoly situation in higher education, but a variety of institutions under different control — a unitary system would surely imply an omniscience which we do not possess.'[35] Others, like Eric Robinson, were prepared to go further in their advocacy of the binary policy:

> Sooner or later this country must face a comprehensive reform of education beyond school — a reform which will bring higher education out of the ivory towers and make it available to all. This will be achieved through a bloodier battle than that for the comprehensive reform of secondary education. In that battle the grammar school was the victim. In the next, the victim will be the university — the commanding height of British education. The shape and the speed of this change to come depends upon the success with which the polytechnics are established. The future pattern of higher education in this country can be set in the development of these institutions as comprehensive people's universities.[36]

Another, and contrary, view is that as a result of the creation of the polytechnics the modern university has belatedly come into its own in Britain (although rather confusingly split down the middle by the binary policy). Taken together, the universities and the polytechnics and colleges of higher education, began to add up to a modern university tradition comparable to those in Europe and North America. But for the creation of a strong and successful polytechnic and college sector in Britain during the 1960s, the higher education system dominated by the universities would have remained trapped in an awkward post-liberal and pre-modern phase. The binary policy has supplied the instrumentalism so typical of the modern university but which British universities have long resisted. It has also supplied the much needed heterodoxy. For many teachers in polytechnics see themselves as having a 'trading' rather than fiduciary relationship with the social and economic systems. They make no claims to be involved in a process of independent critical inquiry, not one at any rate which requires the traditional buffers of institutional autonomy and academic freedom between themselves and society. While there are many polytechnic teachers who see their intellectual and educational responsibilities in terms that are analogous to those of their university colleagues, there are others, in fine-art departments for example, who see their responsibilities as much in aesthetic and moral terms as intellectual ones, as the conscience of an over-mechanistic world; while there are teachers in colleges of higher education, closer to their colleagues in schools and effectively denied the solace of research, who see their role very much in terms of the humanist pedagogy of the liberal university. There have, of course, been attempts to produce some over-arching philosophy of polytechnic education that tries to capture all this heterodoxy in a common gravity and to apply to it a common principle (attempts that go back far beyond Crosland through Lunacharsky to Owen). These attempts have tended to emphasise the intellectual aspect of 'doing', of application, of capability, so offering suggestive evidence of the strong element of instrumentalism in the modern university. To suggest that they have largely failed is not to say that they have not been, and do not remain, a valuable element in the necessary discourse about the purposes of higher education. But perhaps in the end the only adequate 'polytechnic' philosophy of higher education is no philosophy at all, to come to terms with the inevitable and perhaps enriching heterodoxy of cognitive, semi-cognitive, and non-cognitive values that is a feature of the modern university.

It is perhaps against this background that the success of the binary policy must be assessed. Three broad assertions are made about the polytechnics and the colleges. The first is that they have been a conspicuous success, notably adding to the diversity of higher education in Britain by legitimising new forms of it. This is certainly true. The polytechnics and colleges have been successful individual institutions. As a result for the first time in Britain higher education is no longer synonymous with universities, a stage reached in other advanced countries many decades ago if indeed the confusion ever existed. The quantitative expansion of the number of students in the polytechnics has been one of the most remarkable features of higher education development in the 1970s (the 1960s having been the decade of university expansion). And large areas of intellectual activity, whether new or para-professional disciplines or new approaches to more conventional disciplines, and different modes of study, sub-degree qualifications, modular degrees and so on, have been made fully legitimate by the work of the polytechnics and colleges and that of the Council for National Academic Awards (CNAA). Again nothing very remarkable by international standards, but in British terms an important extension of the higher education tradition. The second assertion is that the binary policy has been a failure, confirming and even intensifying an antiquated hierarchy of institutions by continuing the remorseless and ceaseless decapitation of (popular) further education to feed (elitist) higher education. This assertion, although exaggerated, has a sufficient element of truth to be taken seriously. 'Academic drift' is a complex phenomenon reflecting as much a rather snobbish disdain at necessary efforts to raise the intellectual level of subjects regarded as beneath the academic salt, as more legitimate concern about over-academic approaches to practical subjects. But it is possible to observe an occasional tendency to ape the preoccupations of a rather special kind of university education in an inappropriate environment. This is hardly surprising. Academicism is a powerful force through all parts of the modern university. It is also perhaps revealing that the honours degree has remained the predominant model for the proper organisation of a course in higher education. Correct form is clearly a deep-rooted British characteristic. Finally, of course, there is the abiding evidence of the arbitrariness of the binary divide. Who is in one sector and who is in another is almost a matter of accident, at least across a wide borderland. As Martin Trow says of the bureaucratic stratification of higher education in the United States, 'this effort to achieve diversity through prescriptive planning runs against the political forces of equality, the bureaucratic preferences for standardisation, and the academic tendency of institutions to model themselves on the most prestigious'.[37]

The third assertion is that the binary policy has never been tried because universities enjoy superior resources. In fact there never was a clear suggestion that material standards in the polytechnics and colleges should be levelled up to match those in the universities. Indeed, the presumption probably always was that the 'popular' sector of higher education should necessarily be the cheaper sector. This assertion also undervalues the very considerable investment made in the polytechnics and colleges over the past 15 years, investment that but for the binary policy would presumably have been made largely in the universities.

The binary policy does have a crude didactic value. It illustrates through its institutional duality the two main qualities of the modern university that distinguish it from its liberal predecessor, its academicism and its instrumentalism. But the policy is a misleading symbol in two respects. First and less important, it encourages a superficial identification of universities with academicism, and of polytechnics and colleges with instrumentalism that is quite misleading. Second and more important, it may encourage the belief that these two qualities are rivals. In fact they are deeply complementary because both are obverse and converse faces of a single intellectual phenomenon, the belief that knowledge is itself a product and that the modern university's responsibility is to use knowledge 'to invent the future'. It is from this belief that two of the most important characteristics of modern intellectual life can be found, the confusion of intellectual authority and political power and the belief that ideology/technology is a commanding metaphor for society.

Notes

1. A. Flexner, *Universities: American, English, German*, New York, 1930.
2. J. M. Keynes, *The General Theory of Employment, Interest and Money*, London, 1936, p. 383.
3. E. F. Schumacher, *Small is Beautiful*, London, 1973, pp. 155–6.
4. *Technical Education* (White Paper), HMSO, 1956.
5. *Higher Education* (Robbins Report), HMSO, 1963.
6. *A Plan for Polytechnics and Other Colleges* (White Paper), HMSO, 1966.
7. *Higher Education into the 1990s*, Department of Education and Science and Scottish Education Department, London, 1978, Table 5, and O. Fulton, *Access and Demand*, Society for Research into Higher Education, University of Surrey, 1981, p. 72.
8. L. Cerych, S. Colton and J–P. Jallade, *Student Flows and Expenditure in Higher Education*, Amsterdam, 1981, pp. 36–7.
9. Ibid., pp. 74–5.
10. *Development of Higher Education 1950–1967*, Organisation for Economic Cooperation and Development, Paris, 1971, p. 266.
11. Cerych *et al.*, *Student Flows*, pp. 65–6.
12. Ibid., p. 82.
13. Ibid., p. 132.
14. *Social Trends 12*, HMSO, 1982, p. 101, Table 6.1.
15. Ibid., p. 59, Table 3.28 and p. 116, Table 6.22.
16. Cerych *et al.*, *Student Flows*, p. 132.
17. A. N. Whitehead, *The Aims of Education and Other Essays*, New York, 1929.
18. H. Wilson, *A New Britain*, London, 1963.
19. A. Marshall, *Societal Outcomes*, 1930, p. 273.
20. E. Ashby, *Any Person, Any Study*, New York, 1971, p. 101.
21. T. Parsons, and G. Platt, *The American University*, Harvard, 1973, p. 88.
22. Ibid.
23. N. Smelser, epilogue in Parsons and Platt, *American University*, p. 401.
24. C. Kerr, *The Uses of the University*, New York, 1966, p. 4.
25. Parsons and Platt, *American University*, p. 387.
26. Smelser, epilogue in Parsons and Platt, *American University*, p. 399.
27. J. Sparrow, *Mark Pattison and the Idea of a University*, Cambridge, 1967, Chapter 3.
28. M. Archer, *Social Origins of Educational Systems*, London, 1979, p. 494.
29. Robbins Report, p. 6.
30. Quoted in Kerr, *Uses of the University*, p. 5.

31. M. Trow, *Problems in the Transition from Elite to Mass Higher Education*, Carnegie Commission on Higher Education, Berkeley, 1973, p. 12.
32. Ibid., p. 7.
33. *Higher Education into the 1990s*, p. iv, Table 5.
34. J. Mountford, *British Universities*, London, 1966, p. 166.
35. E. Robinson, *The New Polytechnics*, London, 1968, Appendix C, p. 193.
36. Ibid., pp. 10–11.
37. Trow, *Problems*, p. 53 (footnote).

Chapter Four

THE UNIVERSITY IN CRISIS?

Ten years ago the potential achievements of the modern university seemed immense and even awesome. In its infancy Flexner saw the modern university in contrast to its liberal predecessor as 'an expression of the age'. Forty years later, in its prime, Daniel Bell in his influential book *The Coming of Post-Industrial Society* came close to seeing the age as the expression of the university:

> In descriptive terms, there are three components [of post-industrial society]: in the economic sector, it is the shift from manufacturing to services; in technology, it is the centrality of the new science-based industries; in sociological terms, it is the rise of the new technical élites and the advent of a new principle of stratification. From this terrain, one can step back and say more generally that post-industrial society means the rise of new axial structures and axial principles: a changeover from a goods-producing society to an information or knowledge society; and, in the modes of knowledge, a change in the axis of abstraction from empiricism or trial-and-error tinkering to theory and the codification of theoretical knowledge for directing innovation and the formulation of policy.[1]

Clearly, under such conditions the university as the leading intellectual institution in society would become a commanding institution of political and economic life also. It would be power in as actual and realisable a form as oil under the deserts of Saudi Arabia and the waters of the North Sea. Indeed, it would be a superior form of power. Bell even speculates about whether such changes in the social, economic, and intellectual bases of modern life might lead to a revolution in social consciousness and personal sensibility. Reality, he suggests, is no longer nature as it was in pre-industrial society, or 'technics' (machines in a broad sense) as it is in industrial society, but the social world. 'Society itself becomes a web of

82

consciousness, a form of imagination to be realized as a social construction,' he writes.[2]

Today it is difficult to feel the same excitement and optimism about the future of the university. Certainly within the modern university the shift from empiricism to theory is a well-established intellectual trend in most disciplines, but its immediate relevance to the economy and lay society seems much less sure than it did in 1973. Two other interpretations of its significance are equally plausible: that it is essentially an intellectual phenomenon which reflects the logic of scientific discovery within academic disciplines and has no straightforward social significance; or that it has as often taken the form of ideology which has been of more ambiguous benefit to political society, especially in the liberal democracies, in contrast to that of technology, which has been of more obvious benefit to the economy. If it is fair to equate Bell's 'codification of theoretical knowledge' with the modern university's academicism, and his 'directing innovation and the formulation of policy' with its instrumentalism, then the events of the 1970s have eroded rather than strengthened the conviction that these two characteristics have a cause-and-effect relationship. Although both characteristics appear to have common roots in the development of the modern university, it is less possible to be confident that their effects will preserve the same mutuality. It is just as likely that they will come into conflict. Indeed, the most plausible interpretation may be that there is no common and straightforward relationship between academicism and instrumentalism, but that this relationship will range from mutual through neutral to hostile across the disciplines.

In the natural sciences the codification of theoretical knowledge is clearly a precondition of better technology and so of greater productivity and thus, it is to be hoped, of greater wealth. In the case of the natural sciences academicism within the modern university has increased its instrumentality. But even in this best case it has to be remembered that the relationship although straightforward in intellectual terms is far from straightforward in the practical world. The difficulties over nuclear energy are perhaps the best contemporary demonstration of the social, political, and even economic barriers to progress as conceived in perhaps too narrowly scientific terms. In the applied sciences, paradoxically, the link between academicism and instrumentality seems much weaker. To the extent that the codification of theoretical knowledge approximates to scientific abstraction, it is far from clear that engineering has benefited either itself or the economy by becoming engineering science, or that medicine has gained by its enthusiasm for high technology. With the social sciences the relationship becomes more ambiguous still. Common-sense issues have often been intellectualised by the academicism of the modern university in ways that make them less rather than more accessible to the judgement of policy-makers. Has the rise of monetarist theory really led to more sensible management of the economy? Has the intellectual enthusiasm for quasi-Marxist social theory encouraged the development of a Welfare State securely founded on, and so funded by, a broad popular consensus? There is a strong, practical not intellectual, case to be made for saying that in areas like economic and social policy the contribution of the necessarily inexact social sciences is as well made through empiricism as through theory.

In the case of the humanities also it is not clear how growing academicism has increased their instrumentality to lay society (however necessary this development may have been for more purely intellectual reasons). Indeed, it can be argued that the trend towards abstraction in the humanities has undermined the ability of these disciplines to serve as part of a general culture of civilisation and so in a significant sense impoverished lay society. In their case academicism seems to have been an enemy of instrumentality. To be fair to Daniel Bell, he, of course, had in mind not simply the codification of 'higher' theoretical knowledge such as is found in universities but all knowledge amenable to codification. Indeed, the computer codes on cans and shelves in supermarkets are perhaps a better motif of his knowledge society than fusion research. But naturally enough his and similar views of the early 1970s were interpreted as an intellectual endorsement of the growth and success of the modern university. Ten years later it seems much less clear that the trajectories of academic knowledge, especially but not exclusively in non-science disciplines, will naturally and closely coincide with the trajectories of society and the economy; still less that the former command the latter; and least of all that even in the knowledge society of the future the university will necessarily become a central institution because it produces nearly all the science and most of the technology on which such a society would need to depend.

Another assumption made ten years ago that would not be made so blithely today was that the higher education system would continue to expand. Indeed, because the events of the 1960s seemed to show that the planners, and the magisterial Robbins Report itself, had erred on the side of caution, the most common assumption at the beginning of the 1970s was that, if anything, expansion would be more rapid in the future than in the past. In its prime the modern university was an almost imperial institution, constantly expanding its frontiers by incorporating parts of post-secondary education that hitherto had been quite separate, and by exploring new territory among school leavers and to a much lesser extent mature students.

In the United States these twin processes of incorporation and exploration went much further than in Britain. Community colleges had always been firmly incorporated in higher education, the very category of further education having been squeezed to death between a secondary school system enrolling virtually universal student populations up to the age of 18, and a college system enrolling 50 per cent and upwards of the relevant populations of young people and large numbers of older learners. In some social classes and in some States, college attendance became a virtually universal experience. Here in Britain the expansion of higher education was insufficient to abolish the distinction between higher and further education, but the territory of the former was remorselessly expanded at the expense of the latter first through the promotion of the CATs, then the establishment of the polytechnics, and most recently through the incorporation of teacher training (and its spin-off diversifications in liberal arts and social studies) into the mainstream of higher education. This process created for the first time in Britain a distinctive higher education system, centred on the universities, with values and priorities separate and even different from those of the rest of the education service, now centred on secondary schools. This would have been inconceivable in the time of the liberal university when a much greater identity of interests was assumed through all levels of the system.

Both the United States and Britain, and indeed all the developed countries of Western Europe, Australasia and Japan, shared this belief in the near-inevitability of the exponential expansion. After all, between 1960 and 1975 the number of students enrolled in OECD countries (excluding Yugoslavia) had increased from 6.3 million to 17 million.[3] The annual growth rate in student enrolments had been 7.2 per cent compared with 2.1 per cent for all education.[4] So when Martin Trow wrote in 1973, the same year as the publication of *The Coming of Post-Industrial Society*,

Despite the problems that the growth of higher education brings in its train and despite the arguments one hears from various quarters that the growth should be slowed or stopped, it seems to me unlikely that any advanced industrial society can or will be able to stabilize the numbers going on to some form of higher education any time in the near future[5]

this assessment was not at all controversial. A year before, the target of 750,000 students in British higher education in 1981/2 announced in the White Paper *Education: A Framework for Expansion*[6] was regarded as much too modest and was strongly criticised as a retreat from a target of more than 800,000 tentatively suggested in a planning paper published by the Department of Education and Science three years earlier at the end of the 1960s.[7]

The social and economic arguments that were used ten years ago to justify this nearly universal expectation of further substantial expansion have not, of course, lost any of their intellectual force. Nor have any reasons emerged to doubt the basic outline of Daniel Bell's analysis of the, at any rate technical and structural, direction of social and economic development. Yet neither carry quite the same political conviction that they did in the early 1970s. It is not entirely clear why this should be. After all, the last decade has seen an explosion in information technology of the kind anticipated by Bell in 1973. The use of computers has pervaded industry and commerce, not simply as accounting and control tools but as instruments of production. Microprocessors have brought computing capacity within the range of the mass of the population for either serious or leisure purposes. Bell's information technology is now displayed in shop windows in every High Street. Similarly, the 1970s have seen the rapid growth of service occupations in general and of a technical intelligentsia in particular. Much of the technology and much of the technical intelligentsia are the products of the modern university.

At a more practical level higher education has expanded throughout the 1970s at a pace which would have appeared unprecedently fast had it not followed the 1960s. An increase of a quarter in a single decade only appears slow in comparison with the truly explosive growth in the number of students from 179,000 in 1960/1 to 446,000 in 1970/1. Admittedly, the pace was set in the 1970s by the polytechnics rather than by the universities, which had set the pace of expansion in the 1960s. But in a higher education system moving rapidly away from its origins in the liberal university this emphasis on more instrumental and less elitist institutions appears entirely natural and proper. Yet when all the pleas for mitigation have been entered, it has to be admitted that the modern university, certainly in Britain and probably elsewhere, has entered a period of depression and even of crisis. No one in 1984 is likely to be looking forward to post-industrial society with as much enthusiasm as Daniel Bell ten years ago; nor assuming so easily the centrality of the university to any knowledge society of the future. Nor is anyone at the start of the 1980s anticipating any substantial growth in the system of higher education. There has been a decisive shift towards pessimism.

This shift has three dimensions, supply (of money), demand *Unearly*. (from potential students), and reputation (in both political and civil society). The first and most important of these is certainly the declining willingness of the state to invest public expenditure in higher education as generously as in the 1960s. This is not an especially new phenomenon; it has been apparent in Britain since the mid-1970s, although it has in the early 1980s passed from the chronic to the acute phase. Nor is it an isolated phenomenon; in most OECD countries it is possible to observe a sharp decline in the rate of growth of public expenditure on higher education and in many a levelling-off to reach an expenditure plateau. The broad pattern of this increasing constriction on resources is also clear. Until the winter of 1973/4 expenditure continued to grow at the rates familiar in the 1960s. It then suffered a sudden and catastrophic decline, partly as a result of direct cuts made by the government, but mainly as a result of the rapidly rising inflation rate for which the government could not or would not compensate. There then followed a gradual and incomplete restoration of expenditure between 1975 and 1979 to the levels, if not of the early 1970s, at least of the mid-1960s. Current expenditure for each full-time student in universities in 1976/7 was £2,400, only £50 less than it had been in 1966/7.[8]

A second qualification that must be made is that the polytechnics were much less affected by the cuts of the mid-1970s than were the universities. In the polytechnics current expenditure per full-time student increased from £1,900 in 1973/4 to £2,260 in 1975/6, although it then fell back almost to its 1973 level in the next year. At the beginning of 1979 this first wave of public-expenditure reductions seemed to have been absorbed by the higher education system without too much damage. The outlook for the succeeding five years was almost bright. According to that winter's public-expenditure White Paper higher education could look forward to an increase of 9 per cent in real terms in its income from public expenditure in the years up to 1983/4.[9] It has to be emphasised, especially in the light of the very different outcome, that this was not particularly generous. In the case of both universities and polytechnics it implied a further small erosion in income per student. The universities, for example, were being expected to take 18,500 (or 6.3 per cent) more students by 1981, while their grant from the government would have risen by only 5.7 per cent.

In fact events have turned out very differently. The election of a Conservative government in May 1979, determined to reduce radically public expenditure, led to a second and more serious wave of reductions in the income of higher education. After a first and probably tolerable round of cuts the universities were first promised 'level funding'. This was far less generous than it sounded for two reasons. First, the number of students assumed for the calculation of the appropriate level of expenditure was certainly below the actual number of students enrolled in universities; and secondly, 'level funding' was accompanied by a new policy towards overseas students under which they were obliged to pay much higher fees for tuition. This policy led not only to further losses of income, but also created serious distortions within the university system. In any case the precarious promise of 'level funding' was abandoned within a year, and a new round of cuts was imposed in the public-expenditure White Paper of the winter of 1980/1.[10] These reductions were applied selectively to individual universities by the UGC in July 1981, with some suffering very small reductions in grant income over the next three years, while others had to face the prospect of cuts of up to 40 per cent. Without further growth in the number of students and with an academic profession that has a 'bulge' of 35 to 50-year-olds as the result of the expansion of the 1960s, the universities are not in a position to absorb these reductions in income through increased productivity, whether of the positive or negative variety (in any case, in a university system which spends 70 per cent of its income on staff salaries, greater productivity is too close to the risk of lower quality for comfort). The result must be that up to 3,000 university teachers could be made prematurely redundant as a result of this second wave of cuts. The impact on the polytechnics and colleges of higher education has been very similar, although in their case the number of potential redundancies ranges up to 5,000. Expenditure on advanced further education (that is, higher education outside the universities) has been, rather messily, disaggregated from general local authority expenditure on education. This has allowed the Government to control the total amount spent on polytechnics and colleges (with a few minor exceptions), as it does the total grant to the UGC, so ending these institutions' relative immunity from public expenditure reductions that was apparent at the time of the first wave.

Serious as these reductions in public expenditure are likely to be for the future development of higher education in Britain, at least as important in the medium and long term are likely to be the structural changes which these reductions have, if not caused, at any rate reinforced. The first of these has already been mentioned, the creation of a more distinct demarcation line between higher education outside the universities and further education. Although this has come about principally for reasons of financial control, it corresponds closely with the internal and normative momentum of the polytechnics and colleges. Its consequences are also important. The need to establish reasonably logical criteria to distribute the new restricted total grant (the advanced further education 'pool'), if possible informed by academic judgements, has placed greater emphasis on central and professional (academic and bureaucratic) decision-making at the expense of local and political decision-making. It is difficult to estimate the precise significance of these important structural changes for the future trajectory of the polytechnics and colleges. But it may be worth noting that in the United States the existence of a firm demarcation line between further and higher education is seen as inconsistent with the creation of a mass system of higher education, and that considerably more room has been found for the expression of local and political influence than has been the case historically in Britain. In a more restricted British context it is possible that these structural changes may inhibit the development of the colleges of higher education as a vital 'third force' in higher education, and especially perhaps those with proto-community college ambitions; and that they may shrink rather than expand higher education's constituency, with unfortunate results in terms both of student demand and public reputation.

The second change brought about by the cuts since 1973 is likely to have even more important consequences. It is the substantial erosion of the tradition and practice of university autonomy, first through the destruction of the system of quinquennial financing and

later through *both* the explicit selectivity of the UGC in its distribution of the shrinking total grant from the Government *and* the
undermining of the UGC's status and authority by outspoken critics
of the committee's selectivity policy. It is not an exaggeration to say
that the destruction of the quinquennial system between 1973 and
1975 was more serious for the universities than the cuts themselves
during the first wave. At a practical level the disarray caused by
these cuts was compounded many times by the disappearance of the
planning 'horizon' provided by a fixed quinquennium. But the disappearance of the quinquennium, which with automatic compensa-
tion for inflation provided universities with a guaranteed level of
income for five years, was not only an occasion for diseconomy but
also a most important erosion of institutional freedom. From now
onwards the universities and more especially the UGC were subject
to both immediate political pressures and to the vagaries of the
public-expenditure system. For a brief period after 1977 it seemed
just possible that a modified quinquennium might be restored. But
after 1979 this faint possibility disappeared, probably for ever.
'Rolling' triennia and indications of provisional grant for future
years may help to avoid the worst of the planning difficulties caused
by the collapse of the quinquennial system, but as instruments of
political interference they are much more powerful than no indication at all because they describe the direction in which the state
would like the system of higher education to travel.

It is perhaps redundant to mourn the collapse of the quinquennium. No doubt it became inevitable when Whitehall adopted the
practice of regular reviews of public expenditure in the late 1960s,
and the great expansion of the 1950s and 1960s had made it probable
even earlier. There was no way in which universities could expect to
be insulated from the general fortunes of public expenditure once
they became almost entirely dependent on it for their income and
began to consume a significant share. It can also be argued that with
the transition from the liberal to the modern university the quinquennial system allowed universities an unacceptably large degree
of freedom from political influence (especially as, in Britain and
most of Europe, universities were equally insulated from the
influence of private markets). Nevertheless, its collapse remains one
of the most important consequences of the cuts in public expenditure. Nor, of course, has the UGC, that other prop of university
autonomy in Britain, been unaffected by these cuts. The model of
British universities as a collegium of independent institutions

presided over by a benign and barely executive chairman in the shape of the UGC has been gradually replaced by a new model of a bureaucratic system in which the UGC has increasingly been forced by circumstances to play the part of managing director. In 1963 the Robbins Report considered most carefully whether there was, or should be, a 'system' of higher education and concluded cautiously that perhaps there should. Today the emphasis is on the system at the expense of its constituent institutions. Decisions about priorities, which in times of growth can safely be dispersed, have become increasingly centralised as growth has been replaced by constriction.

Again it is difficult to see how it could have been otherwise, although there is room for doubt about whether the UGC by virtue of its rather archaic constitution and its necessarily limited administrative and technical expertise is, as at present constituted, the most appropriate body to undertake such large-scale planning. Its legitimacy to a considerable extent rests on its articulation of the consensus among and within the universities, but its effectiveness as a prescriptive planning body may depend on its ability to resist the present consensus in the name of future needs. Yet the alternative to the UGC is still unclear and would face perhaps more acute problems of acceptability and effectiveness. The reductions in public expenditure have also greatly encouraged the trend towards the more explicit stratification of British higher education not only between but within sectors, a trend which had probably been made inevitable by the expansion between 1955 and 1975. Again it is naive and unfair to regard the UGC's selective distribution of the much reduced university grant in the summer of 1981 as an example of elitist, or simply eccentric, malevolence, rather than in the context of long-term stratification. But stratification, like centralisation, represents an important departure from the traditional pattern of British higher education. Although recent cuts have certainly accelerated both processes, they are the cause of neither. So it may not be entirely accurate to include them as components of the present crisis — or if they are included, it has to be firmly recognised that the crisis is one of much more general application that goes beyond the recent cuts in public expenditure. What seems to have happened in Britain is that the cuts have brought forward problems and issues which we did not expect to experience until a state of mass higher education, with a quarter and more of the age group enrolled, was at least being approached. Martin Trow refers to this as 'the possibility

that an élite system can acquire some institutions and characteristics of mass higher education without growth much beyond
present levels'.[11]

Perhaps one of the most important and ominous of these characteristics is that the university may atrophy not just as a liberal institution but also as an effective and autonomous one. Under present
conditions both its bureaucratic and intellectual authority are being
drained away; the former 'upwards' to system-wide planning
agencies and the state, and the latter 'downwards' into academic
disciplines that find it increasingly difficult to communicate with
each other, and to discipline-based agencies like research councils. It
now seems to be accepted that the university itself, largely because
of the centrifugal consequences of the modern university's academicism, no longer possesses a common intellectual language for
the purposes of setting new institutional directions (in times of
growth) or setting priorities (in times of cuts). Even if a university,
against the odds, does manage to establish rigorous yet acceptable
priorities, there is still no guarantee that these institutional priorities
will add up to sensible priorities for the system, priorities which
inevitably are decided by political as much as academic criteria.

Bureaucratisation, therefore, joins centralisation and stratification as one of the apparently inevitable characteristics of modern
higher education systems. Yet the individual university (or polytechnic or college) remains the institutional context in which
students are taught (and, to a lesser extent because it crosses institutional boundaries more easily and has other foci of loyalty, and
resources, research is conducted). It is also the form in which
academic freedom has been most completely and satisfactorily institutionalised in our society. So the atrophy of the university can
hardly be regarded as of little consequence. Again, the recent cuts
have accelerated and distorted an apparently inevitable tendency.
The UGC's practice of regarding the university system in terms of
subjects rather than of institutions was once a practice that respected institutional autonomy by declining to make such comparisons and by confining the criteria to the strictly academic in any
exercise in discrimination. Today, because of the cuts, this same
practice has the opposite effect. It ignores, and so degrades, the
institutional element in the university system, although the criteria
for discrimination have become to some extent politicised.

It is unclear whether the second component of this shift to pessimism, demand from potential students, is truly an independent

factor or whether it is simply a distorted reflection of the first component, the constriction of resources because of cuts in public expenditure. It is certainly true that the number of students entering higher education increased much more slowly in the 1970s than in the 1980s, even though the size of the 18-year-old age group increased from a trough of 741,000 at the end of the 1960s to 881,000 at the end of the 1970s.[12] The result of this slower growth was that the age-participation rate, the most popular although by no means the most reliable indicator of the social demand for higher education, declined from a peak of 14.2 per cent in 1972/3 to less than 13 per cent at the end of the decade.[13] However, this picture of apparently flagging demand needs to be qualified in several respects. First, the run-down of teacher education and the closure of some colleges of education during the 1970s to reduce the supply of new teachers to a shrinking primary and secondary school system substantially affect the overall picture. The number of full-time students in teacher training in England and Wales fell from 118,000 in 1972/3 to 45,000 in 1978/9.[14] Some but by no means all of these places were replaced by the expansion of other parts and types of higher education. In contrast, during the 1960s the expansion of the colleges of education played a substantial role in the overall expansion of higher education. The expansion of the number of students in universities, from 218,000 in 1972/3 to 286,000 in 1980/1, and in advanced further education apart from teacher training, from 86,000 to 128,000 over the same period, was much closer to the growth rates of the 1960s.[15] Secondly, there was a significant shift away from school leavers towards overseas students (a bubble that has since burst as the result of the decision to charge such students full-cost tuition fees) and towards mature students (a trend that continues and deepens).

Thirdly, the number of part-time students grew rapidly during the 1970s, in the case of men from 142,000 to 190,000 and in the case of women from 22,700 to 81,400.[16] In a system still very much preoccupied with full-time students the weight of part-time students is consistently and inevitably underestimated. Fourthly, qualifications with lower entry requirements like the certificate of education were abandoned in the course of the decade to be replaced by substitute qualifications with normal, and higher, entry requirements such as the B Ed and the Diploma in Higher Education (Dip.HE). Similarly, although less dramatically, the Higher National Diploma (HND) (now in the process of becoming the Business and Technician

Education Council (BTEC) Higher Diploma) with a one A-level entry qualification was frequently replaced by a degree with the conventional two A-level or equivalent entry requirements. So the scope of higher education was actually narrowed rather than widened during the course of the 1970s, as higher education became in a minor way the victim of the process of credentialisation which it had done so much to advance. Fifthly, in a system in which nearly all home students receive a 'student wage', however inadequate, in the form of grants, their value as determined by the government has a direct and powerful impact on the attractiveness of higher education to the potential student. During the 1970s the real value of student grants fell considerably, a process that still continues. For a minority of courses students do not qualify for mandatory grants, but must instead rely on the discretion of their local authority. The successive reductions in central government grant to local authorities, together with inflation and political conservatism on the part of many local authorities, has meant that such discretionary awards have virtually dried up, again significantly depressing demand. Sixthly, the slower growth of the economy during the 1970s has slowed the rate at which the number of graduate jobs has increased, so reducing the economic rate of return on higher education. This slower growth has also probably affected the social reputation of higher education in ways that may be difficult to measure but can still be influential.

Finally, of course, the reduction in public expenditure on higher education has limited the capacity of the system to undertake rapid growth on the scale of the 1960s. Only in a very few areas has the insufficiency of demand rather than the restriction of resources acted as the inhibitor of growth. Certainly, this did not apply to the system as a whole. So throughout the 1970s and up to the present the possibility that the growth of higher education in Britain might be frustrated by a lack of demand remained entirely hypothetical. In the context of restricted public expenditure it is likely to remain so. This is not to say that the appearance of slackening, or better still insubstantial, demand is not a useful alibi for any government already determined to reduce public expenditure on higher education. Still less is it to say that the shifting pattern of student growth during the 1970s does not impose on the modern university difficult choices. For example, it is not clear that the new students of the 1980s can be accommodated as easily as the new students of the 1960s and early 1970s within the framework of values developed by the modern university and its particular emphases on academicism and instrumentalism. But it would probably be wrong to see the grounds for the present pessimism about demand in any anticipation of these difficult future choices. Indeed, to conclude at all that British higher education has at present a 'demand' problem seems to go beyond the evidence of the actual experience of entirely sufficient demand during the last ten years.

The third component in the shift to pessimism in the modern university, the belief that the status and reputation of higher education has seriously declined in recent years is the most insubstantial, but also probably the most influential. This belief that in some fundamental way society has turned against higher education and that reductions in public expenditure on universities and colleges — which are undeniably being made — and the slackening of demand — which is a much more contestable phenomenon — are symptoms of this revulsion is certainly strongly held. It is supported by self-justifying anecdotal evidence but not by the semi-scientific evidence that exists in the form of opinion polls. The mass of the population does not appear to reject and disapprove of higher education to anything like the degree to which higher education itself feels rejection and disapproval. Perhaps to some extent the intellectual class which is so firmly entrenched in higher education has fallen the victim of its own disposition to believe in crises where more pragmatic people simply see difficulties. Perhaps the academicism of the modern university with its preference for theory over empiricism has also made a contribution to this mentality by encouraging those who work in higher education to see their present condition within an ideological framework. Certainly, at a more atavistic level there is a tendency to regard the present reduction in public expenditure on higher education as an attack on the system's values, to an extent that would not be recognised, consciously at any rate, by those most responsible for ordering these reductions. In a similar way there seems to be a desire to over-interpret the evidence about student demand and to fit this over-interpretation into some general theory about the role of higher education, when in fact the evidence is much less clear-cut than appears at first and can be adequately explained by (purely) pragmatic and unconnected causes. For all these reasons it is probable that the sense of pessimism and even crisis that is certainly widespread in the modern university tends to be exaggerated.

However, it has some substance. In the early 1960s a Prime

Minister clearly felt it would add to his political credit if he established a major inquiry into the future of higher education, and had no hesitation in endorsing its carefully considered but nevertheless expansionist conclusions. Although a politician would acquire no political credit for too direct an attack on higher education even today, it is difficult to imagine him (or her) believing that support for an expansion of higher education on the scale recommended by the Robbins Committee would be politically wise. It is fashionable today to suggest that higher education over-sold itself during the great expansion. Suggestive theories about possible connexions between investment in higher education and faster economic growth were put forward, and in a more altruistic mood the expansion of opportunities for higher education was regarded as the culmination of an educational revolution stretching back to the 1870s and beyond, again with suggestive implications for social justice and equality. In both senses the modern university appeared to be a central institution in the creation of a modern society. As 'the expression of an age' it could hardly fail to share the ambitions and the conceits of the society in which it was placed. Criticism with the benefit of hindsight of a pattern of behaviour to which there was no valid alternative hardly seems fair. It is, of course, fair to question the more detailed internal development of the modern university, particularly at the level of its intellectual values. But it seems unrealistic to suggest that these are the grounds for any loss of public reputation, although they may very well be grounds for believing that the modern university may find it difficult to adapt to necessary change in the 1980s and 90s. The only safe conclusion seems to be that higher education, in common with all institutions that did well in the optimistic 1960s, suffered a relative loss of esteem in the more pessimistic later 1970s; that this loss is more symptom than cause of the reductions in public expenditure on higher education that are hurting so much; and that furthermore this loss of esteem is more keenly felt within than without higher education.

So far the evidence for believing that the modern university, at any rate in its British form, is in a state of crisis has been examined in terms of any actual symptoms that have emerged during the past ten years. The result is ambiguous; a crisis of resources plainly exists, a crisis of reputation is too subjective and secondary a phenomenon to be defined satisfactorily. But there is also a need to consider the state of the modern university in terms of both underlying trends in finance, demography, the labour market which will influence the shape of the higher education system in the next ten years, and of its intellectual values. This consideration can be divided conveniently into three parts; structural trends, superstructural trends, and intellectual trends. Among the structural trends two are especially important, the development of the economy in terms both of public expenditure and of graduate employment, and the pattern of demography. The shape of public expenditure on higher education in the recent past has already been discussed and its future shape, of course, can only be a subject of speculation. In the same way economic policy in general is beyond the scope of this book. Nevertheless, there are two questions that are worth asking; is it reasonable to assume that higher education's fortunes would improve with faster economic growth? (and its converse, has the slow-down in growth been sufficient to justify the reductions in public expenditure already made?); and is there evidence that higher education's relative position in public-expenditure priorities is likely to change?

It would, of course, be comforting to believe that the present difficult circumstances in which higher education finds itself are entirely the result of the economic troubles of the 1970s, that higher education had been an entirely accidental and therefore innocent victim of the OPEC oil-price rises, the consequent inflation and slower growth, and now of the deepest recession since the 1930s. If that were the whole story the appropriate response would be a mixture of fatalism and optimism, the former because higher education would simply be a cork tossed about by the great economic waves of growth and recession, inflation and cuts, and the latter because higher education's present troubles could not be regarded as a direct judgement by society on its usefulness. In fact, although it is most of the story, it is not the whole story. Britain's economic performance during the 1970s was not as terrible as is often supposed. If the level of 1975 is taken as 100, GDP rose from 92 in 1971 to 110 in 1979 (falling to 108 in 1980).[17] The increase in household income was even higher. Again, taking 1975 as 100 real household disposable income per head rose from 90 in 1970 to 115 in 1980.[18] Although Britain's economic performance in the 1970s was still inferior to that of other advanced industrial countries, their respective growth rates tended to converge during the course of the decade, no doubt reflecting the relatively greater impact of the OPEC-induced recession on countries without the cushion of North Sea oil. France, for example, in 1971 enjoyed a growth rate about double that of Britain, 4.4 per cent in that year compared to Britain's 2.3 per cent, but over the

decade as a whole France's superiority was reduced to less than half,
3.1 per cent annual growth as opposed to Britain's 2.1 per cent.[19]
So although economic growth in the 1970s was slower than in the
1960s, it was still sufficient to allow for substantial real increases
in the resources devoted to higher education. It is clearly an
exaggeration to suggest that as a result of the economic troubles of
the 1970s Britain cannot afford to expand and improve its higher
education system. Even if expenditure on higher education had
increased at a rate considerably below the increase in GDP, it would
have had to suffer none of the cuts and dislocations it is in fact
suffering. But even this modest improvement did not happen.
Instead, public expenditure as a whole, including debt charges and
transfer payments, remained virtually constant in real terms and as a
result declined as a proportion of GDP from 46.5 per cent in 1974/5,
to 41.5 per cent in 1979/80. Although it has since risen to reflect the
burden of mass unemployment.[20] Within this relatively declining
total there has been a significant shift away from services like
education and towards social security payments made necessary
by rising unemployment. The result is that current expenditure on
higher and further education has declined by 5 per cent in real terms
between 1974/5 and 1981/2.[21] Even within this shrinking total the
decline would have been more precipitate if extra expenditure on
student awards had not been incurred from 1977 onwards to compensate parents of students for the phased withdrawal of child tax
allowances. To sharpen the focus once more, if expenditure in
1979/80 is taken as 100, current expenditure on universities declined
from 119 in 1974/5 to 98 in 1981/2, and on further education and
teacher training (which covers the polytechnics and colleges) from
106 to 90. In both cases further reductions for the subsequent two
years have been announced which are even more serious.

It is important to emphasise that during most of the period covered by these figures a Labour government, ostensibly at any rate
sympathetic to the development of the social state, was in power.
With its replacement in 1979 by a Conservative government actively
committed to the reduction of public expenditure and a radical shift
towards private expenditure in both personal and corporate forms,
it is reasonable to expect that these trends will not only continue but
intensify. So the answers to the two questions posed earlier are
comparatively clear. No, there is no guarantee that expenditure on
higher education would increase in pace with faster economic
growth (because in the past eight years it has fallen in real terms even

though there has been a modest gain in national wealth); and yes, higher education does appear to have slipped in the priorities of public expenditure. Clearly, its present troubles are a part of the general crisis of the social state now that Britain has reverted, as a result of the shocks of the 1970s, to being a low public expenditure country like the United States rather than following the example of the rest of Europe. But it also faces its own particular crisis of resources.

The second aspect of economic activity which has a substantial effect on the prospects of higher education is the labour market for graduates. A buoyant demand for graduates is likely to lead to the political conclusion that higher education should continue to expand, while any evidence of significant slackness in the market for graduates is likely to undermine any case higher education can make for increased public support. Whether such conclusions would always be justified is unclear, however, because of the necessary ambiguity of the labour market which simply measures outcomes rather than revealing causes. The main problem is theoretical; to what extent is the possession of qualifications gained in higher education of intrinsic value to graduates and employers, in the sense that the qualifications represent knowledge and skills that add to the value of the individuals who possess them; and to what extent are such qualifications simply of extrinsic value, important to the individual mainly because they remain comparatively scarce and useful to the employer as a sieve to discover 'natural' talent? In one sense this question, which of course can never be given anything remotely resembling a definitive answer, may not appear relevant or important. After all, it is difficult to argue with the particular value the market places on a particular skill without rejecting free exchange. As a description the labour market, like other markets, is difficult to fault.

So in these straightforward terms a straightforward conclusion is possible. In 1975 A.B. Atkinson concluded:

> The human capital theory leads to the prediction that earnings differentials depend on the degree of training required, in terms both of formal education and of on-the-job training, and are just sufficient to compensate for the cost of this training.[22]

The first part of this statement would be true whether the extra value of the education and training was intrinsic or extrinsic, and the second part should always apply in broad terms if the labour market is working efficiently. Neither statement, however, is much use in trying to establish the value of higher education to the national economy through its output of graduates. For if higher education acts in the labour market mainly as a sieve, its value to individual graduates and their employers is bound to decline as the production of graduates increases. Under these conditions the questions are whether, from a purely economic standpoint, it is more useful to have a finely grained sieve that allows, say, 5 per cent of the population to pass through it or a more coarsely grained sieve that allows, say, 25 per cent to pass; and whether there is a cheaper form of sieve available than the present system of higher education. The answers to these questions are not necessarily harmful to the interests of higher education. It can indeed be argued in the first case that as the secondary school system, essentially for social and political reasons, has become much less differentiated, higher education must take over the schools' role as a sifter and grader of talent. It can also be argued that in a modern economy the skill deficiencies and mismatches occur most damagingly not at the elite but at the semi-elite levels, among technologists, technicians, and middle managers, so this first argument is not even a barrier to the further expansion of higher education. On the second argument it can be said that Britain by international standards has an exceptionally modest higher education 'sieve', and that when considerations of political quietism and cultural renewal are taken into account its present size cannot be regarded as excessive. Equally if higher education acts not as a sieve but actually adds to the productive skills of both individuals and of the nation, this absolute addition to the sum of the nation's capacity would not necessarily or even probably be reflected in higher earnings or demand for graduates. In this sense the labour market can measure relative shifts while leaving absolute gains unacknowledged. There is a series of interesting theoretical questions that arises from this but cannot be gone into here. But it remains important to recognise the inherent limitations of the labour market as an indication of the value of higher education.

There are two more practical qualifications that must also be included in any consideration of the graduate labour market in recent years. The first is that economic growth has been much less rapid during the 1970s than in the 1960s, and unemployment has increased throughout the decade. Althouh there is no evidence to suggest that the advantages which graduates enjoy over others entering the labour market have been significantly eroded, inevitably there has been some softening of demand. The proportion of graduates either unemployed or in temporary employment at the end of the year in which they graduated has risen from 6 per cent in 1970 to 11.3 per cent in 1979 (although this is a fall from a peak of 12.3 per cent in 1977).[23] Within this total arts graduates experienced a significant worsening of their prospects, with 16.2 per cent still seeking permanent employment in 1979 compared with only 6.8 per cent in 1971, while the position of engineering graduates weakened only marginally from 3 to 4 per cent. This is not perhaps surprising in view of the trends in public expenditure and GDP growth reviewed earlier. Arts and social science graduates have always been much more likely to become employed in the public sector than science and engineering graduates. In 1974/5 22.2 per cent of university graduates were employed in central and local government and a further 13.9 per cent in education. In 1978/9 these had been cut to 13.3 per cent and 10.2 per cent respectively.

So it can be argued that in the last seven years the higher education system has had to go through a process of adaptation in its relationships with the labour market, away from meeting the employment needs of the social state so typical of the 1960s and 1970s, and towards satisfying the more traditional manpower needs of industry and commerce. Arts and social studies graduates have naturally found this process most difficult. However, it would be difficult to prove that in general there had been any softening of the graduate labour market during the last ten years. Indeed, when proper allowance is made for much higher rates of unemployment and lower rates of economic activity, it can be argued that the reverse has taken place because unemployment among school leavers has risen at a faster rate than among graduates. This suggests that in a tight labour market the premium on qualifications rises, which is what we would expect if the higher education system was used mainly as a sieve of available talent rather than as a producer of new talent. But this phenomenon cannot be regarded as evidence that such qualifications are in greater demand in a recession-ridden economy; indeed common sense suggests an opposite conclusion. All it proves is that with rising unemployment employers can pick and choose. The paradoxical result is that if there is a generous surplus of labour the 'sieve' quality of higher education can be used to greater effect and so the apparent value of higher education may rise, even though higher education's contribution to the national economy through the production of highly skilled labour may rise, fall or stay the same.

The second qualification is that during the last ten years the output of graduates has continued to rise although more slowly than in the 1960s. The number of first degrees awarded by universities increased from 59,900 in 1970/1 to 76,000 in 1975/6 and the number of higher degrees from 13,300 to 17,000.[24] The number of graduates entering employment increased from 27,500 in 1975/6 to 34,500 in 1979/80.[25] This is a process with a momentum that is not always appreciated. The result of the post-war educational revolution and more especially of the very substantial expansion of higher education between 1960 and 1975 is that the level of educational attainment in the general population has been substantially increased. Ten per cent of 25 to 29-year-olds have degrees or their equivalent compared with less than 2 per cent of 65 to 69-year-olds.[26] This means that even if no further expansion occurred, the number of graduates in the labour force would go on rising for the next 35 to 40 years as the older and less well qualified retire and are replaced by younger and better qualified entrants to the employment market. To the extent that education is a positional good its relative value must decline as more of the population is better educated. This process must have been at work during the ten years following the great Robbins expansion. What is remarkable is that it was not more obvious in terms of the relative decline in graduate earnings. But this process probably has as little relevance to the real value of graduates to the national economy as the contrary process of a more pronounced 'sieve' effect during a labour surplus.

Perhaps in the end there are only two safe statements that can be made about higher education and the labour market for graduates. The first is that although firm conclusions can be reached about the supply and demand for graduates in particular professions and in particular areas of the labour market, it is almost impossible to aggregate them sensibly. The output of graduates is too heterogeneous, and too many enter unspecific occupations not obviously linked with their areas of study. It is therefore almost impossible to answer in a reasonably scientific manner the question of whether Britain is producing too many or too few graduates. Both are essentially political statements rather than objective judgements. The second is that it is still not clear whether the aggregate demand for graduates is truly an independent variable or whether like student demand it is controlled, consciously or not, by the state through other non-higher education policies. After all the state is not only a substantial direct employer, especially of graduates, but also has a major voice in economic policy generally. It is quite impossible to disentangle the demand for graduates from the action of the state. In the end a country needs as many graduates as it feels it needs. So long as large areas of economic activity in which graduates are engaged remain within an essentially national framework, no prescriptive demand can be established, although labour economists of course can describe the present pattern of demand. In those areas of economic activity that are genuinely international suggestive indications of the demand for graduates can be made. These are that there seems to be a correlation between a high demand for graduate and other highly skilled manpower and high productivity, and that this is better understood abroad than at home. But again it falls far short of proof. In conclusion it is difficult to believe that the shifting pattern of demand for graduates has been a serious or an important factor in contributing to the modern university's sense of crisis and depression. Perhaps in a mass system like that in the United States where going to college is more clearly a consumption good, the inevitable decline in the personal rate of return on higher education may act as a disincentive to some potential students.[27] But even in the United States there is little evidence of employers resisting this drift towards credentialisation. In Britain it certainly seems that while there is a danger of reversion to a low public-expenditure state, there is little danger of reverting to a pre-credentialising state.

The declining number of 18-year-olds in Britain after 1983 was at the centre of discussions about the future of higher education in the late 1970s. The government produced two discussion papers on this subject: *Higher Education into the 1990s* in February 1978,[28] and *Future Trends in Higher Education* in March 1979.[29] Both rehearsed familiar facts: the decline in the 18-year-old cohort from a peak of 941,000 in 1982/3 to 622,000 in 1995/6 and the decline in the age-participation rate in the 1970s from 14.1 to 12.8 per cent, and offered a range of 'models' for future policy. These 'models' are now redundant in the strict sense that the problem they set out to solve, how to use spare resources available from the mid-1980s onwards after the peak cohorts had moved through the system, is no longer a problem because far from providing extra resources to cope with these peak cohorts the government has decided to cut the resources already available. But in a more general sense these 'models' remain relevant to the broad issues of whether the demand for places in higher education can be maintained in the face of this demographic decline, and of whether and how higher education should change to stimulate demand if it does not. Clearly, these issues are an important element in the modern university's sense of crisis. Naturally it is demoralising to suspect that the market for what one produces is likely to decline. If the reductions in public expenditure are the largest element in higher education's crisis in the short and medium term, in the long term it is the possibility of a decline in the number of students that causes the most concern.

The conservatively inclined fear that universities in particular will be forced to follow a consumerist path that may compromise their intellectual integrity and erode academic freedom. They may feel that the semi-desperate recruitment of overseas students, willing to pay the new higher fees, that has taken place in some institutions in the past two years is a foretaste of worse to come when the supply of home students becomes equally insecure. The more radically inclined fear that a declining system will be a conservative system, one that in a practical sense will have little margin for innovation and in a wider sense will move further and further away from the semi-liberal, semi-populist values so absent-mindedly acquired during the 1960s and 70s. The polytechnics and colleges, although less alarmed than the universities about the potential threat of new types of students to their intellectual integrity, fear that in the inevitable competition between institutions the universities will use their historical prestige and their freedom from time-consuming bureaucratic procedures to gain an unfair advantage by offering new courses. The research community fears that the research capacity of the universities will be undermined by shrinking student numbers in a system in which resources follow students.

That such a decline is nevertheless inevitable is widely accepted within higher education. In 1981 John Farrant wrote, 'Altogether, within the limits of policy initiatives likely to be taken by either the present government or its successor, there is little prospect of averting a decline in the total size of the higher education system by 1990.'[30] This assessment is based on the authoritative work done from 1977 onwards by the Conference of University Administrators' group on forecasting, and so must be respected.[31] In any case there is no space here to review what is as technical an issue as the demand for graduates. However, two general points should perhaps be made that to some extent qualify this gloomy prospect of decline. The first is that the character of recent growth has not always been fully and properly appreciated. As has already been pointed out, growth in the 1970s was not as meagre as is normally supposed. The apparent decline in the age-participation rate has to be qualified in several respects. The rapid increase in the number of women students was a notable feature of the later 1970s, and it had the accidental effect of making higher education more exclusive in terms of social class. In broad terms what seems to have happened in the 1970s was that middle-class girls caught up with the participation rates achieved by middle-class boys in the 1960s, while working-class participation in higher education, whether by boys or girls, increased very slowly. An objectionable outcome in social terms, in demographic terms this phenomenon was significant in two ways: first, it indicated that participation in British higher education was possible on something like a semi-mass scale (although sadly at present on a distinctly class-biased pattern), so exploding the assumption that higher education should, and could, only attract the very able; secondly, because the decline in the birth rate in the late 1960s and 70s was very much more marked in the working class than in the middle class. Higher education, with its student population still predominantly middle class, will suffer far less from this demographic decline than the aggregate figures suggest.

The second point is that the higher education system is likely to change substantially during the next 10 or 15 years and most probably in directions that will generate new student markets. Already in the 1970s the number of mature full-time students was growing much faster than the total number. In 1966/7 there were 17,700 and by 1979/81 this had grown to 35,200, or 24 per cent of that year's entrants.[32] The Open University produced its first graduates in the 1970s and in 1978/9 had 70,000 students. Although the number of part-time students increased only modestly during the decade, from 18,000 in 1968 to 28,000 in 1978, in the polytechnics and colleges there was much more notable growth, from 117,000 in 1972/3 to 170,000 in 1980/1. None of these trends is decisive in itself, and even together do not become sufficient to compensate for a serious decline in demand for conventional full-time higher education. But they do add up to an interesting move away from a higher education system based predominantly on students who are studying full-time and have come straight from school towards a system with a much more heterogeneous student body. The favourite model in the 1978 discussion paper was 'Model E', which postulated much greater commitment to part-time students, less rigidly structured courses, and to the principles of continuing education.[33] This model was popular because it seemed the best way to keep the money and the students as well. As a brave new future it seemed to lack credibility, but in a more modest way as a gradual shift of educational values and bureaucratic practices it makes some sense. That is certainly the direction in which the system has travelled in the 1970s and will continue to travel. Whether it can travel fast or far enough to avoid an overall decline in the size of the system in the late 1980s is not, of course, clear. The fear that it might not, with all the damaging consequences of substantial contraction, and the fear that it might, with its unknown consequences for standards, values, even integrity, are both part of the modern university's sense of crisis.

The superstructural reasons for higher education's shift to pessimism are much less easy to specify because they are concerned with the values and even 'mood' of society. Yet this difficulty cannot be used as an excuse to ignore them, because they make up the social and political context in which more direct and structural factors like public expenditure and student and employer demand have to be considered. Four main bundles of changing values can perhaps be identified, which although they are by no means consistent have all contributed to higher education's present mood of crisis. The first is the influence of the student troubles of the late 1960s and early 70s in particular the growth of youth culture, and the development of the 'New Left' as a social as well as a purely intellectual phenomenon. The influence of these events on the external reputation of higher education was almost certainly negative. Politicians, employers, school teachers, all of whom had a strongly positive attitude towards the university up to that point, became much more critical in the 1970s. But their influence on the internal character of the modern university was equally significant. Many scholars and teachers saw these disturbing events as a direct threat to the intellectual and cultural integrity of the university. This revolt by educated youth seemed to challenge not only the academicism so valued by those within the university — what other interpretation could be placed on its anti-intellectualism and frequent irrationality — but also the instrumentalism so valued by the politicians who had argued for the expansion of higher education, the taxpayers who had paid for it, and the employers who had consumed its products. Many in the mid-1970s saw the main threat to higher education as the submergence of cognitive by affective and political values, the displacement of rationality as the commanding principle of the university by a new enthusiasm for experiments in life-styles masquerading as politics.

Norman Birnbaum has criticised this as 'socialization by induction into a limited form of intellectual technique, or in the most vapid case, by exposure to a form of peer-group culture'.[34] Parsons and Platt managed to end *The American University* on a note of conditional optimism, but only after raising, although rejecting, a semi-Spenglerian speculation about the possibility of a destructive undermining of the academic system and through it a repeal of the educational revolution which they saw as a key characteristic of modern society.[35] It would be wrong to underestimate the contribution this apparent threat to rationality made to the gathering gloom in higher education during the 1970s. Long after the memory of the actual events themselves had faded, the power of the threat remained. Although in Britain this threat to the integrity of the modern university was never as intense or as persistent as in the United States or the rest of Europe, and although the abrupt end of growth as a result of recent cuts in public expenditure has made such an eventuality much more remote than it appeared in the early 1970s, it probably continues to be a major if unacknowledged factor in the pessimism, conservatism, and timidity of many of those in higher education today. They have seen the future — and it does not work.

The second bundle of changing values is the, highly dubious, rise of 'post-materialism'. In broad terms this is the tendency for public opinion, especially its younger and richer components, to place a higher value on non-material qualities like freedom of expression and a greater say in political decisions rather than on purely material causes like the fight against inflation or the maintenance of public order. Bernard Cazes in a recent paper to an OECD conference on social policies interprets this movement towards 'post-materialism' as potentially highly beneficial to the future prospects of the Welfare State because those who emphasise qualitative rather than quantitative advance in society are likely to see the activity of the Welfare State as especially relevant. After all, the supply of services outside the normal market processes of exchange, the making of regulations and the setting of standards by public authority, and the redistribution of income through progressive taxation and transfer payments, are all methods of public policy that seem appropriate to achieving communal and qualitative goals. Indeed Cazes sees this as a benign coincidence.

> It is as if the emergence of new values and new types of scarcity was precisely timed as a fresh stimulus to take the place of the impetus which used to be generated by the availability of a substantial budgetary dividend for distribution each year.[36]

Nor is he discouraged by the fact that 'post-materialist' values appear to be most strongly entrenched among the young and the rich, who in any case we would expect to be less preoccupied by immediate material needs. He writes:

> If it is assumed that the Welfare State still, at least potentially, represents a break with the logic of a bourgeois-capitalist order, the link we have observed between middle-class membership and the espousal of new values would be an element of support for the optimistic interpretation, since in the past the members of the middle class have been the defenders of traditional values.[37]

Others have disputed not only this relatively optimistic interpretation of the influence of 'post-materialist' values on social policy, but also whether such values have become more influential, and Cazes himself is sceptical of the claims for the importance of 'post-materialism' put forward by Roland Inglehart in *The Silent Revolution*.[38] Nevertheless, there are two broad factors that support the argument that such values have become more important: first, post-war prosperity has inevitably moved the preoccupations of most of the population away from basic material needs towards, at the very least, optional consumerist needs which might include qualitative and cultural needs (this trend, of course, could well be in the process of being reversed by the present recession); secondly, the growth of a substantial intellectual class, based largely in the non-market public sector, has greatly increased the number of people whose cultural bias is likely to be towards 'post-materialism'.

But even if such values have increased in importance, their influence on the modern university remains ambiguous. Structurally as part of the Welfare State the university could only benefit from any change in social values which made it less likely that the Welfare State would be reduced as economic growth declined or stopped.

However, to the extent that 'post-materialism' is another way of describing those disturbingly affective and non-cognitive values already so familiar from the student troubles of the late 1960s and early 70s, this phenomenon is likely to be seen as a threat to academic integrity. A tentative conclusion would be that the latter aspect is likely to be of much greater influence than the former on the development of the modern university. If 'post-materialism' exists at all, its influence on public policy seems not only negligible but negative, at any rate in Britain. Public expenditure on services has been cut more than can be justified by the slow-down of economic growth not less as this hypothesis would suggest. It is difficult not to conclude that 'post-materialism' does not represent a change of heart in society at large, but is a particular aspect of the formation of a strong intellectual class. In other words, because this intelligentsia is very much based in higher education itself, 'post-materialism' is an internal experience of the modern university more than it is an external phenomenon. As such it is not necessarily grounds for optimism, because it continues to carry, at a low level, the threat of an undermining of rationality by non-cognitive values, and, at a higher level, presents the risk of a growing gap between the still essentially materialist values of lay society and the arguably 'post-materialist' values of higher education. As the first would be a threat to the academicism of the modern university and the second would be a threat to its instrumentalism, 'post-materialism' is better regarded as a contributor to higher education's present crisis than as its potential salvation.

The third superstructural element in this crisis is a by-product of the successful expansion of higher education in the 1950s, 60s and 70s. This is that as higher education has become much more widely available, it has inevitably become less precious, in a precise economic sense and in a more general social and cultural sense. The first of these is easy to understand: the more graduates there are, the smaller will be the economic value of a degree to the individuals who possess them. The decline in the rate of return on higher education therefore is an entirely predictable phenomenon. It is also a very old phenomenon. In the eighteenth century Dr Samuel Johnson complained 'the indiscriminate collation of degrees has justly taken away that respect which they originally claimed as stamp, by which the literary value of men so distinguished was authoritatively denoted'.[39] This argument has been developed in a more systematic form by Fred Hirsch in *Social Limits to Growth*.[40] Hirsch argues that an increase in demand for superior jobs can be expected to accompany the growth of the material economy because with their material needs better satisfied people are readier to devote more resources to improving their work situation. This is likely to increase the resources devoted to formal education, but this in turn will reduce the efficacy of education in securing access to higher level jobs. 'One man's higher qualification devalues the information content of another's.'[41] To the extent that education is a positional good from the perspective of the individual, or a sieve from the perspective of employers, more of it is needed to produce the same effect. However, a general expansion of educational opportunities does not help to allocate individuals to scarce superior jobs. The result is an intensification of the screening process. Hirsch comments,

> the expansion of educational credentials. . .has probably increased the attention paid to presumed differences in their quality. Expansion of new universities in England has not weakened the hold Oxford and Cambridge graduates have on particular professions and instead may have increased the value set by employers on the Oxbridge degree.[42]

According to this interpretation the expansion of higher education since 1945 has led not only to a systematic devaluation of degrees and other qualifications, but has also encouraged systematic stratification to ensure the system's continued effectiveness as a sieve. Ordinary unclassified degrees are superseded by classified honours degrees which in turn are capped by postgraduate qualifications. Hirsch argues that the 'inflation' of educational credentials involves social waste in two ways: first, resources are absorbed by the increasingly elaborate screening process, and secondly, individuals are disappointed and frustrated because they have to accept jobs which do not make full use of their education. But there is apparently no way in which this waste can be avoided, because as the average level of educational qualifications in the labour force rises 'a kind of tax is imposed on those lacking such qualifications, while the bounty derived from possessing a given qualification is diminished.'[43] In other words, more education is needed simply to stand still on the occupational ladder.

This process has had important consequences for the modern university, not all of them by any means benign. First, because of the post-war expansion of higher education and the growth since the

1960s of a much less differentiated system of secondary education, the modern university has been forced to operate more explicitly and more effectively as a sieve. As a result there has been a substantial development of the university's role as a job broker. Secondly, the same pressure to act as a sieve has encouraged the stratification of higher education, a process not only of administrative complexity and political difficulty, but also one which undermines the essentially collegial values of the university. Thirdly, the inevitably declining unit value of degrees can easily be misinterpreted as a decline in the value of higher education to society. Fourthly, as expansion of the system has placed greater and certainly more explicit emphasis on the sieve effect, correspondingly less emphasis is placed on the extra-economic and even altruistic aspects of higher education. Fifthly, the declining personal dividends paid by higher education create serious difficulties for reformers who find that to widen opportunity is also to dilute it. All five consequences have had at the best an ambiguous effect on the morale of the modern university.

A sixth consequence has had a more positive influence. This is the acceleration of demand through this process of credentialisation, but even this must be qualified in two ways. First, this demand is driven more by the fear of the consequences of not having higher education than by the positive attraction of higher education itself, and therefore in this important sense is external to the system and its values. Secondly, the importance of higher education in Hirsch's positional economy, combined with the general failure to devise legitimate principles for the equitable rationing of such socially scarce goods, is a source of ambiguity and tension within the modern university which the 1970s have done little to resolve.

The fourth superstructural element in the modern university's sense of crisis is the simplest, the vaguest, but perhaps the most influential. It is the spirit of the age, which since at least 1973 has been depressed and troubled. The modern university as the expression of its age, in Flexner's phrase, is much less insulated from the mood of society than was its liberal predecessor. There can be little doubt that there has been a decisive shift towards pessimism in Britain since the early 1970s and higher education has shared in this mood and been a victim of it. In the first place low growth and lower morale have led to a situation in which investment has been crowded out by consumption. As higher education is still properly regarded in Britain as an investment good rather than as a consumption good, it has suffered from this process. Secondly, the perhaps naïve faith of the 1960s in the benefits of science has been replaced by suspicion and semi-hostility. 'The white hot heat of the technological revolution' has been succeeded by Harrisburg and Sizewell. The modern university, as the largest single producer of scientific knowledge, has seen its public reputation modified as a result. Finally, this social pessimism has been often accompanied by political recidivism, most prominent on the right but also apparent on the left. Modernism in all its forms has become suspect, and this will be discussed in greater detail in the final chapter. Just as the natural sciences are regarded as the ultimate sources of high technologies, such as nuclear energy or genetic engineering which do not enjoy unconditional social support, so the social sciences are seen as responsible for Keynesianism or Fabianism, which seem to be in temporary political eclipse.

The third set of trends, changes in intellectual value, are probably a more important element in the modern university's shift towards pessimism than either the structural or superstructural trends that have been described already. Both the academicism and the instrumentalism that are almost defined characteristics of the modern university have continued to intensify, the former as a result of the apparent logic of the creation of knowledge itself, and the latter because of external pressure on higher education to service the intellectual and training needs of modern society. Although academicism and instrumentalism had a common origin, and although there are strong and interesting parallels between the formation through credentialisation of a new intellectual/professional division of labour and the fracturing of the modern university's knowledge base, more recently tension has developed between these twin characteristics. Finally, the shape of the academic profession has started to shift in ways that are not reassuring, and this factor is the most straightforward. Because of the exceptional pace of expansion during the 1960s the bulk of university teachers in Britain are aged between 35 and 45. Only about 10 per cent are aged over 55, and because of the reductions in public expenditure on higher education in the second half of the 1970s very few new appointments have been made. The age distribution of polytechnic and college lecturers is similar but less pronounced. The tenure enjoyed by most university teachers, the prospect of redundancies, and low mobility between the academic and other professions, mean that almost no new people will come into university teaching and the few that do will be concentrated in temporary or part-time posts. The prospect therefore is for a slowly ossifying core of university teachers surrounded by a semi-proletarianised penumbra of temporary lecturers and researchers on short-term contracts which present plans for 800–900 extra 'new blood' posts cannot really modify. This situation would not be relieved until the final years of the century when the number of new academic appointments will rise, so holding out some hope of a resurgence of intellectual excitement. This prospect of an inexorably aging academic profession is not only an important contribution to the present mood of pessimism within higher education, but is also likely to have important consequences for the intellectual output of the system. There is probably no better argument against the viability of the 'steady state' university than this.

The growing tension between academicism and instrumentalism is also a source of pessimism about the future of the modern university. Increasingly, it is expected by the political order and by civil society to justify itself in more and more explicitly instrumental terms. At the same time its own internal values push it towards a more and more explicit academicism, or concentration on as purely cognitive values as possible. In the early days of the modern university this presented no problem because both appeared to be the processes of intellectual specialisation and even professionalisation that had superseded the elitist amateurism of which the liberal university, a little unfairly perhaps, had been accused. Today disciplines have become so specialist and professions so technical that they can hardly be said to share any common values. The fracturing and refracturing of the natural sciences has been carried over into the social and even the human sciences. Professional education has inevitably been caught up in this movement towards greater and greater specialisation, most especially in those professions with a high technology content. A generation ago the scholar and the senior administrator still had a great many common values, intellectual as much as social. Today the professional academic working away in the factory of his discipline and the practitioner in one of the technologised professions are likely to be at the best ignorant and at the worst actively hostile to each other's values.

This has had four main consequences. The first is the growing tension between academicism and instrumentalism itself. After all, the practical issues that modern society must face are unlikely to fit neatly into the disciplinary compartments designed by professional scholars. Those with professional skills must remain in an abiding sense generalists, while the same restraint on specialisation does not apply to scholars and scientists. Perhaps this tension is at the root of complaints about engineers or doctors being too scientific. For if the professions and other highly skilled occupations are to retain their political status they must not only keep up with the technology that is being produced by the advance of science, but also retain a knowledge of that 'meta-language of command' which implied a generalist or integrative element. Secondly, there is the equally prominent tension between 'knowledge' and pedagogy. After all, academicism in the sense of placing the highest and hegemonic priority on the codification of theoretical knowledge does not have an unchallenged right to be regarded as the primary value of the university in any proper historical perspective. The rather broader concept of the cultivation of rationality in a specific cultural context has as good a claim. Yet this traditional but also liberal purpose has been superseded in the modern university by the instrumentalism and the academicism that are really of more recent origin. But just as there is a growing tension between the specialist and generalist demands of professional education, so a new conflict may be on the point of arising between those values associated with the formation of the intellect in a broad sense and those associated with the advancement of a particular discipline. The growing competition between research and teaching especially in the natural sciences is a symptom of this conflict. In a much wider sense this raises once more the fundamental issues of the relationship between political power and intellectual authority and of the contrasting views of knowledge as a technological product and as a pedagogical process. The answers that are available today are much less categorical and confident than they were a generation ago. This is certainly an important element in the crisis of the modern university.

Thirdly and more speculatively, there may be a conflict within some disciplines between the accumulation of empirical knowledge and the formulation of theoretical knowledge. The former is increasingly and necessarily specialist, while the latter must maintain to some extent a generalist or integrative element. There may therefore be a contradiction between the increasingly detailed and specialist knowledge base of some disciplines and the drive to be more theoretical. Both, of course, are aspects of the modern university's academicism, but they are not necessarily harmonious. At a more practical level there are centripetal as well as centrifugal forces in intellectual life. In more than one discipline the exciting areas of inquiry are to be found not in its cooling core but at the periphery, in the borderland with other disciplines. So perhaps such nuclear attraction can glue disciplines together (and so to reintegrate the university?) with greater force than the electrical repulsion of fracturing disciplines will force them apart. Certainly there is a case for saying that the formulation of revolutionary new paradigms in Kuhn's sense is likely to occur in these intellectual borderlands where the weight of tradition and orthodoxy is less oppressive. If this is ever true, the modern university's commanding assumption that knowledge is best advanced through a process of concentration rather than of generalisation appears much more doubtful.

Fourthly and finally, the process of disciplinary specialisation in the modern university has led to its loss of a common intellectual language. The different branches of knowledge find it increasingly difficult to regard the modern university as in any sense an organic academic society rather than simply as a shared bureaucratic environment, a common material framework of buildings, jobs, careers, and equipment which can be exploited for a variety of more or less cognitive activities that have little in common with each other. If this is true, it has important and depressing implications for the ability of the university to maintain its traditional autonomy and so for the ability of society to organise its intellectual effort under conditions of freedom. It may also mean that the university itself will increasingly be controlled by knowledge bureaucrats who possess a meta-language of bureaucratic command which has filled the vacuum created by the disappearance of a common intellectual language. In a strange and disturbing inversion of the natural order of the liberal university, essentially administrative values would then become superior to intellectual values.[44] The crisis of the modern university, if such is a fair description, is to found much more in these conflicts and tensions within intellectual life than in the present cuts in public expenditure on higher education or the future threat of demographic decline. Certainly, it is in the context of these conflicts and tensions that the resolution of this crisis will be discovered.

Notes

1. D. Bell, *The Coming of Post-Industrial Society*, New York, 1973, p. 487.
2. Ibid., p. 488.
3. *Future Education Policies in the Changing Social and Economic Context*, Organization for Economic Cooperation and Development, Paris, 1979, p. 94, Table 1.

4. Ibid., p. 95, Table 3.

5. M. Trow, *Problems in the Transition for Elite to Mass Higher Education*, Carnegie Commission on Higher Education, Berkeley, 1973, p. 40.

6. *Education: A Framework for Expansion* (White Paper), HMSO, 1972.

7. *Student Numbers in Higher Education in England and Wales*, Education Planning Paper Number 2, HMSO, 1970.

8. *Statistics of Education 1976*: volume 5 (Finance and Awards), HMSO.

9. *The Government's Expenditure Plans 1979–80 to 1982–83*, HMSO, 1979.

10. *The Government's Expenditure Plans 1981–82 to 1983–84*, HMSO, 1981.

11. M. Trow, 'Comparative Perspectives on Access' in O. Fulton, *Access to Higher Education*, Society for Research into Higher Education, 1981, p. 118.

12. *Higher Education into the 1990s*, Department of Education and Science and Scottish Education Department, 1978, p. vi, Table 5.

13. Ibid., p. vi, Table 5.

14. J. H. Farrant, 'Trends in Admissions' in O. Fulton, *Higher Education*, p. 69, Table 2.1.

15. Ibid., p. 69.

16. *Social Trends 12*, HMSO, 1982, p. 54, Table 3.20.

17. Ibid., p. 101, Table 6.1.

18. Ibid., p. 79, Table 5.1.

19. Ibid., p. 102, Table 6.2.

20. Ibid., p. 118, Table 6.25.

21. Ibid., p. 59, Table 3.28.

22. A. B. Atkinson, *The Economics of Inequality*, Oxford, 1975, p. 84.

23. Fulton, *Higher Education*, p. 17, Table 2.8.

24. L. Cerych, S. Colton and J-P. Jallade, *Student Flows and Expenditure in Higher Education*, Amsterdam, 1981, p. 49, Table 6.

25. *Social Trends 12*, p. 55, Table 3.21.

26. Ibid., p. 55, Table 3.23.

27. R. B. Freeman, *Over-educated America*, Academic Press, 1976.

28. *Higher Education into the 1990s*.

29. *Future Trends in Higher Education*, Department of Education and Science, 1979.

30. Farrant, in Fulton, *Higher Education*, p. 65.

31. Conference of University Administrators, Group on Forecasting and University Expansion, *Interim Report 1977*, Glasgow. Conference of University Administrators, Group on Forecasting and University Expansion, *Final Report 1978*, Norwich.

32. Fulton, *Higher Education*, p. 55.

33. *Higher Education into the 1990s*, pp. 8–9.

34. N. Birnbaum, 'Students, Professors and Philosopher Kings' in C. Kaysen (ed.), *Content and Context*, New York, 1973, p. 446.

35. T. Parsons and G. Platt, *The American University*, Harvard, 1973, pp. 386–8.

36. *The Welfare State in Crisis*, Organization for Economic Cooperation and Development, Paris, 1981, p. 155.

37. Ibid., p. 156.

38. R. Inglehart, *The Silent Revolution*, Princeton, 1977.

39. S. Johnson, *A Journey to the Western Islands of Scotland*.

40. F. Hirsch, *Social Limits to Growth*, London, 1977.

41. Ibid., p. 49.

42. Ibid., p. 48.

43. Ibid., p. 51.

44. T. Becher and M. Kogan, *Process and Structure in Higher Education*, London, 1980.

Chapter Five

THE ROBBINS ACHIEVEMENT

Apart from Oxford and Cambridge and the four ancient Scottish universities of Edinburgh, Glasgow, Aberdeen and St Andrews, the British universities are the product of the nineteenth and twentieth centuries. They were created to meet the new intellectual demands stimulated by the growing elaboration of science, the new vocational demands of a rapidly industrialising economy, and the new social demands produced by the development of a liberal democracy and the educational revolution that was its inevitable accompaniment. The University of London has its own peculiar history in which religion played an early prominent part, but most of the great civic universities of the North and Midlands were established through the efforts of local civic and commercial elites. So from their earliest days most British universities were very much part of modern society. Indeed, it is possible to be more positive, and to argue that the universities of the nineteenth century were key instruments of modernisation. This must be emphasised because at the time of their foundation the forms and rituals adopted by the universities, with their echoes of venerable tradition, and subsequently the growing independence of the academic profession encouraged by national policy in the twentieth century, created the misleading impression of universities standing apart from contemporary society.

The comparatively recent origin of the British university system also needs to be emphasised. More than half of our present universities had not been established in 1900. Indeed, almost half have only become universities since 1945, although some of these had much earlier and deeper roots within technical education. If the total number of students is the measure, the British university appears an even younger institution. As there were still only 25,000 full-time students in higher education in 1900 (20,000 in the universities), it is almost possible to regard our university system as a twentieth-century creation. Indeed, a case can be made for

117

regarding our present universities as very much post-war institutions. In 1938/9 there were still fewer than 70,000 full-time students in higher education (50,000 in the universities). In 1980/1 there were more than half a million students, 307,000 of whom were in universities. Although clearly it would be misleading to ignore the influence of tradition, it would be equally misleading not to acknowledge that our present system of universities was largely created during the 1950s and 60s. It happened just yesterday, not a century or more ago. The typical British university today is the product of the UGC's plans for development made during the 1950s, and of the Robbins Committee's blueprint for expansion that was so spectacularly executed during the 1960s and 70s.

This perspective makes it easier to demystify the development of British universities, and so to measure their achievement in more pragmatic and categorical terms. If universities are a largely modern creation, there is less need to uncover the hidden layers of meaning represented in the university tradition and so try to reconstruct some semi-metaphysical purposes and objectives. Instead it is possible to examine the intentions of those responsible in the 1950s and 60s for the effective creation of our modern university system, and to construct from these intentions a set of pragmatic purposes. These, unlike the rhetorical or metaphysical purposes that are so often attached to universities, can then be tested. In this way an analysis of the universities' record can be reduced to manageable proportions: the objectives of the UGC development of the 1950s and the Robbins expansion of the 1960s can be defined, the extent to which the universities have met these objectives can be measured, and some conclusion can be reached about whether these objectives were right and/or realistic (and so the universities could be said to have failed to the extent to which they have not met these objectives), or alternatively whether these objectives were unsound (and the universities right to modify them in the light of the experience of expansion).

There are three important sources which help to reveal the objectives for university development which those who were most influential in pressing for this development had in mind. They are the Robbins Report, with its 178 recommendations and its six appendix volumes; the various publications and pronouncements of the UGC from the mid-1950s to the mid-1970s; and the evidence, inevitably more anecdotal and personal, from those who wrote about the future of the universities, especially those who were actively engaged in building the post-war university system. The sources therefore cover those who proposed, those who disposed, and those who interpreted. Between the three a fairly comprehensive picture can be obtained of the range of objectives the modern British university was expected to meet.

The Objectives of Post-war Development

The first objective was the expansion of the universities. But why? This general desire to support a larger university system needs to be unpicked because it embraced many, often divergent, motives. Some, paradoxically perhaps, saw expansion as a conservative policy — in two senses. First, they argued that because of rising standards in the schools and wider expectations of social mobility after 1945 entry to university was in danger of becoming much more competitive. Sir James Mountford wrote in 1966:

> Before 1945 an intelligent pupil who wished to go to university had no serious problem to face, apart from the often decisive one of finance. There were indeed minimum academic requirements to be satisfied, but there was no lack of places: no college or university was overflowing.[1]

The Robbins Committee itself used this argument, although it moved far beyond it in its support for expansion. The Robbins principle — 'all young persons qualified by ability and attainment to pursue a full-time course in higher education should have the opportunity to do so'[2] — was translated into an operational policy which in practice meant that entry into higher education for those with A-levels should by and large not be allowed to become more competitive than it had been at the beginning of the 1960s.

As the 1950s went by the belief grew that universities were facing a crisis, a damaging excess of demand over supply, all too reminiscent of the housing shortage of the immediate post-war period. Well before Robbins the UGC in 1958 had remarked on the consequences of the rise in the birth rate after the war and the growing tendency of young people to stay on at school and to obtain the qualifications for entry to higher education. The committee added:

> The increase in the number of applications for admission to universities in the last two years [i.e. 1956 and 1957] has been

much greater than the increase in the capacity of the universities to admit students, and this has led to difficulties for candidates, for the schools from which they come, and for the universities themselves.[3]

By 1963 the problem seemed much more urgent. The Robbins Committee entitled its final chapter 'The Short-term Emergency', and suggested that radical expedients such as evening-only degree courses and correspondence courses might be necessary to beat the bulge.

The second sense in which expansion could be regarded as a conservative policy was that any other policy would lead to a substantial change in the position of the universities within higher education. To suppress growing student demand would lead to a perhaps irreversible rise in entry standards. The likely outcome would be to place greater and greater emphasis on academic standards narrowly conceived when admitting students, and so devalue those broader extra-academic qualities to which the liberal university tradition attached considerable importance. Under these conditions the universities might become, in the view of an influential segment of opinion within them, over-academicised; they would certainly be very different from the pre-war universities. To divert student demand into other, non-university, institutions would present a double danger: universities would not only become over-academicised, but they would also lose their hegemony over higher education as a whole.

Certainly, this alternative of keeping the university sector small and exclusive was never seriously considered by the Robbins Committee, although its members were criticised then and later for adopting a policy of expansion that was bound in the end, critics said, to lead to the spread of mediocrity. Lord Annan has argued that the thesis on which this criticism was based did not stand up to examination.

The model on which it is based is higher education in the USSR where there are proportionately few universities and many specialised institutes; a pattern that follows logically in a country which puts faith in manpower predictions and national plans.[4]

For all these reasons even conservatives had little choice but to support the post-war expansion of the universities. Whatever the long-term dangers, the failure to expand would in the short term both jeopardise the internal character of the university and undermine its external status within higher education as a whole. Academic hot-houses by-passed by expansion and pushed to the margin of society could hardly appear an attractive future for institutions that traced their ancestry, however remotely, to the *studium generale* of the Middle Ages, and which in Britain at any rate had acquired particularly incestuous links with the administrative elite.

Others supported the expansion of the universities for less defensive reasons. Renewing the nineteenth-century theme of the universities as instruments of modernisation, they placed particular emphasis on the urgent need to relate university development more closely to post-war social and economic demands. These can for convenience be divided into social demands which naturally took the form of pressure to extend opportunity for higher education, and economic demands which were expressed through the demand partly for theoretical knowledge that could be productively employed and partly for highly skilled manpower. In practice these two sets of demands were very much confused. Both went back to the 1940s. The first was summed up by R. H. Tawney in 1943 when he wrote in a draft for the Labour Party's education sub-committee of 'throwing the universities wide open to ability as distinct from wealth'. The second was as tersely summed up by Clement Attlee when he wrote to Ernest Bevin in 1945 that university expansion was 'a very serious matter, as we cannot hope to solve our post-war problems unless we increase the supply of trained men and women in the various departments of our national life'.[5] The Barlow Committee on scientific manpower took up this theme in its report in 1946. Seven years later the UGC in its quinquennial report predicted that the growth of scientific knowledge would lead to a continued increase in university expenditure. The committee argued that such an increase would be found to be in the national interest

> not only because the dependence of this country on manufactured exports makes it essential for it to keep in the forefront of scientific and technological development, but more generally because its success in solving its internal problems and maintaining its position of responsibility in world affairs is inseparably bound up with its standards of higher education.[6]

Both these themes were taken up strongly in the Robbins Report, which contained what is still probably the best statement of the 'social' case for higher education, and paid far more attention to the parallel 'economic' case than many of its critics have been prepared to concede. The committee saw its task in clear terms:

hmmm ?

> It has come about that, seventeen years after the passing of the great Education Act of 1944, which inaugurated momentous changes in the organisation of education in the schools, we have been asked to consider whether changes of a like order of magnitude are needed at a higher level.[7]

The historical perspective of the Robbins Report is still impressive. The committee saw its responsibility in the context of an unfolding education revolution that reached back at least to 1870. Nor did it shrink from occasional grandiloquence. Having conceded that its plan required a perhaps difficult revaluation of national priorities, the committee wrote:

> Not only is it a probable condition for the maintenance of our material position in the world, but, much more, it is an essential condition for the realisation in the modern age of the ideals of a free and democratic society.[8]

To Robbins the 'economic' case for expansion was always secondary, or perhaps more accurately it was subsumed in the broader 'social' case. The committee believed that, however much general importance needed to be attached to an adequate supply of highly skilled manpower, it was difficult to translate this into detailed operable policies. Having drawn a perhaps over-sharp contrast between manpower planning and student demand as the alternative engines of higher education expansion, the committee chose the latter with perhaps too few qualifications. Yet the Robbins Report made a series of recommendations which showed that it was far from immune from the contemporary enthusiasm for science and technology: it proposed that five Special Institutions for Scientific and Technological Education and Research (SISTERs) along the lines of the Massachusetts Institute of Technology should be established, that the colleges of advanced technology should be promoted to full university status, and that the CNAA should be created, so ending the universities' monopoly of awarding degrees. The committee also believed that some of the regional colleges of technology (now incorporated into the polytechnics) should become universities. If the full Robbins package had been accepted, it would have led to a significant injection of the values and practices of technology into the university system. It is also possible to argue that, if Britain was regarded as being in some kind of technology race with other advanced countries, the Robbins recipe for reform particularly the creation of SISTERs would have been at least as effective a policy as the binary solution adopted a few years later. Perhaps technological excellence at the highest level was, and is, needed as much as technological expertise at the level of advanced further education. Whatever view is taken of this question, it is difficult to sustain the criticism that Robbins ignored technology and the wider 'economic' case for the expansion of the universities.

However, perhaps the most significant achievement of the Robbins Report was to convince most people in universities that substantial expansion of the system could take place without significant erosion of academic standards. The committee was clear that excellence had to be maintained, but it denied that this was incompatible with expansion. First, the report pointed out that past expansion had not damaged standards: 'recent increases in numbers have not been accompanied by an increase in wastage and the measured ability of students appears to be as high as it ever was'.[9] Then it considered in detail the concept of a, limited, pool of ability only to conclude

> we think there is no risk that within the next twenty years the growth in the proportion of young people with qualifications and aptitudes will be restrained by a shortage of potential ability. . . If there is to be talk of a pool of ability, it must be a pool which surpasses the widow's cruse in the Old Testament.[10]

The committee was profoundly convinced of the possibility of improvement without disturbance, and was largely successful in spreading this Whiggish confidence through the universities. Expansion, therefore, became not a threatening prospect but a semi-moral duty.

The expansion of the universities therefore was supported by such an overwhelming majority of those within them largely because of this rich and revealing diversity of motives. Five deserve special emphasis:

*If the universities were not expanded they would become more and more exclusive in their student intake. If this led to their becoming academic hot-houses many of the broader pedagogical goals of the liberal university tradition would have to be abandoned.

*If the main thrust of expansion took place in non-university institutions the university would lose its position as the dominant model for a mature institution of higher education.

*The expansion of the universities was the natural culmination of the educational revolution which had led to a public system of elementary schools after 1870 and to the extension of this system of secondary education after 1944. The progress of this educational revolution was closely allied with the building of a liberal democratic society.

*The advance of science and the growing demand for highly skilled manpower made it essential to expand the universities if Britain was to keep up in the economic race with rival nations.

*A substantial expansion of student numbers could be achieved without any significant erosion of standards because the pool of available talent if it was limited at all was very deep.

These motives carried different weight with different groups and at different times. For the Robbins Committee, and probably the contemporary members of the UGC, the third was particularly important: for successive governments the fourth was perhaps the most influential: for those within the universities the first, second, and fifth were certainly very important. In the course of the 1960s and 70s more and more emphasis was placed on the 'external' third and fourth motives for expansion and correspondingly less on the 'internal' first, second, and fifth motives.

The second objective of the post-war development of the universities was to encourage more liberal forms of higher education. In practice these were largely interpreted in terms of broader first-degree courses. This was a persistent and powerful theme in most of the reports of the UGC in the 1950s and early 60s, although it became significantly weaker after the mid-1960s. It was, of course, a commanding motif of the Robbins Report itself. In 1958 the UGC stated: 'But the acquisition of specialised knowledge is not the only, or the most important, benefit which a student should derive from his course. It should also give his mind a cutting edge.'[11] And a little later:

> The danger, at a time when the volume of available knowledge even in narrow fields is so enormous, is that the utilitarian purpose of the special subject will drive the student to memorise as much as

possible of this knowledge in the limited time available, leaving him no time to develop his power of thought or to acquire any knowledge outside this subject. We fear that the drive to acquire a maximum of specialised knowledge to the exclusion of other things is too often abetted by the teacher, himself perhaps the victim of excessive specialisation.[12]

After the committee's visitations to universities in 1960/1 it again drew attention to the need to guard against the dangers of excessive specialisation. In its 1964 quinquennial report the UGC commended the academic planning boards of the new universities for their determination to achieve breadth in the undergraduate curriculum.[13]

The Robbins Committee had no doubt that this was the right approach. The second of its objectives for higher education eloquently addressed this issue

> While emphasising that there is no betrayal of values when institutions of higher education teach what will be of some practical use, we must postulate that what is taught should be taught in such a way as to promote the general powers of the mind. The aim should be to produce not mere specialists but rather cultivated men and women. And it is the distinguishing characteristic of a healthy higher education that, even where it is concerned with practical techniques, it imparts them on a plane of generality that makes possible their application to many problems — to find the one in the many, the general characteristic in the collection of particulars. It is this that the world of affairs demands of the world of learning.[14]

So it is hardly surprising that the Robbins Report recommended that a higher proportion of students should receive a broader education in their first degrees. Indeed, the committee emphasised that this was central to the philosophy of its report: 'We regard such a change as a necessary condition for any large expansion of universities.'[15]

This broader undergraduate education would take two forms, more degrees that combined two or more subjects and more pass degrees 'at a less arduous level'. Perhaps one of the weaknesses of Robbins was that at this stage the argument for general undergraduate education faltered. The committee did not explain the suitable content and structure of such education in sufficient detail to allow effective policies to be developed. It insisted that it was not arguing for breadth as such, regardless of the suitability of the combinations of subjects, and also that students should not be made guinea pigs on 'experiments with totally new subjects without textbooks or a commonly accepted core of methods of thought', a considerable caveat. The committee was equally cautious in its detailed remarks about pass degrees. It expected the number of such courses and of students on them to remain small, and that the majority of students would still embark on honours degree courses despite the blight of specialisation. The pass-degree route was consigned to 'the slower and less able student'.

Both the commitment of the Robbins Committee to the principle of general undergraduate courses and their ambivalence about their detailed implementation echoed the contradictory opinions on this question within the universities. First, the commitment, which had three discordant elements. The first was a perhaps reactionary sentiment, a longing for the integrative disciplines that had played such a creative role in the elite pedagogy of the liberal university. The second, in contrast, was almost futurist, a prediction that in the future the turnover of theoretical knowledge would be so great that those with an over-specialised higher education would be saddled with obsolescent information and skills. So the acquisition of adaptable, and necessarily general, intellectual skills had to have a higher priority than the acquisition of detailed information and specialised skills. The third was the discreet recognition that a substantial expansion of the universities would in time suck in students who although not necessarily 'slower and less able' might lack the sharply focused intellectual commitment of students in a smaller and more selective system. All three elements came together to make up this sustained commitment to more general undergraduate education.

The ambivalence of Robbins about the details is equally interesting. For the enthusiasm of the committee, and of the UGC, for general courses was tempered in three ways. First, both contemplated a substantial expansion of postgraduate courses, although they attached a low priority to extending the length of first degree courses. The need for this was clear to Robbins. The expansion of knowledge had made it impossible for a student to master a subject within the limits of a first degree. Attempts to do so had led to serious overloading which had not only made first degrees too specialised, but failed to achieve this objective. The worst of both worlds in fact. The committee was also concerned to extend and improve professional education, but believed that in most cases this could best be done at a postgraduate level on the firm foundations of a coherent general first degree. The second qualification was that considerations of manpower planning were never entirely banished even from the Robbins Report. The committee paid considerable attention to the split between arts and sciences, and half-recommended, half-predicted that the proportion of students studying science and technology subjects (excluding medicine) in universities should rise from 45 per cent in 1962/3 to 56 per cent in 1980/1, and that within this increase there should be a relative shift from science to technology. From the late 1960s the UGC became increasingly absorbed with this kind of macro-manpower planning in general and the arts/science split in particular. Of course, this concern did not directly contradict the enthusiasm for more general undergraduate education. General science courses could be conceived as well as general non-science courses, but in practice because of the greater fragmentation of scientific knowledge were much more difficult to implement. So it is probably fair to regard the concern with the arts/science split, to the advantage of the latter, as subversive of the enthusiasm for more general degrees.

The third qualification of this enthusiasm was really also the third objective of university development: it was knowledge itself, or in the words of Robbins 'the advancement of learning'. For, as has been emphasised in Chapters 3 and 4, the modern university placed the codification of theoretical knowledge at the centre of its enterprise. Even the Robbins Committee, in many ways a body very much attached to the older values of the liberal university, was prepared to concede this although rather grudgingly. The advancement of learning was the third of its four objectives for higher education. 'The search for truth is an essential function of institutions of higher education and the process of education is itself most vital when it partakes of the nature of discovery.'[16] By accepting that this search for truth, which in the inevitable form of research would be almost wholly determined by the theoretical preoccupations of specialised disciplines of knowledge, was an essential function of the university, *and* that the teaching of students had to be conducted in close association with research the Robbins Committee made it unlikely that its scheme for general degrees would be developed on any scale. The committee was constrained by its conviction that 'it is the essence of higher education that it introduces students to a world of intellectual responsibility and intellectual discovery in which they are to play their part. . .an ounce of example is worth a pound of exhortation'.[17] Although uneasy, the members of the committee did not break with this orthodoxy. In a significant sense the interests of the 'slower and less able' student who was most likely to benefit from a broad undergraduate education were sacrificed to the high-flyers who aspired to 'a world of intellectual responsibility and intellectual discovery'. It made the binary policy inevitable.

For the advancement of learning no longer took place within the liberal context of integrative human disciplines but in the amoral chaos of specialised, disintegrative disciplines. It was through this increasingly complex division of intellectual labour that the modern university had become an efficient knowledge machine. Both the members of the UGC and of the Robbins Committee were aware of two persuasive facts. The first was that this division of labour had been much more forcefully followed through into a parallel differentiation or stratification of higher education in rival nations than in Britain. In the USSR, very much in the mind of the Robbins Committee because of the recent successes of Soviet science, research and the training of the ultra-skilled had been segregated into specialist institutions. In the United States the much greater diversity of the system had allowed the so-called research universities to concentrate on science and scholarship and relatively to degrade undergraduate teaching. In contrast to both, Britain's more homogeneous universities seemed a more primitive knowledge machine. The second was that the greatly increased public expenditure on universities was regarded by successive governments as an investment in science, technology and other useful knowledge. They were the advance factories of ideas that would invent the future, or at any rate prevent our falling too far behind the Americans and Russians (or, a decade later, the French and Germans).

In any case neither UGC nor Robbins could reverse the priority that the universities themselves had given to the codification of academic knowledge as the hegemonic purpose of higher education. They now saw themselves primarily as intellectual rather than pedagogical institutions. The specialisation of knowledge first stimulated the divorce of teaching and research, and then was in turn stimulated by the new independence, even dominance, that the preoccupations of research came to enjoy within the academic profession. The 'visible college' of institutions which had been formed to teach students waned, and the 'invisible college' of academic disciplines which transcended these institutional boundaries waxed. This priority among university teachers could be measured: at the beginning of the 1960s 47 per cent of them had PhDs, and 59 per cent had first-class honours degrees. The trend also seemed to be plain. In its appendix on teachers the Robbins Committee stated: 'By and large, the junior staff in each faculty devote more time to research than lecturers, and lecturers more than senior staff,'[18] a clear indication of a growing preoccupation with research.

It is of course difficult to measure the development of this research culture except in anecdotal and impressionistic terms. Yet its growing force was unmistakable in the 1950s and 60s. In 1958 the UGC quoted, with plain regret for their passing, the reported views of Jowett on research:

> Research, he seems to have thought, was more often than not a self-indulgence, an agreeable escape from more urgent, if more tedious, duties. . .If teaching was their function they must put their pupils first and do their research in their spare time.[19]

The committee then described the new priority that research had come to enjoy at the end of the 1950s.

> Since Jowett's time the wonders of scientific discovery and technological achievement have created an atmosphere in which it is almost taken for granted that to take part in scientific research is the highest destiny of man. We have heard it suggested that the standard of a university institution is measurable by the amount of research which is done there.[20]

By 1963 the Robbins Committee seemed to have shed most of the nostalgia that still affected the UGC in the 1950s on the issue of research, although it did recommend that promotion to senior lecturer should depend on other factors besides published work. When the committee came to consider the future evolution of the colleges of education and the regional colleges of technology, both of which it recommended should be incorporated eventually within the university system, it readily assumed that they too would become more involved in research. 'Where the will and the capacity for original work exists it should be encouraged, and rewarded.'[21] Throughout the 1960s the strength of this preoccupation with research increased. The UGC forgot whatever nostalgia it had once felt for more traditional pedagogical preoccupations. By 1964 the committee felt able to emphasise with apparent equanimity the dual functions of the university 'about half of their activities are devoted to the spreading, and about half to the advancement, of knowledge'.[22] At the end of the next quinquennium in 1968 the strength of the research culture had become such an established fact that the committee felt no need to make general observations on the proper balance between research and teaching and confined its attention to managerial issues raised by the universities' research effort.[23]

The fourth broad objective of university development since 1945 was to establish a new relationship with lay society. The Robbins Committee had no doubt about the solemn obligation of universities to contribute to a broader mission of cultivation than simply educating students to fulfill socio-economic roles after graduation and advancing the frontiers of knowledge. The committee's fourth objective of higher education was 'the transmission of a common culture and common standards of citizenship'.[24] It was the responsibility of higher education, in partnership with the schools and the family, to provide 'that background of culture and social habit upon which a healthy society depends'. But in the course of the 1950s and 60s this traditional view of the university's obligation to sustain high culture was modified in two important respects. The first was the growing self-confidence of the academic profession. The phrase 'donnish dominion' is A. H. Halsey's, and it accurately and eloquently evokes the power that the academic profession in Britain came to enjoy after 1945 and especially during the 1960s. Yet this outcome would have been difficult to predict in the middle of the nineteenth century when the development of a modern university system got under way. With the exceptions of Oxford, Cambridge, the four ancient Scottish universities, and, more arguably, Durham and the first London colleges, British universities were the products of civic or industrial initiatives in which the academic profession itself played almost no part. Universities were established by lay society even if they were later to come under the commanding influence of the dons. Until well into this century they suffered from a chronic financial insecurity which inhibited the early or easy consolidation of the academic profession, because only a few senior professors could be offered secure jobs and properly rewarded careers, and universities remained dependent on philanthropy, industrial sponsorship and student fees. For this reason they remained for a long time subservient to industrial and other lay benefactors, whose expectations were very down to earth. Only Oxford and Cambridge had the social eminence and so independence to pursue the more elevated roles of scholarship and pedagogy. For the rest it was 'useful' science and technical training. As in the rest of Europe and the United States the theoretical sciences grew out of the practical sciences rather than the other way round — artillerymen became mathematicians and later physicists (and back to artillerymen, some would add, in the nuclear age) — but in Britain two special factors intensified the practical bias of the early modern university. The first was the pragmatism of the British intellectual tradition; the second the fact that universities, although sponsored by the state, were not maintained or controlled by the state, and their teachers were not as in so many countries civil servants. This made them chronically dependent on private subsidy, and so left them with little freedom to insist that the practical sciences should be subordinated to the theoretical.

In the nineteenth century both these factors discouraged the consolidation of the academic profession; in the twentieth they had the opposite effect. The pragmatism of the British intellectual tradition inhibited the development of an oppositional intelligentsia which might make its natural home in higher education and so provoke the suspicion of established society. As a result the state saw no reason to distrust the growing autonomy of higher education which was a precondition of the 'donnish dominion'. This may help to explain a puzzling paradox: the exceptional autonomy enjoyed by British universities, and the almost as exceptional degree of solidarity between higher education and political society. The second factor had a similar effect. The state's lack of a strong financial interest in the early universities allowed them to develop remarkably autonomous forms of government, which have been maintained even though the state has become the only serious source of income for most universities. If, for instance, all university teachers had been civil servants, it is difficult to imagine how the academic profession could have established so successfully its 'donnish dominion'.

The outcome was that in the twentieth century the state and the academic profession became allies, even if they did not always recognise each other's support. The keys to the successful consolidation of the academic profession in Britain can perhaps be found in the two factors already mentioned. Higher education's commitment to practical sciences, which was reinforced by the pragmatism of the British intellectual tradition, not only meant that the forms of knowledge being produced by the early modern university were not seen as at all dangerous or subversive but as an essential support for an industrialising society. In the twentieth century this latter aspect received even greater emphasis because of the growing importance attached to scientific knowledge of all kinds, and to its technical application. So the state had a growing incentive to give a growing subsidy to such an obviously beneficial activity. The First World War was perhaps especially decisive. In 1919 H. A. L. Fisher, President of the Board of Education, wrote that at the start of the war 'there was a most inadequate apprehension of the results which might be derived from the laboratories and brains of the universities'.[25] During the war the DSIR, the forerunner of today's research councils, had been established.

This heightened appreciation of the potential contribution of higher education led naturally to much increased state subsidy. Already in the early years of this century R. B. Haldane's *ad hoc* University Colleges Committee had recommended the creation of a permanent Advisory Committee on University Grants which became in 1919 the UGC. These last two were composed almost entirely of members of the academic profession or close allies, and the last was made responsible to the Treasury rather than the Board of Education so emphasising official acknowledgment of the profession's growing status. By 1938 a third of university income came from state grants and by 1951 two-thirds. The effect of the state's financial intervention was not to reduce the autonomy of the universities but rather to enhance it. For state grants not only introduced an alternative source of income to industrial subsidy, but also encouraged industry to redouble its support for higher education for reasons very similar to those which the state had found so persuasive[26]. The universities found that their services, which were now regarded as much more valuable, were being bid for by both state and industry. So the strategic position of the academic profession was immensely improved. It could begin to pick and choose which services it cared to provide, and at the same time now had the financial security and prosperity that could offer most teachers in higher education a proper career structure and reasonably well-paid jobs.

The second modification to the traditional view of the university's responsibility to and relationship with lay society, the much closer engagement of the university with immediate social issues, seemed at first sight to contradict the first, the rise of the 'donnish dominion'. For through the 1950s and 60s public expectations of the practical utility of universities increased. A large part of this was the new enthusiasm for science and technology. Universities as the producers of nearly all the science and a good part of the technology inevitably became the focus of greater public attention. At the same time Robbins' 'background of culture and social habit', for which universities bore a tripartite responsibility with the schools and the family, underwent a social democratic revision. To the extent that post-war British society accepted that the creation of greater equality had become a legitimate and overriding aim of public life, the universities were expected to adapt to this new priority. Just as the late Victorian university had had to accept that lay society expected it to produce the future *cadres* of administration and empire, so the post-war university had to accept that the creation of greater equality had to be incorporated in some way within the traditional goals of the university. As the thrust to equality was most obviously expressed through improved access and faster expansion, objectives which the majority of the academic profession shared, this presented little difficulty.

So the conflict between these two modifications, autonomy and engagement, was probably much less than might have been expected. The 'donnish dominion' was largely based on the ability of the universities to satisfy the scientific and manpower demands of both the state and of industry. It had been established with the acquiescence of rather than in opposition to lay society. In no sense did it represent a successfully contested claim to stand aside, either as the critic or conscience of bourgeois society or as the guardian of high culture in the face of mass society. So the new relationship that developed between universities and society after 1945, the fourth objective of university development, had two prominent features. First, the universities not only accepted but welcomed the view that they should be, in Flexner's phrase, 'an expression of the age'. Far from discouraging public expectations of their utility, they encouraged them. But, secondly, the academic profession believed that it possessed the authority and the expertise to control the terms on which these very welcome exchanges should take place.

The broad objectives of post-war university development therefore can be summarised in the following terms.

Expansion Without Tears

The number of students of universities must be expanded because of the new demands of science and technology, because it was the natural culmination of an educational revolution reaching back to 1870, and because it could be accomplished without lowering standards. If the universities were not expanded, awkward rival institutions might be created and universities themselves might become over-academic hot-houses.

The Liberalisation of Undergraduate Education

The structure and content of courses must be reformed because the proliferation of knowledge had overloaded the first degree, because the specialisation of knowledge had begun to undermine the broader pedagogical ambitions of undergraduate education, because the increasing turnover of knowledge had increased the dangers of obsolescence, and because students from less intensely academic backgrounds might be attracted into the universities.

The Development of a Strong Research Culture

The new emphasis on science and technology, the growing autonomy of the academic profession, and the sophistication of theoretical knowledge made it inevitable that universities should give a higher priority to research than in the pre-war period. Universities came to be seen as intellectual machines rather than pedagogical institutions.

Autonomy and Engagement

Universities should be more exclusively controlled by the academic profession itself, not to distance them from lay society but to maximise their utility.

Expansion Without Tears

The first of these objectives was half-achieved. On the one hand the universities successfully accomplished a most spectacular expansion of student numbers. In 1957/8 there were only 97,851 full-time students in British universities; ten years later this had more than doubled to 205,195; and ten years after that in 1977/8 the total stood at 277,000. According to the latest available figures there are 309,000 full-time students in the universities. So in less than a generation there has been more than a three-fold expansion in the size of the system. There has also been a large increase in the number of universities. In 1957 there were still only 24 institutions on the UGC list; by 1982 there were 53 institutions. Some of this increase is explained by the fact that the constituent colleges of the University of Wales have come to receive their grant directly from the UGC. But most of it is accounted for by new foundations — East Anglia, Essex, Kent, Lancaster, Sussex, Warwick, York, Stirling and Coleraine (which is now being amalgamated with the Ulster Polytechnic) — and by the promotion of the former colleges of advanced technology — Bath, Bradford, Brunel, City, Loughborough, Salford, Surrey, Heriot-Watt, Strathclyde and Chelsea (which became a school of London University rather than a separate institution).

This spectacular expansion was not achieved at the cost of lower standards, so justifying the optimism of the Robbins Committee and disproving the well-publicised fears of those who cried that 'more means worse'. In October 1963 8.6 per cent of first-year students in arts subjects had obtained three D grades at A-level or worse.[27] Nineteen years later in 1982 4.6 per cent of newly admitted arts students had found places through the clearing scheme operated by the Universities Central Council on Admissions (UCCA) and their A-level scores ranged from 9 (the equivalent of three C grades) to 6 (the equivalent of three Ds).[28] Although the comparison is not exact, it certainly suggests that there has been no decline in the level of achievement of successful candidates despite the three-fold increase in the number of places. A similar pattern can be seen in social studies, in which 11.6 per cent of successful candidates in 1963 had only D-grade passes at A-level, compared with only 6.1 per cent of successful candidates admitted through UCCA clearing in 1982 (who had A-level scores in the range 10 to 7). With most subjects the same broad pattern prevails. A final comparison will underline the evidence. In 1963 54 per cent of all candidates in non-technology subjects and 68 per cent of those in technology were admitted. In 1982 45 per cent of all candidates (77,752 out of 171,496) were similarly successful.

However, the success of expansion has to be qualified in two respects. First, its scale did not in the end make it unnecessary to establish rival institutions in the form of the polytechnics with consequences that will be discussed in Chapter 6. The pattern of expansion tells the story. The decade from 1958 to 1968, before the polytechnics got under way, was a period of unrestrained university expansion with a growth of 110 per cent in student numbers. The next decade, in which the polytechnics successfully established themselves, was a period of much slower growth: a 35 per cent increase in the number of university students between 1968 and 1978.

Second, although the strongest motive for university expansion in the first instance may have been the desire to enhance Britain's effort in science and technology, the most rapid growth was not in science and technology but in social studies. In 1960/1 39.6 per cent of university students were in science and technology compared with 28.3 per cent in arts, 17.3 per cent in medicine and agriculture, 10.8 per cent in social studies, and 4 per cent in education.[29] Twenty years later in 1980/1 science and technology's share had fallen a little to 37.4, arts and medicine fallen more sharply to 20.4 per cent and 12.6 per cent respectively, education stayed the same at 4.1 per cent, and social studies increased to 25.4 per cent.[30] Of course, this proportional decline in science and technology students masks the very substantial increase in their actual number. It is also misleading if it leads to the conclusion that universities deliberately held down science and technology's share. In fact there were empty places in science and technology departments in most universities throughout this period, and universities consistently admitted science and technology students with lower entry qualifications than those possessed by arts and social studies students.

Liberalising the Curriculum

The second objective of university development, the broadening of undergraduate education, has not been met. It certainly has not been met by the universities. What progress has been made, and much of that has been precarious and conditional, has been made in the polytechnics and other non-university colleges. In universities the overwhelming majority of undergraduates continue to be enrolled on degree courses. In 1980 of the 70,461 who successfully completed courses 94 per cent were awarded degrees. The overwhelming majority of these were honours degrees in single subjects awarded after full-time study. In 1980/1 only 20 per cent of university undergraduates were studying more than one subject, and only 17 per cent were not on honours degree courses. Yet two of the reforms proposed by the Robbins Committee had been the more general adoption of mixed-subject and general degrees, and of pass degrees that avoided the excessive concentration so often involved in study at honours level. The evidence appears to show that universities have resisted both reforms. A further recommendation made by Robbins has enjoyed as slight a success: the committee recommended that more postgraduate courses should be developed to prevent undergraduate courses becoming overloaded. Yet the proportion of students who are undergraduates is actually higher today (84.2 per cent) than it was in 1961/2 (82.9 per cent). The one qualification that must of course be made is that many postgraduate courses today are taught rather than research courses, another reform which Robbins proposed. Yet overall there has been almost no significant change in the pattern of undergraduate education, although the arguments employed by the Robbins Committee twenty years ago to support such a reform are stronger than ever.

At first sight this conservatism is puzzling. During a period when Britain developed an at least semi-mass system of university education, the hegemony of the honours degree has been virtually without serious challenge. Indeed, it can be argued that it has been reinforced by the development of degree courses in the polytechnics and colleges under the auspices of the CNAA. Part of the explanation is simply banal. There was in the 1950s and 60s a large, unsatisfied demand for higher education places, as the subsequent successful expansion so clearly established. As the universities were largely in the business of offering specialised degree courses it was almost inevitable that much of this expansion would flow into that channel.

However, a major reason must be the values of the academic profession and the traditions of the universities which are reflected in the practice of honours degrees. One does not need to be a conservative to accept that honours degrees occupy a particularly sensitive and influential place in British universities. This cannot be explained simply in terms of institutional inertia or fear of change. They also embody important and for many eloquent values about the intentions of undergraduate teaching, which are related to both the commitment to excellence, a duty which the Robbins Committee took particularly seriously precisely because it was recommending such a radical expansion of the system, and the pedagogical traditions of the liberal university and its strong commitment to high public culture. Although there is not room here to discuss these underlying values in any detail, four general points may perhaps be made.

The first is that because British universities have continued to enrol only on balance the brightest students, who if they are immediate school leavers will have passed through an intensive and rigorous education in the upper secondary school. University teachers have high expectations of their students; they believe that they should be able to master subjects in detail and in depth, an expectation that would be less in other countries. Secondly, there is still a strong assumption that conceptual skills are best acquired through the sustained study of a specialised subject. This may reflect the pragmatism of the British intellectual tradition with its instinctive distrust of too explicit a theoretical structure or teaching method, and also the assumption that bright students can in any case be expected to develop cognitive skills by themselves without being over-organised by their teachers.

Thirdly, the hierarchy of the academic profession continues to be largely determined by prowess in research, and there is still no serious division of labour between teachers and researchers. One result is that teachers, however devoted they may be to good undergraduate teaching, always have to pay considerable attention to the developing theoretical preoccupations of their disciplines. This may produce a bias towards specialisation of subject matter, and an ignorance of teaching methods and curricular organisation that is difficult to eradicate. Indeed, this bias may be intensified by the fact that there are powerful research institutions that can command the attention of individual universities directly through grants and indirectly through the influence of discipline-based networks, while the process of teaching undergraduates has no such powerful external focus. The existence of the CNAA modifies this pattern in the non-university half of higher education, but the universities remain free of all external validation or accreditation. Fourthly, British universities are exceptionally autonomous. Neither the state nor the market has much influence over what goes on inside individual universities. So the hegemony of the honours degree may simply be a reflection of the 'donnish dominion' described earlier.

The Culture of Research

The third broad objective of post-war university development, the growth of a more persistent research culture, has to be measured against two distinct sets of criteria: the statistical and the normative. The results of the first test do tend to support the view that research has become much more important within universities. In 1954/5 universities had a research income of £1,951,000 (£1,096,000 from the government), which represented 5.5 per cent of their total income.[31]

In 1956/7 their research income had grown to £2,683,000 (£1,377,000 from the government) or 6.5 per cent of their total income.[32] By 1961/2 the universities' income from research of £8,228,000 represented 11.1 per cent of their total income, and six years later these figures had increased to £21,630,000 and 12.4 per cent.[33] By the beginning of the 1970s 14.6 per cent of university income was for research, and in 1978/9 it had edged up again to 15.3 per cent, £123 million out of £800 million.[34] These figures, of course, cover only identifiable research income and not the research element in the normal recurrent grant from the UGC.

It has been suggested that since the mid-1970s this trend has been reversed and that expenditure on research has been squeezed as universities have had to readjust to reduced income. In 1982 the Merrison Report on the support of scientific research in universities stated quite categorically: 'The economies that universities were required to make during the seventies have tended to have a disproportionate effect on the support of research.'[35] It is certainly true that the number of university teachers has increased more slowly than the number of students, so leading to less generous staff/student ratios and so, potentially at any rate, to greater concentration on teaching. Yet this has been offset by two factors. The first has been the growth in the number of academic staff in universities solely concerned with research, the majority on short-term contracts. These research-only staff increased from 17 per cent to 21 per cent of all academic staff between 1976/7 and 1981/2.[36] The second is that, although the universities' share of the science budget may have declined from its mid-1970s peak, the science budget itself has continued to grow much faster than general university income. So the true picture may be not that research is on the defensive in universities, but that it is being conducted under different conditions that make much greater use of contract labour rather than mainstream university teachers.

The second test for the growth of a research culture is more difficult to apply. For it carries the discussion far beyond the conventional frontiers of research and its place within the university. It requires an examination of the important changes in the construction of knowledge and the shifting preoccupations of those in intellectual professions. The question therefore becomes whether the development of the post-war university has stimulated not only a powerful research culture but also spawned an intelligentsia. Some people, of course, would argue that such changes simply reflect the rather more solid changes in the social and political conditions to which people in intellectual occupations are subject, and so steer the discussion back to the statistical. Yet it does not seem unreasonable to regard changes in knowledge and in its organisation as having an independent and substantial reality for those engaged in such occupations, or to believe that such changes may influence the way in which they see their role in society. Three intellectual movements of the twentieth century appear to be of such fundamental importance that they transcend not only advances within individual disciplines, but have changed the map of knowledge in a way that may modify social reality. The first of these movements, of course, is the continuing revolution in the natural sciences. No other word but revolution is appropriate to describe advances in knowledge that seem more rapid and more extensive every year. The main intellectual consequence of this revolution has been apparently to free knowledge from the constraints of culture. Of course, it cannot be argued that the pace and priorities of scientific advances are not profoundly influenced by the social, economic and political environment as was argued in Chapter 2. Nuclear research is encouraged by governments convinced of its central importance for the exercise of political power (bombs to keep the Russians in their place, power stations to keep the miners in theirs), but occasionally slowed by environmentally conscious public opinion. Research into racial differences is taboo for entirely legitimate liberal principles. But the results of scientific advances are not determined by their environment, although their interpretation may be heavily influenced by political considerations. When all the very necessary qualifications have been made, however, the revolution in the natural sciences apparently established for the universities and the intellectual class in general a new model of knowledge — independent, objective, scientific knowledge, superior to the culturally constrained knowledge of the past. This new and more powerful form of knowledge granted intellectuals as its guardians a potential social power that their faint ancestors in the medieval universities had once exercised as part of the universal church. In this way advances in the natural sciences established the intellectual basis for the social importance of the intelligentsia, or at any rate its leading scientific members, and for the less inhibited development of a research culture.

The second movement is the pervasive influence of high technology which has been such a powerful stimulus to post-war university development. This is not, of course, the near-monopoly of intellectual institutions in the same way as the revolution in the natural sciences on which it ultimately depends. Instead it is the result of a partnership between intellectual and entrepreneurial institutions, the co-product of the application of theoretical knowledge, usually from the natural sciences, and of the industrial and social organisation of advanced economies to the solution of problems which either the state or the market has identified as of immediate priority. Its main intellectual consequence is simply its success. No problem seems to be able to resist the assault of the mechanistic instruments of technology. Nothing seems to be impossible. Reflection is subordinated to action. So high technology has increased human arrogance, and especially of the technical intelligentsia, and intensified his alienation by demonstrating just how absolute man's command over nature has become. This sense of intellectual omnipotence that has been stimulated by the successes of technology, therefore, is the second quality which the modern intellectual class has absorbed. Just as the potential objectivity of scientific knowledge created a necessary detachment and separation from both political power and civil society, this second quality has provided the intelligentsia with an alternative form of power, a mechanistic power that is not rooted in culture and tradition. Again, a stronger research culture has been a key by-product.

The third movement is the rise of the social sciences and the 'scientification' of the humanities. Although both these are part of the same intellectual movement, they have had different social consequences: the first has led to a notable extension of the scope of the modern intelligentsia and provided it with its most conspicuous and most criticised intellectual tools, while the second has led to a process of professionalisation. This shows the paradoxical influence of the changing shape of knowledge which has played such an important part in the creation of an intellectual class — at once to popularise and to mystify. The intellectual thrust of the social sciences, of course, has been to apply the principles of scientific knowledge derived from the experience of the natural sciences to human affairs and to link them with man's apparent ability to manipulate and control his environment, an ambition derived from the success of high technology. The thrust of the academicised humanities is more modest and is confined to the first of these objectives, which has the effect of reducing the potential social utility the humanities enjoyed in their older, pre-scientific and literary forms.

The attempts in both the social sciences and the humanities to capture scientific objectivity approximate to that achieved in the natural sciences naturally makes use of similar intellectual techniques, above all greater use of conceptualisation and a new readiness to construct theories. The enthusiasm for semiotics, or structuralism, or Annales-style history shows this development clearly, if anecdotally. But while in the natural sciences a theory can usually be reduced to a testable mathematical model, in the social sciences and humanities it can easily degenerate into untestable but hugely influential ideology if not handled with care and integrity. Such ideology appears also to have an intellectual solidity to which intuitive pragmatism could never aspire. Finally, of course, the rise of the social sciences and of the academicised humanities has been more ambiguous intellectual phenomena than the revolution in the natural sciences and the achievements of high technology. They have not produced the same success story. Scientific knowledge has been aspired to but rarely achieved; man's command over his own affairs as opposed to his material environment has not been significantly increased, and theories have often degenerated into ideologies and even into dogmas. One consequence may have been to introduce a strain of pessimism into intellectual life.

Yet it would be misleading to end this discussion of the growth of a research culture, and more widely the development of a discernible intelligentsia, in universities at this point. For compared with other nations' universities what is remarkable about British universities and the academic profession is their instinctive resistance to adopting this new and controversial role. The degree to which universities were able to go their own way. A. H. Halsey's 'donnish dominion' again, continued to be limited in two respects. First, it was externally limited by the concordat with the state, industry, and more broadly lay society which was described earlier in this chapter.

The first limit implied in this concordat was that paradoxically perhaps the first effect of the state's enthusiastic subsidy of the practical sciences offered by higher education was to increase the negotiating strength of the academic profession and so allow it to pursue its natural inclination to place more emphasis on theoretical sciences. In the 1920s and 30s university teachers had a new freedom to pursue academic as opposed to practical preoccupations. But if they led to the splitting of the atom or the invention of penicillin who could really complain? However, the profession had to use its new bargaining strength with discretion. In the 1960s it seemed to push

CROOM HELM LTD.

51 Washington Street
Dover, New Hampshire 03820

Please mention our address in your review, as we are not yet listed in Books In Print.

FOR REVIEW

THE CRISIS OF THE UNIVERSITY

by Peter Scott

$28.00 cloth   ISBN 0-7099-3303-7   277 pages

$14.50x paper   ISBN 0-7099-3310-X

Publication Date: June, 1984

For more information contact: Martha Goelzer

We would appreciate receiving two copies of your review when it appears.

its luck too far. The great expansion of higher education triggered by the White Paper on technical education in 1956 and by the Robbins Report seven years later was clearly seen by government as an investment in scientific invention and technological excellence. Yet the resources given to higher education were directed instead, perhaps inevitably, into an expansion of the social sciences. No doubt there were sound intellectual reasons why this should have been so. But the 'donnish dominion' had been tolerated, even encouraged, by the state because of the universities' instrumental potential, not because of their broader intellectual role. In recent years the universities seem to have half-forgotten the social reasons for the development of the 'donnish dominion', and imagined that its autonomy existed in a vacuum without legitimate constraint.

The result has been a backlash, often polite and disguised but the unmistakable object of which has been to curb the power of the academic profession. Its roots perhaps can be traced as far back as 1946, when the UGC's terms of reference were revised to include a specific commitment to meeting 'national needs'. But its full force was not registered until the 1960s: the creation of the polytechnics under 'greater social control' rather than the further expansion of the universities, the growing if incoherent demands for manpower planning, the emergence for the first time of national higher-education policies that were not synonymous with the priorities of the academic profession, perhaps even the unduly harsh treatment of higher education within the cuts in public expenditure ordered by the present Conservative Government — all are evidence for such a backlash. The position of the UGC is particularly revealing. Much of the recent criticism of its priorities in sharing out the reduced university grant has been myopically misplaced. Far from being an alien agency imposing alien priorities, the committee seems to reflect all too accurately the values of the universities themselves. If it is reformed or even abolished, it will not be because it has interfered insensitively with the autonomy of the universities, but because it is a bulwark of the 'donnish dominion' that lay society has come increasingly to distrust.

The second external limit on this dominion has been treated with much more respect by the academic profession. It has already been argued that the state allowed universities exceptional autonomy because they could be trusted not to exploit this independence for ideological causes that might be hostile to the interests of the state. On the whole the profession has accepted this invisible but powerful restraint. Teachers in higher education in Britain have kept to the role of the academic and eschewed that of the intellectual — which may just be another way of saying that they have been warry of following theoretical preoccupations through to their social or political implications — to a much greater extent than their colleagues in other countries. This may even account for the strain of philistinism that runs through parts of the academic profession in Britain. Any tension that has existed between the state and higher education can be much better explained by the desire of the latter to establish the conditions for professional autonomy than by any particular enthusiasm for a left-wing critique of capitalism. The failure of British higher education to establish enduring examples of general education with a broad mission of cultivation, a very different phenomenon, can be explained in similar terms. This could only have been achieved by abandoning the pragmatic commitment to practical sciences and moving into politically sensitive territory where uncomfortable questions might have to be asked. Again, the advance of the social sciences in the 1960s seemed to begin to compromise the apolitical values of the academic profession. The phenomenon of student revolt, feeble as it was in Britain, touched a raw nerve because it might be interpreted as an attempt by higher education to break this concordat of apolitical autonomy. In the end neither had this effect, but the sensitivity remains.

It would probably be wrong to put too much emphasis on the check which the universities has received since 1975, and most painfully 1979. Although there are reasons why lay society should be less ready to believe that the highest possible degree of autonomy for the profession is mutually and unconditionally beneficial, two important qualifications have to be made. The first is that there is no evidence of any sustained desire to roll back the gains made by the academic profession since 1919 and most spectacularly since 1945. It is probably a case of 'so far but no further'.[37] The second is that the status of the profession is being undermined for practical not ideological reasons. Academic tenure, for example, is being questioned not because lay society places a lesser value on the preservation of academic freedom than in the past, but because it is an obstacle to both making sensible savings and encouraging flexibility to meet new student needs. Indeed, it is possible to be more positive, and to argue that the present doubts surrounding the status of the universities and the academic profession are a symptom as much of success as of failure.

The second limit on the unconstrained growth of an unqualified research culture, and so of an intellectual class, has been internally imposed. The extent to which British universities and the teachers within them have been prepared to accept that more traditional values should be subordinated to those of the new research culture, still less of a burgeoning intelligentsia, has been as decisively limited by the traditions and practices of the academic profession itself. By international standards the academic profession in British universities displays strong and perhaps surprising solidarity which some would describe also as conservatism. Only in a few other countries where higher education has been developed under British influence does the academic profession share this characteristic to the same degree. The symptoms of this academic solidarity are a considerable equality of privileges and influence between senior and junior staff, the lack of any significant division of labour between teachers and researchers, the absence of any serious stratification of institutions, and a remarkable homogeneity of intellectual and broader cultural values within the profession. Most of these features are absent in other European systems of higher education where tension between senior and junior staff is common, research and teaching are often separately organised, the roles of institutions are sharply and sometimes formally differentiated, and intellectual and cultural values are sometimes bitterly contested within the academic profession.

All four features deserve to be emphasised. For what appears as normal in Britain is in fact exceptional by international and even European standards. First, the comparative equality of status between senior and junior staff. The tyrannical professor is a rare figure outside a few single-professor departments. Indeed, in Oxford and Cambridge university professors enjoy considerably less prestige than college tutors, especially in non-science subjects. In many other universities the office of head of department is rotated among the academic staff and is not confined to professors. This strong tradition of collegiality was reinforced during the 1960s by two new developments: the growing strength of trade unionism in the academic profession, and the reform of academic government which increased the voice of junior staff within departments, faculty boards, and senates.

In contrast in the polytechnics and other non-university colleges the academic hierarchy has retained greater vigour. Heads of department have remained permanent posts that do not rotate, partly because they represent established points on a salary scale that cannot be abandoned without loss, and partly because they fulfill a strong academico-administrative role that in universities would more normally be filled by professional administrators. There is also a significant difference of ethos between the universities and the rest of higher education. In the latter the principal or director and his chief lieutenants can take advantage of a more authoritarian tradition. Yet even in the polytechnics and colleges their practices have been largely assimilated to those in the universities. Here too, academic self-government has been strengthened and trade unionism has spread among lecturers. The balance between these two factors may be a little different, with more emphasis on academic democracy in the universities and on trade unionism in the polytechnics and colleges. But the outcome is similar: the erosion of hierarchy within the academic profession.

The second symptom of academic solidarity is the absence of a significant division of labour between teaching and research which might separate the professor into a lecturing proletariat and a research-minded professoriate. All university teachers are expected to engage in scholarship and research, as well as teaching. This expectation is reflected in what are still by international standards generous staff/student ratios despite their erosion since 1975, and in the general allowance for research that is included in each university's grant from the UGC. Recently there have been suggestions that this grant should be disaggregated into teaching and research elements[38] but this was opposed in a recent official report from the Advisory Board for the Research Councils.[39] The budget of the five research councils has been protected while the general university grant has been reduced, so tipping the balance from uncommitted research expenditure to earmarked research grants. This is significant because the former complements while the latter often competes with teaching. The research councils have also adopted more directive and interventionist policies. Yet both the principle and the practice of the traditional system under which all universities, and so most university teachers, are provided with a basic research capacity have continued to be respected.

The third symptom is the lack of significant differentiation between institutions in British higher education. Within the universities, of course, the comparability of standards and so of institutions is an article of faith that is enshrined in the doctrine of the 'gold standard' which holds that all degrees are of equal academic merit, and in the practice of external examiners which is intended to achieve this object. Not only are teaching standards equalised in this way, but there is also a reluctance to acknowledge either that research should be concentrated in a small number of elite institutions (as with the research universities in the United States), or hived off into separate research institutes (as is common in the rest of Europe). One sign of this is that unlike the academies of sciences in other countries the Royal Society and British Academy confer academic dignity but have almost no role in the management of research. Similarly, the research councils have been reluctant to establish extra-university research institutes, but have preferred to operate within the framework of the university (although industrial relations have been a significant factor here).

The fourth symptom is the exceptional homogeneity of academic and cultural values across the whole British academic profession. It has become a truism to argue that the real institutions of British higher education are not the 'visible college' of individual universities or polytechnics, but the 'invisible college' of physics, sociology, history, or engineering. Britain shares this characteristic presumably with all other countries. But in Britain these specialised disciplinary webs that bind together teachers in different parts of higher education are reinforced by broader bands of shared values, about the intentions of undergraduate education, the collegial structure of the university, the cultural dimensions of a higher education, and the location of the university in modern society.

All these symptoms of the almost anachronistic solidarity of the academic profession in Britain have been modified to some degree in recent years. The equality of senior and junior staff within a strong tradition of collegiality has been seriously compromised by the growth in the number of short-term contract teachers and research staff who do not enjoy the normal privileges of the established teacher. Once the expansion of higher education was able to ensure that these under-privileged members of the profession were soon absorbed into permanent jobs and their total number remained small. With the end of expansion their under-privileged status has become more permanent and their number has grown. The same phenomenon has also begun to open up a fissure between teaching and research. As the budgetary balance has shifted from the general research funds of universities to specific grants made by research councils, there has been an increase in the number of academics whose salary, and so loyalty, is dependent on these specific projects.

They, therefore, have correspondingly less commitment to their university or polytechnic as a whole, and so can display less solidarity to their profession.

It is also difficult to deny that British higher education has become more formally differentiated. The selectivity exercised by the UGC in the distribution of the general university grant has tended to encourage the development of first, second, and possibly third divisions within the university sector. The first dim outline of a super-league of research universities, ten or twelve in number, can perhaps now be discerned. Finally, of course, the traditional autonomy of the institutions themselves has come under growing pressure, partly because of reductions in public expenditure on higher education, partly because the expansion of the system has taken it into areas in which lay people can make more sensible judgements. Yet the abiding impression is of a continued strong commitment to traditional values and practices.

Autonomy and Engagement

The final objective of post-war university development, the moulding of a new relationship between the universities and lay society, has already been discussed within the context of the growth of a research culture. The broad pattern is clear: in intrinsic terms universities became more autonomous; lay participation in their government declined still further. It is interesting to note that the representation of lay interests is much less adequate in the constitutions of the new universities established during the 1960s than it had been in the case of the civic universities established a century earlier. No doubt this devaluation of the lay voice within universities merely represented the increased status of the academic profession, which no longer saw itself as so dependent on the opinions of those outside the universities, a conceit some would argue in the light of more recent events. Yet it is as interesting to note that recent cuts in public expenditure on universities have not led to a resurgence of lay influence. Instead the crises of contraction within individual universities have been managed by tightly knit groups of senior academic leaders. The lay voice has remained as weak as ever.[40]

But that is only half the story. In intrinsic terms universities may have become more autonomous; in extrinsic terms they have become more engaged in or dependent on the practical world, depending on one's view of the merit of this particular phenomenon. In fact equal weight needs to be given to both engagement and dependence. The second has been over-emphasised at the expense of the first. The transfer of responsibility for university funding from the Treasury to the new Department of Education and Science (DES) in the early 1960s, a little later the decision to bring university accounts within the remit of the Comptroller and Auditor General, tougher government policies towards overseas students, the long anticipated *dirigisme* of the UGC (which really only became active in July 1981 when the committee adopted a highly slective policy towards the distribution of the reduced university grant) are well known as symptoms of the growing dependence of the universities on the state. Indeed, this list is far from complete.

Yet this growing dependence, which appears so negative and involuntary to many in the universities, has to be balanced by their increasing engagement in lay affairs, which was more positive and essentially voluntary. Indeed, the development of many technology subjects and many of the applied social sciences can only be viewed in this second context. They were not forced on the university by the state but offered willingly. The whole process of expansion in the 1960s and 70s is comprehensible only in terms of the growing engagement of the universities. The same pattern can be observed in research. It is misleading to claim that the growing enthusiasm for applied as opposed to pure research, and even for Lord Rothschild's customer-contractor principle, came entirely from outside the university. The recent debate within the social sciences about whether the Social Science Research Council (now renamed the Economic and Social Research Council) was right to reorganise its subordinate committees in terms of problems and issues rather than disciplines, has highlighted this process of engagement.

Perhaps this pattern of growing autonomy within the university and increased dependence/engagement in the relationship between the university and lay society can be explained in terms of the development of academicism and instrumentalism as uneasy bedfellows within the modern university, which was discussed in Chapter 3. The expulsion of lay influence from university government may reflect the academicism of the modern university. For the increasing specialisation of academic knowledge sharply reduced the legitimacy of lay views. On the other hand the involuntary dependence of the university on the state and its voluntary engagement with society may reflect the modern university's instrumentalism. If the argument that academicism and instrumentalism have a common root is accepted, the circle is complete. The new relationship between universities, the state and society that has developed in Britain since 1945 no longer seems full of paradoxes and ambiguity, but easily explicable in terms of the fundamental characteristics of the modern university.

The title of this chapter — The Robbins Achievement — is justified in the light of the post-war development of British universities. The great expansion in the number of students and increase in the number of university institutions was undoubtedly a considerable achievement. But it was also a controlled achievement in the sense that its effects were carefully contained. The development of the universities stopped short of that point beyond which fundamental questions would have had to be asked about the purposes of university education. It was precisely because the Robbins achievement, so impressive quantitatively, was comparatively modest qualitatively that the binary policy and the polytechnics became inevitable.

But if, to borrow Martin Trow's dichotomy once more, a lot less happened in the 'public life' of the universities than appeared in the middle of the headlong expansion of the 1960s and 70s, a lot more happened in its 'private life' than many supposed at the time. Universities abandoned their traditional commitment to what can be called elitist pedagogy. In teaching the decline of the integrative disciplines of the past continued and the specialisation of disciplines intensified, despite the misgivings of the Robbins Committee. This process was accelerated by the growth of a strong research culture. It was these movements in the universities' 'private life' that shaped their post-war development as decisively as the apparently more spectacular movements in their 'public life'. The broad picture that emerges, therefore, is rather different from the common view of what has happened to the universities since 1945, and more especially since the great Robbins expansion. Instead of the popular stereotype of tumbling standards, mass teaching and mediocre scholarship and research, the true picture is of an intensification of the academicism of the universities. British universities in 1983 are much more powerful intellectual institutions than they were in 1945 or even 1963, an achievement certainly, but one not without significant consequences for the overall shape of higher education.

Notes

1. J. Mountford, *British Universities*, London, 1966, p. 91.
2. *Higher Education* (Robbins Report), HMSO, 1963, p. 49.

3. *University Development 1952–57*, HMSO, 1958, p. 74.

4. N. Annan, 'The University in Britain' in M. D. Stephens and G. W. Roderick, (eds), *Universities in a Changing World*, London, 1975, p. 28.

5. Quoted in P. Scott, *What Future for Higher Education?*, Fabian Tract, London, 1979, p. 6.

6. *University Development 1947–52*, HMSO, 1953.

7. Robbins Report, p. 5.

8. Ibid., p. 267.

9. Ibid., p. 53.

10. Ibid., p. 54.

11. *University Development 1952–57*, p. 38.

12. Ibid., p. 39.

13. *University Development 1957–62*, HMSO, 1964, p. 106.

14. Robbins Report, p. 6.

15. Ibid., p. 93.

16. Ibid., p. 7.

17. Ibid., p. 181.

18. Ibid., Appendix 3 'Teachers in Higher Education', p. 63.

19. G. Faber, *Jowett*, London, 1957, p. 43.

20. *University Development 1957–62*, p. 43.

21. Robbins Report, p. 185.

22. *University Development 1957–62*, p. 57.

23. *University Development 1962–67*, HMSO, 1968, pp. 138–40.

24. Robbins Report, p. 7.

25. H. A. L. Fisher, *The Place of the University in National Life*, London, 1919.

26. M. Archer, *Social Origins of Educational Systems*, London, 1979.

27. The Universities Central Council on Admissions, *First Report 1961–63*, London, 1964, pp. 21 and 23.

28. *UCCA Twentieth Report, 1981–82*, Cheltenham, 1983, pp. 26–7.

29. Robbins Report, Appendix 2A, p. 23.

30. *University Statistics*, volume 1, 1980, Cheltenham, 1982, Tables 4 and 6, pp. 18 and 22.

31. *University Development 1952–57*, p. 44, Table IX.

32. *University Development 1957–62*, p. 45, Table 18.

33. *University Development 1962–67*, p. 38, Table 19.

34. *Report of a Joint Working Party on the Support of University Scientific Research* (Merrison Report), HMSO, 1982, pp. 16 and 53 (Appendix P).

35. Ibid., p. 8.

36. *University Statistics*, p. 50.

37. M. Archer, *Social Origins*.

38. G. Oldham, (ed), *The Future of Research*, Guildford, 1982.

39. *Report of a Joint Working Party on the Support of University Scientific Research*.

40. 'No Shift in Power Base', report in *The Times Higher Education Supplement,* 1 April 1983, p. 4.

Chapter Six

THE POLYTECHNIC ALTERNATIVE

So far as we have in Britain any policy for higher education, it is the binary policy. For the division of higher education into a university and a polytechnic and college sector not only establishes the political, administrative and financial context in which detailed decisions about both educational and resource priorities are made, but also serves as an influential metaphor about the future shape and direction of the system. The binary policy is the nearest thing we have to an authoritative statement about the purposes of higher education. In this important sense it is both a fundamental and a qualitative policy; other policies that have been developed by the DES or within the system since 1965 have been essentially secondary, because they are concerned with administrative adjustment within the accepted context of the binary structure, or quantitative, because they are concerned with reconciling the resource needs of higher education with the public expenditure available for this purpose.

Has the Binary Policy Failed?

This dual nature of the binary policy, as structural *status quo* and normative metaphor, has often led to confusion and ambiguity. So it has at times become difficult to discuss the advantages and disadvantages of the binary policy without paying very close attention indeed to the terms of reference of the debate: is the binary policy being regarded as an administrative arrangement or as a semi-political statement? This ambiguity causes particular difficulty when the question that must be addressed is — has the binary policy failed? It is, for instance perfectly acceptable to argue both that the polytechnics and colleges have been successful as institutions and even that the present binary structure of higher education provides an essentially sound administrative framework, *and* that the binary

152

policy has failed as normative metaphor or political statement about the future direction of the system. Conversely, it is possible to accept entirely the aspirations for a more accessible and more relevant system which were embodied in the original decision to go (or rather stay) binary, *and* to argue that the present administrative and financial division of the system into two distinct sectors was always or has become an obstacle to realising these aspirations. So there is no natural congruence between the two aspects of the binary policy. It may have succeeded administratively only to fail normatively or — and this is the view that will be supported with qualifications in this chapter — it may have failed or be failing administratively while succeeding normatively.

Although this duality of the binary policy as *status quo* and as metaphor is the most significant complication that must be taken account of in any discussion of its success or failure, there are others. First, it must be emphasised that the binary policy was not created in the mid-1960s by Anthony Crosland as Secretary of State, aided and abetted by Sir Toby Weaver, who was then deputy secretary in the Department. Mr Crosland began his second binary policy speech, at Lancaster University in January 1967, by underlining this point:

> I must begin by mentioning a severely practical reason for this policy and the system of higher education that goes with it. That is that the system already existed. I did not invent it; it had been developing steadily since the turn of the century or earlier . . . This was the plural or binary system — whatever you choose to call it — which we inherited. Were we to convert it into a unitary system entirely under university control? . . . The plain fact is that we did not start off *tabula rasa*; we started off with a given historical situation. A plural system already existed.[1]

Of course at Lancaster, where he was attempting to answer the many criticisms of the binary policy announced at Woolwich almost two years earlier, Mr Crosland adopted a disingenuous position. He defended the policy as an accurate and sensible reflection of the administrative *status quo*, and placed much less emphasis than he had done at Woolwich on the importance of the binary policy as a normative metaphor. He understandably desired to portray the binary structure as the natural order, an interpretation, however, which could be sustained only by ignoring much of the debate that

had taken place since the publication of the Robbins Report in 1963.
Nevertheless, there is a substantial and highly significant truth in
the statement that the binary policy has always existed and probably
always will exist. The effective question has always been not whether
a binary line should be drawn, but where it should be drawn. Indeed,
one of the most important motives for drawing the line where it was
drawn between autonomous universities and maintained polytechnics and colleges, was precisely to prevent its being drawn in
a place that might have made better administrative sense, but would
have caused greater normative offence, between higher education
of all kinds and 'non-advanced' further education and adult
education. The only way in which the need to draw a binary line
somewhere can be avoided is by abolishing entirely the present distinctions between higher, further and adult education. Indeed, with
the present turmoil in upper secondary and lower further education
as a result of the development of the Manpower Services Commission and the growing attraction of tertiary colleges that straddle
both sectors, even that might not be sufficient. What this means is
that under present and foreseeable future conditions there will
always be a binary policy. In this sense the question, 'Has the binary
policy failed?' is inherently implausible. The only realistic question,
therefore, can be: 'Would a different binary policy have worked
better?'

A second complication arises from a widespread confusion about
the nature of the binary policy that was adopted in the mid-1960s
and has remained the administrative framework for British higher
education. This policy is over-interpreted in two crucial respects.
First, it has sometimes been defined in terms that go far beyond the,
at any rate publicly stated, aims of the policy. Some, most notably and most eloquently Eric Robinson in his book *The New
Polytechnics*,[2] have argued that the binary policy should have
become the basis of a radical policy for higher education which
would cast the polytechnics in the role of 'people's universities'.
Others have argued that the binary policy was an unnatural attempt
to restrain the legitimate ambitions of the polytechnics and colleges,
a device to preserve the traditional elitism of the universities from
the consequences of the rather thoughtlessly expansionist mentality
which the Robbins Report had perhaps unwittingly encouraged the
universities to adopt in the early 1960s. Both are interesting and
stimulating points of view which help to illuminate important and
difficult choices facing British higher education. But neither is an

approximately accurate description of the binary policy, the first being very much a plea for the binary policy-that-might-have-been, and the second only sustainable in terms of psycho-history. In fact, the aims of the binary policy were clearly laid out in Mr Crosland's speeches at Woolwich and at Lancaster, in the subsequent White Paper[3] and in the various modifications to the original policy that have emerged in the last 10 to 12 years. It is possible to take these publicly stated aims and to examine to what extent they have been achieved by the polytechnics and colleges since 1965. Such a task may be less exciting than politicised speculation, but it is more useful in terms of both improved policy analysis and the feasibility of reforming the present binary structure. This does not mean, of course, that the binary policy should be judged entirely as an administrative framework without normative content. What it does mean is that the validity of the binary policy as a normative meta-phor must be tested not by indisciplined speculation, but by careful analysis of whether it has encouraged or protected those types, aspects, and styles of higher education which were regarded as espe-cially significant in the promotion of those values which the binary policy aimed to reflect.

Secondly, the binary policy has been misinterpreted by those who confuse the primary principles of the policy with the secondary means of implementation that were chosen to give it effect. The binary policy is not the same thing as the polytechnic policy. The first is ends; the second means. This distinction is important because the binary policy is about both more and less than is commonly imagined. It is about more in the crucial sense that it is a policy for *all* higher education. After all, the binary policy first and foremost was a decision not to establish any more new universities. As a result it embodies a particular view of the correct balance of types of institution and of the styles of higher education which they represent within the total system. In both these respects, the negative and the system-wide, the binary policy is as much a policy for the universities as for the local authority (and voluntary college) sector. But it is about less than many people suppose, because it did not require to be implemented in the way in which it has been imple-mented, broadly through the concentration of advanced courses in a small number of large comprehensive institutions called poly-technics. It has been argued that this process of concentration was mistaken because it tended to create within further education a more systematic split between higher education and the rest, an outcome which the binary policy itself on a wider stage had been designed to prevent. This argument may lack weight because it ignores the difficulty in terms of both the most efficient use of resources and the desire to achieve parity of esteem with the universities of an anti-polytechnic policy which would have made no attempt to concentrate advanced courses. But it does perhaps demonstrate that the detailed implementation of the binary policy was not predetermined. Again, this is an important qualification if the question is, 'Has the binary policy, as opposed to the polytechnic policy, failed?'

The third complication is that 'binary' has come to be used not only as the description of a policy but as the characterisation of a system. We talk as much of the binary system as of the binary policy. This is a misleading habit. It implies a system neatly and symmetrically divided into two homogeneous sectors, which was not an accurate description in 1965 and is even less accurate in 1983. The non-university sector in particular is a heterogeneous collection of institutions which have little in common with each other except the fact that none is a university in the rather precise constitutional sense which we have adopted in Britain. Not only must a distinction in legal, administrative and financial terms be made between maintained local authority colleges and voluntary colleges with their denominational histories, but in terms of educational balance and style it is possible to distinguish four main institutional types within the non-university sector. First are the 30 polytechnics which act as the flagships of this sector; secondly are the 14 Scottish central institutions, centrally funded by the Scottish Education Department, as their name implies, but in other ways more diverse than the English and Welsh polytechnics, with some like Robert Gordon's in Aberdeen and Paisley effectively polytechnics but others specialist monotechnics (the Scottish structure is still further complicated by the presence of polytechnic-style colleges like Glasgow College of Technology which are not central institutions but are maintained by regional authorities). Then there are the 64 colleges and institutes of higher education formed from the debris of the contraction of teacher education in the mid-1970s, which again can be sub-divided into four types — proto-polytechnics like Ealing, Humberside or Derbyshire, liberal arts colleges like Bulmershe, colleges of education still almost exclusively involved in teacher training like North Riding, and embryonic community colleges on a semi-American pattern like Bradford and Ilkley. The fourth of the main institutional types comprises the more than 300 colleges of further education which continue to provide some advanced (i.e. higher education) courses. This last group is sometimes regarded as a residual anomaly. This point of view can be questioned partly because the contribution of ordinary further education colleges to higher education is still substantial, particularly in the important areas of part-time and higher-technician courses, and partly because in many of the best colleges excellence and specialism are defined in terms of areas rather than levels of work.

Alongside the diversity of the non-university sector the 45 universities may appear a homogeneous group of institutions. But again it would be a mistake to place too much emphasis on this quality. The technological universities, the former CATs, have always stood a little apart from the other universities, protective of their peculiar histories and highly, even hyper-conscious of their distinctive mission. Their presence within the university sector has often acted as an irritant to the conventional and convenient symmetry of the binary system (although not necessarily of the binary policy). Within the rest of the university system the ebb and flow of subject preference among students and the not always harmonious ebb and flow of 'knowledge formation' within disciplines have both encouraged an institutional volatility which is not sufficiently recognised. Most recently the selectivity practised by the UGC in July 1981 in its distribution of a much reduced grant to universities has intensified this accelerating process of differentiation and even stratification between universities. The less visible and so more acceptable selectivity that is practised by the research councils has had a similar effect. The result is that even among the universities the appearance of homogeneity tends to dissolve the more closely it is examined. When this growing differentiation among the universities is set against the historical diversity of the non-university sector, the tidy symmetry of the binary system so often relied on by macro-policy makers disappears almost completely. This conclusion, of course, says nothing about the success or failure of the binary policy. Indeed, it is possible to argue that the diversity of British higher education in 1982 is an outcome of that policy, or more modestly that this diversity would have been much less had the recommendations of the Robbins Committee been put into effect. But this conclusion does mean that to talk of a binary system of higher education is a nonsense Mr Crosland, it should be remembered, preferred the adjective 'plural' even in the mid-1960s, and this is an even more appropriate adjective today. The most accurate formula, therefore, is to talk of a binary policy within a plural system.

In any discussion of the success or failure of the binary policy, therefore, these four complications, or reservations, have to be constantly recognised:

1) The binary policy is not only a simple description of the past, present (and future?) administrative framework in which British higher education operates, but a normative metaphor for the creation of a more accessible, diverse, and relevant system. The congruence of these two aspects cannot be taken for granted.

2) The active policy issue is not whether a binary line should be drawn, but where such a line should be drawn. So the effective question is not 'Has the binary policy failed?' but 'Would a different binary policy have worked better?'

3) The public aims of the binary policy were described with sufficient clarity when it was first introduced to allow them to be tested. And assessment of the performance of the policy should be based on the results of such tests, not by attempting to measure its performance against objectives attributed to it by others (i.e. 'people's universities', keeping the universities purely elitist, or concentrating all advanced courses in polytechnics).

4) A binary policy does not imply a binary system. Higher education in Britain was a plural system in 1965 and is even more plural today. The concern of the binary policy was with the balance within a plural system, not to create the arbitrary dichotomy of two homogeneous sectors.

The Five Objectives of the Binary Policy

The first objective of the binary policy was to prevent the total domination of the higher education system by the universities. The Robbins Committee, it must be remembered, had recommended that, in addition to the transfer of the CATs to the universities and the establishment of the new universities which had already been planned, a further six universities should be founded and the colleges of education should be brought under the wing of the universities. If the Robbins pattern of expansion had been followed, of the 558,000 full-time students expected in 1980/1 346,000 would have been studying in the universities and a further 146,000 in the 'client' colleges, leaving only 66,000 in further education. The government decided that this balance would be quite wrong, and announced that no more new universities would be created and that the colleges of education would remain either local authority or voluntary institutions. These two decisions made up the initial and the essential binary policy.

In this first form the policy was both radical and conservative. It was radical in the sense that once the government had concluded that the universities could not be allowed to become the semi-monopoly instruments of the expansion of higher education which everyone desired in the first half of the 1960s, it was obliged to go on to conclude that the university was not the only conceivable model for a fully mature institution of higher education. In 1963 this was an unfamiliar idea. Although it was recognised that non-university institutions made an important contribution to higher education, such institutions, particularly those in further education, were regarded as either peripheral or half-formed. If the natural pattern of institutional development was followed, the further education caterpillars would evolve into university butterflies. The Robbins Committee, for instance, carefully considered proposals for the creation of new, non-university institutions only to reject them all.

We have given serious attention to these proposals [for 'university colleges' that would be rather less than universities but rather more than technical colleges or training colleges] and are in sympathy with many of the educational objectives they are designed to achieve. We fully accept the need for experiment in the planning of courses, whether these are courses of general education or have a specific vocational aim. But the question is whether new kinds of institution should be founded specifically to carry out such experiments. We reject this proposal.[4]

The committee put forward three reasons for its rejection; new, non-university, institutions would be too static; innovation should be encouraged within established institutions; and it would be difficult to estimate the number of students who would prefer to study outside universities. All three reasons remain important ones in any discussion of the success of failure of the binary policy. But the general attitude of the Robbins Committee was clear from the start of their report; they disapproved of attempts to 'perpetuate irrational distinctions and rigid barriers between institutions'.[5] The binary policy was conservative in the sense that it represented an attempt to hold the balance that existed in the early 1960s between universities, colleges of education, and further education within the total system of higher education, a balance which the Robbins recommendations if accepted threatened to upset. In this perspective the binary policy can be seen as a successful attempt to preserve the *status quo* in the face of the university imperialism fomented by Robbins. Even in its first stages, therefore, the policy exhibited the duality between administrative *status quo* and normative metaphor. What Robbins was proposing was conservative in normative terms, because it could envisage no other model for a fully mature institution of higher education than the university, but radical in administrative terms, because this myopia led inexorably to the conclusion that a much expanded system of higher education would naturally be a system even more entirely dominated by the universities. In contradiction, the binary policy was conservative in an administrative sense, because it sought to preserve the existing balance between university and non-university components of higher education, but radical in normative terms, because this affection for the administrative *status quo* led equally inexorably to the need to 'invent' new types of institution.

The second objective of the binary policy was to encourage the development of vocational or 'relevant' courses within higher education, a task which it was felt the universities were not well equipped to undertake or alternatively with which they should not be expected to bother. This point of view was expressed with least equivocation by Mr Crosland in his first binary speech at Woolwich Polytechnic in April 1965 when he said:

> We live in a highly competitive world in which the accent is more and more on professional and technical expertise. We shall not survive in this world if we in Britain alone downgrade the non-university professional and technical sector. No other country in the western world does it — consider the *grandes écoles* in France, the Technische Hochschulen in Germany, Zurich, Leningrad Poly in the Soviet Union. Why should we not aim at that sort of development? At a vocationally oriented non-university sector which is degree-giving and with an appropriate amount of postgraduate work with opportunities for learning comparable with those of the universities and giving a first-class

professional training. Let us now move away from our snobbish, caste-ridden, hierarchical obsession with university status.

The same view had been expressed more concisely and carefully in the same speech:

> There is an ever-increasing need and demand for vocational, professional, and industrially based courses in higher education — at full-time degree level, at full-time just below degree level, at part-time advanced level and so on. This demand cannot be fully met by the universities. It must be fully met if we are to progress as a nation in the modern technological world. In our view it therefore requires a separate sector, with a separate tradition and outlook within the higher education system.[6]

Mr Crosland later admitted that he regretted parts of his Woolwich speech, and the first of these two passages must surely have been among those he regretted. In an interview in 1970 he admitted that he had accepted the advice of his civil servants to make a major speech on higher education at a time when he had only a superficial knowledge of the subject, and that 'every change I made in the draft of the speech made it worse'.[7] But he added that the more he had thought about it the more he had become convinced that the binary policy was right, and that he had set out the real arguments for it in his second binary speech at Lancaster. This is an interesting and revealing comment because it makes it possible to compare the two speeches and see which bits were missed out of the second speech. The most obvious omission in fact is this second objective of the binary policy, the need to have an alternative sector which will offer a distinctively vocational and 'relevant' form of higher education. Clearly, on reflection Mr Crosland felt that the contrast between university-style and polytechnic-style higher education in this respect was less than he had at first disposed. Yet it is not clear whether his greater reticence at Lancaster reflected a significant decline in his, and the DES's, belief that the non-university sector could provide more relevant and more vocational courses than the universities, or simply a recognition that this idea had been crudely and antagonistically expressed at Woolwich.

Certainly, the idea that in some important sense the polytechnics offer a more relevant form of higher education has not gone away. The 1966 White Paper *A Plan for Polytechnics and Other Colleges* naturally enough followed the emphasis of the Lancaster speech because it was almost a contemporary document. It justified the binary policy and the creation of the polytechnics in more administrative and less ideological terms. But the objective of greater 'relevance' in the non-university sector surfaced again in the 1972 White Paper *Education: A Framework for Expansion*, which stated:

> The motives that impel sixth formers to seek higher education are many, various, and seldom clear-cut. A minority wish to continue for its own sake the study in depth of a specialised subject to the top of their bent. It is crucial for the world of scholarship, research and invention that their needs should be met. This has always been a leading function of the universities and must remain so. Some students have a specific career in mind. A larger number are anxious to develop over a wider field what the Robbins Committee called the general powers of the mind, but not without questioning whether a specialised honours degree course is the best way to achieve it. Some ask for no more than a stimulating opportunity to come to terms with themselves, and to discover where their real interests and abilities lie. Others have no better reason than involuntarily to fall in with the advice of their teachers and the example of their contemporaries. But not far from the surface of most candidates' minds is the tacit belief that higher education will go far to guarantee them a better job. All expect it to prepare them to cope more successfully with the problems that will confront them in their personal, social and working lives.
>
> It is important that the last and most widespread of these expectations should not be disappointed. The Government have sympathy with the sincere desire on the part of a growing number of students to be given more help in acquiring — and discovering how to apply — knowledge and skills related more directly to the decisions that will face them in their careers and in the world of personal and social action. This is what is meant by 'relevance'. . .[8]

Mr Crosland's first formulation of this objective for the binary policy in his Woolwich speech may have been crude. Certainly it begged many questions. His comparison with the grandes écoles and the Technische Hochschulen in particular was dubious support for his argument that a new, non-university sector needed to be created: the Robbins Committee no doubt would have pointed out that their proposal to establish SISTERs would probably make a serious contribution to the fostering of really high-level technological education in Britain, and moreover would have been a more logical extension of the policy laid down in the 1956 White Paper on technical education which had led to the creation of the CATs. After all, in France the grandes écoles enjoy resources and esteem far superior to those enjoyed by the universities, and there was no suggestion in the original binary policy that so radical an inversion of priorities was ever contemplated by Mr Crosland or Sir Toby Weaver in their wildest moments.

An unfortunate result of Mr Crosland's second thoughts after Woolwich was that this second objective of the binary policy, to foster a more relevant form of higher education through the polytechnics and other non-university colleges, was never properly developed. It was raised at Woolwich and then dropped from sight, never to be properly debated or even articulated. But nevertheless, it remained immensely influential in the popular interpretation of the binary policy. A most interesting debate could have been developed about the appropriate educational level for the most effective intervention to remedy Britain's apparent technological inadequacy: Robbins, and previous government policy, suggested that such intervention should be at the highest level through CATs and SISTERs; Crosland and Weaver seemed to be suggesting rather clumsily that intervention should take place at a lower level (ordinary degrees? technician diplomas and certificates?) International comparisons would suggest that they were right and Robbins was wrong. The same kind of issue is at the heart of the present inchoate debate between 'Cambridge' engineering and 'Salford' engineering within the university sector. But, sadly, this debate has never taken place within the all-important context of the binary policy. Instead the argument about 'relevance' in higher education has often taken place on what might be called the socio-sentimental plane rather than in terms of a coherent policy of scientific and technological manpower. At times even it has drifted perilously close to the shoals of personal fulfilment ('the world of personal and social action') far from the deep channels of economic need. No doubt the growing presence of the social sciences within the non-university sector and the gradual assimilation of colleges of education to the maintained sector mainstream have contributed to this drift. But an important reason was the failure in the mid-1960s to address the issue of relevance with sufficient rigour and directness.

The only other context in which the differences between university-style and polytechnic-style higher education can be discussed is that of philosophical abstraction, as higher education for knowledge-generation on the part of the universities and higher education for practical problem-solving on the polytechnic and college side. Or finally, it may be seen in the context of a Manichean struggle between Lord Robbins, strongly committed to the extension of liberal forms of higher education, and Sir Toby Weaver, equally strongly committed to higher education for capability. None of these perspectives is at all useful to the policy-maker. To see the binary policy in terms of Cardinal Newman v. Karl Popper may be the basis for an interesting conversation, but it is not only unprofitable in the context of practical policy but also a misleading over-interpretation of that policy. This second objective of the binary policy, although immensely influential, has remained ill-defined and undebated. Yet it cannot for that reason be ignored. Leaving aside treacherous concepts such as 'applying knowledge to the solution of problems, rather than pursuing learning for its sake',[9] it is possible to identify certain characteristics of higher education courses that might be regarded as more 'relevant' than those traditionally offered by universities. First, it should be possible to study less traditional subjects at degree level (this was frequently not the case in 1965). Secondly, such courses might be more likely to be sandwich courses. Thirdly, such courses might have a more flexible structure than that of conventional degrees. All three characteristics were mentioned by Mr Crosland in his Woolwich and Lancaster speeches. They, and other characteristics which he did not mention such as the nature of the student intake, student perceptions of the differences between university-style and polytechnic-style courses, and any differences in the pattern of the employment of their respective graduates, may help to provide a framework in which the success or failure of this second binary objective can be tested without summoning Cardinal Newman or Sir Karl Popper as witnesses.

The third objective of the binary policy was more closely defined and is much more straightforward. At both Woolwich and Lancaster Mr Crosland placed particular emphasis on the need to sustain both full-time sub-degree courses, and part-time advanced courses of all descriptions. At Woolwich he said of the first category:

Their [the further education colleges'] second function, of vital importance today, falls outside the scope of normal university work. They have the primary responsibility for providing full-time and sandwich courses which, while falling within the higher education field, are of a somewhat less rigorous standard than degree-level courses. It is here that the colleges meet the needs of the thousands of young people who will occupy the all-important intermediate posts in industry, business and the professions — the high-level technicians and middle managers who must support the scientists, technologists and top managers in a modern economy. These students, both for their own sake and for obvious social and economic reasons, must have a full share of the resources of the colleges and not be neglected through pre-occupation with the first category of students [full-time degree students].

Of the second group he said:

There are tens of thousands of part-time students who need advanced courses either to supplement other qualifications or because for one reason or another they missed the full-time route. There are immense fields of talent and aspiration here; common justice and social need combine to demand that they should be harvested.

In his Lancaster speech if anything he placed even greater emphasis on these two groups of students as a justification of the binary policy. He referred to them as an issue 'of great immediacy', insisted that the universities could not cater for such students 'without a complete transformation . . . which would not be practicable for many years ahead', and placed more weight on them than on full-time degree students in 'relevant' subjects. At Woolwich sub-degree and part-time students had been placed after full-time degree students in importance; at Lancaster the order was reversed, with the presence of full-time degree students in the non-university sector being largely justified because it was essential to sustain sub-degree and part-time courses.

This emphasis on these last two groups of students was continued in both 1966 and 1972 White Papers, and became a common even stale ingredient in all subsequent ministerial statements on the binary policy. The 1966 White Paper, for instance, stated:

> The Government believe it to be of the utmost significance that the leading colleges concerned with higher education should be comprehensive in the sense that they plan their provision of courses to meet the needs of students in all three categories [i.e. full-time degree, full-time sub-degree, and all part-time advanced].[10]

However, an important qualification must be made. It was not intended that all non-university institutions should be equally committed to all three categories of students. The White Paper made it clear that the government would like to see the concentration of full-time courses in the polytechnics so far as practicable. Although it specifically stated that full-time courses should continue to be offered in non-polytechnic colleges when there was adequate student support, it also stated that colleges not already engaged in full-time higher education should not embark on it except in the most exceptional circumstances. But the White Paper also made it clear that a much wider distribution of part-time courses was both inevitable and proper, although this liberalism was qualified by the subsequent statement that

> proposals for part-time courses will not be entertained from colleges which have no full-time higher education courses unless the course is to be conducted in close association with a polytechnic or other college that is offering degree courses in the same field.

So two areas of ambiguity remained. Did the government expect full-time sub-degree courses to be concentrated to the same extent as full-time degree courses in polytechnics and other major colleges? And did the government believe that part-time courses should be more widely dispersed than full-time courses, or did it believe that a tight association between the two was necessary for both educational and efficiency reasons? Neither was clear in the mid-1960s, and rather than gradually being answered by the pressure of events they have tended during the 1970s to become more obscure. Yet in broad terms this third objective of the binary policy seems fairly straightforward; the polytechnics and colleges were intended to be comprehensive institutions offering not only full-time degree courses but also (and perhaps more so) full-time sub-degree and part-time degree and sub-degree courses.

The fourth objective of the binary policy was to keep a substantial

part of higher education 'under social control and directly responsive to social needs', to borrow the phrase used by Mr Crosland at
Woolwich. In his Lancaster speech he elaborated on this objective
by emphasising that he had not intended to suggest that the
universities were not socially responsive, but that 'given the high
degree of autonomy which they enjoy, there is a sense in which the
other colleges can be said to be under more direct social control'.
What precisely did Mr Crosland mean by social control? It is clear
both from his Lancaster speech in which he gave as two examples
the (then) recent 20 per cent productivity exercise in colleges of
education and the control over courses and class sizes in further
education, and from his 1970 interview with Maurice Kogan[11] that
what he intended was the whole panoply of administrative controls
exercised by regional advisory councils for further education,
regional staff inspectors, and the DES itself. One of the objectives
of the binary policy was therefore an essentially negative one, the
fear that with the drift to university status that would have taken
place under the Robbins scheme for the future a series of important
control levers would have been lost by the government. An important advantage of the non-university sector in the eyes of the government was that it would remain subject to detailed administrative
control. In this sense 'social control' was a rather limited and even
negative concept. The course-approval system after all is basically a
mechanism for assessing the proposals put forward by colleges in
the light of national or local need, likely student demand, and so on.
It is not a mechanism for generating proposals in the first place. So
'social control' should not be confused with democratic control.
The need in the mid-1960s did not appear to be to stimulate new
proposals for courses, many of them 'directly responsive to social
needs', from institutions, but to regulate and direct these proposals
so that specific national needs could be satisfied and that in general a
well-balanced higher education system was produced. The danger at
that time appeared to be that the very rapid expansion of higher
education which nearly everyone supported or believed was inevitable would be disorganised and even anarchic. Hence the need for
firm administrative control.

It is certainly important to distinguish between 'social control' in
this sense and a closely related objective of the binary policy,
which was to retain a substantial local authority stake in higher
education. It is clear from both the Woolwich and the Lancaster
speeches that Mr Crosland saw them as distinct objectives. At

Woolwich he said: 'It is further desirable that local government, responsible for the schools and having started and built up so many institutions of higher education, should maintain a reasonable stake in higher education'; and at Lancaster he stated: 'It is in my view a valuable feature of our democratic tradition that elected representatives and local authorities should maintain a stake in higher education'. Apart from this general principle of democratic accountability, three other reasons were advanced for maintaining this local authority stake. First, it was argued that at a time of rapid expansion and changing ideas it was better to have a variety of institutions under different control rather than a monopoly (Mr Crosland said at Lancaster that 'a unitary system would surely imply an omniscience which we do not possess'). This argument for pluralism was particularly applied to the colleges of education, which in the mid-1960s were in the middle of a particularly rapid expansion and which it was felt would suffer from 'a change of horses' in mid-stream.

Secondly, it was argued that both local authorities and voluntary bodies were willing to allow liberal changes in the government of colleges to reflect their new status. Thirdly, the need for close links with the schools was emphasised (although interestingly the same emphasis was not placed on the organic links between non-advanced and advanced further education). But there is nothing to suggest that the government intended to encourage a more active involvement of local authorities in setting institutional priorities. The notes of guidance on the government and the academic organisation of polytechnics issued in 1967 made it clear that local authorities were expected to adopt a 'hands-off' policy towards their polytechnics and colleges. The notes stated quite clearly that

> the Secretary of State believes that these objectives can only be achieved by delegating the main responsibilities for conducting the affairs of the polytechnics to suitably constituted governing bodies with a large measure of autonomy, and, under the general direction of the governing body, to the director and academic board[12]

and again

> It is important that within the limits necessitated by national policy and their dependence on public funds for financial support,

they (the polytechnics) shall be given all possible freedom in managing themselves with the minimum of detailed control by the maintaining authorities.

The role of local authorities in the non-university sector seemed to be envisaged in terms of good financial housekeeping by the institutions and as guarantors of pluralism, variously and confusingly defined as maintaining the *status quo*, and encouraging the development of a more diverse system to meet more diverse needs. It was the Regional Advisory Councils (RACs), Regional Staff Inspectors (RSIs) and the DES which were to exercise the 'social control' recommended by Mr Crosland.

The fifth objective of the binary was only half an objective. It was not mentioned at all in the Woolwich speech and mentioned only obliquely in the Lancaster speech. This was the potential capacity of polytechnics and other non-university colleges to attract students from a less restricted social constituency than the universities. This capacity had two aspects. First, the polytechnics and colleges because of the more populist tradition of further education would act as an alternative route into higher education for those potential students who would be dismayed by the university route. At Lancaster Mr Crosland placed particular emphasis on this aspect:

The inclusion of full-time degree work carries on the historic and invaluable FE tradition of providing opportunities for educational and social mobility. The colleges have always catered amongst others for the students who cannot on entry show that they are of university calibre, and for those who can profit from a university course but cannot give their whole time to it. Technical-college teachers could quote hundreds of examples of students in these categories who have been helped by good teaching and their own strong motivation subsequently to tackle a full-time degree course. Perhaps they left school early, perhaps they were late developers, perhaps they were first generation aspirants to higher education who were too modest at the right moment to apply to a university, perhaps they had started on a career and thought that a technical-college course would more directly improve their qualifications for doing it. The important thing is that the leading technical colleges, by their capacity to provide for students at different levels of ability and attainment (and that is why I call them comprehensive), provide a chance for students of these kinds not only to tackle degree level work part-time or full-time, but also to develop their latent capacity to do so. This range of opportunity is a precious part of our educational heritage that we would be mad to abandon. No wonder some other countries envy what has come to be called the open-ended role of the technical colleges — the role of providing the second chance, the alternative route.

It is sometimes assumed that the polytechnics and colleges were intended to be a 'working-class' form of higher education to complement or compete with the 'middle-class' form provided by the universities. In fact there is little in the official formulations of the binary policy to support such an assumption. The passage just quoted is perhaps the strongest, official, statement of the 'egalitarian' objectives of the binary policy. Yet with the exception of the reference to first-generation aspirants to higher education, there is little in it which could be called a specific reference to social class. However, it does provide a more modest check list of the kinds of students which the non-university sector was designed to help: (i) under achievers at school who have not demonstrated that they are of university calibre; (ii) those who do not come to higher education straight from school because they left school at 16 (and then spent some time gaining qualifications in non-advanced further education?); (iii) mature students; (iv) first-generation students who probably for social reasons did not want to apply to a university. It may of course be that there is a correlation between such groups of students and social class. But this was not made explicit in any formulation of the binary policy, however common it may have become subsequently in populist interpretations of this policy.

The second aspect of the capacity of the polytechnics and colleges to meet the needs of new types of students was more structural. It was the belief that if universities were given a virtual monopoly of degree-level work by creaming off either the relevant courses in further education or the further education institutions themselves, this would create a socially and educationally damaging '18 plus' divide. In Mr Crosland's words,

it would be truly 'binary' with a vengeance, converting the technical colleges into upper-level secondary modern schools and dividing the 18-year-olds into a privileged university class of full-time degree students with the remainder in FE. I can imagine nothing more socially or educationally divisive.

This belief that an 18 plus of this nature would be undesirable was clearly closely linked with the subordinate beliefs in the need to maintain diversity in higher education, and to maintain the non-university colleges as comprehensive institutions offering a wide range of courses, full-time, part-time, and sub-degree.

The binary policy was clearly a complex set of practices and attitudes, prejudices and aspirations which add up to more than the formal objectives of the policy as enunciated in the middle and later 1960s, and which are equally distinct from the specific development of the polytechnics and other colleges during the 1970s. Yet to test these objectives against outcomes is an essential precondition to bringing some order and coherence to what it is admitted must be a wider and more ideological debate. So, to summarise, the main objectives of the binary appeared in the 1960s to be:

1) *Pluralism*
To maintain a balance between an autonomous university sector and a maintained (or voluntary college) non-university sector, rather than following the Robbins road to a university-dominated system of higher education.

2) *Relevance*
To encourage courses in subjects, structure, and modes that were relevant to students with more specifically vocational expectations of higher education.

3) *Comprehensiveness*
To maintain within (large?) comprehensive institutions a range of full-time degree courses, full-time sub-degree courses, and part-time courses both degree and sub-degree.

4) *Social Control*
To keep a substantial part of higher education subject to the administrative controls exercised through RACs, RSIs and the DES: and secondarily to maintain a local authority stake in higher education.

5) *Social Justice/Mobility*
To cater for new kinds of students such as underachievers, early school leavers, mature students and first-generation students; and to discourage the growing up of an 18-plus divide.

The Outcomes of the Binary Policy

The first outcome of the binary policy neatly fits the first objective of the policy. However radical in a normative sense, this first objective was conservative in administrative terms; it was to maintain the existing, 1962/3, balance between university and non-university components within the expanding system of higher education. This objective has been achieved with considerable accuracy. In 1962/3 130,000 of the 216,000 full-time students were in universities, or 60 per cent. In 1980/1 297,200 of the 516,300 full-time students in higher education were in universities, or 58 per cent.[13] Although in 1962/3 there were five students in colleges of education for every three in advanced further education, and 19 years later there were almost five times as many students in advanced further education as there were in the much shrunk colleges of education, the proportion of all students in higher education studying in the non-university sector had remained almost the same, creeping up from 40 to 42 per cent. So in these global terms the binary policy succeeded in freezing the balance between university and non-university components of higher education.

There is a more considerable and a less conservative achievement than it appears. If the recommendations of the Robbins Committee had been followed the number of students in higher education would have been divided as follows: 346,000 in universities (63 per cent), 146,000 in colleges of education which would by then have had a much closer relationship with the university sector (26 per cent), and only 66,000 in advanced further education (12 per cent), making a total of 558,000 full-time students in higher education.[14] If this Robbins projection is adjusted in the light of the unforeseen contraction of teacher education during the 1970s, and the actual total of 41,000 is substituted for the 146,000 assumed by Robbins, the drive towards a system dominated by the universities in the Robbins proposals is even starker. This revised Robbins projection would be: 350,000 in universities (77 per cent), 41,000 in colleges of education (or successor institutions) (10 per cent), and 66,000 in advanced further education (13 per cent), making a new total of 457,000. So if the Robbins projection, with this adjustment, had been followed, the binary split would have been 77:23 in favour of the universities. In fact as a result of the rejection of Robbins and the substitution of the binary policy the split is 58:42. Or to put it another way, the non-university sector has enrolled more than 100,000 'extra' full-time students than it might have been expected to have enrolled under previous policies, half of their gain being represented by the universities' 50,000-student 'shortfall' compared to the Robbins projection, and half by the 50,000 extra students the higher education system has enrolled above the adjusted Robbins total. To what extent this latter gain was achieved by substituting full-time for part-time students will be discussed later.

The success of the binary policy's second objective, the promotion of courses in subjects that are more vocational and 'relevant' than those offered in universities, is almost impossible to assess. Is vocational relevance to be measured in relation to the input, the intentions of the student when he/she starts a course; to the process, the content of the course which presumably reflects the intentions of those who designed it; or to the outcome, the use to which the qualification eventually gained is put in the labour market? Depending on the answer rather different interpretations of vocational relevance will be preferred. Nor is it possible to express simply the contrast between the university and non-university sectors in terms of vocational relevance by pointing to those clearly vocational subjects which are only offered in the latter, and those equally clearly academic or liberal subjects that are offered only in the former. For the spectra of subjects offered in the two sectors largely coincide. Where they do not — medicine is a university monopoly, and art and design is (almost) a polytechnic and college monopoly — such exceptions prove little. The difficulty still experienced in the early 1960s whereby certain subjects could not be studied to degree level because of the conservatism of the universities, then the only degree-awarding bodies, has dwindled away to insignificance as a result of the success of the CNAA. So the need for a non-university sector to be strengthened because in important areas of study of considerable vocational relevance the award of a degree was impossible has disappeared. Indeed, the criticism is sometimes the other way round: that universities have been more liberal or even sloppy in their approach to validating courses in other institutions than the CNAA.

However, although no simple or satisfactory evidence is available to settle this question of whether the polytechnics and other non-university colleges offer more 'relevant' courses, it is possible to apply some suggestive tests as to whether such a claim is true or not. The first is the input to the non-university sector, in broad terms the characteristics and perceptions of their students. The characteristics of polytechnic and college students will be discussed later in this chapter in the context of the binary policy's record on part-time and sub-degree students and on allowing greater social mobility. However, there is evidence that polytechnic and college students do regard their institutions as more 'relevant' than universities. A survey conducted among students at the (then) Enfield College of Technology (now part of Middlesex Polytechnic) in 1970 found that 67 per cent of those who replied agreed with the statement that 'polytechnics give an education which is more relevant to the needs of society than that of universities', while only 2 per cent disagreed. This belief, however, was somewhat qualified in their answers to another question; only 14 per cent thought that polytechnic graduates would be able to obtain entry to the career of their choice more easily than university graduates, with 30 per cent believing that university graduates would have the advantage in this respect.[15] Similar results were produced by a survey at the Polytechnic of Central London in 1972.[16] In it 62 per cent of students felt that polytechnics had greater contact with industry and commerce, and 77 per cent believed they offered more practical courses, with only 3 per cent believing that universities were superior in these two respects. However, universities were seen as superior in offering better career opportunities, opportunities to meet a greater variety of people, better tuition, and better social and accommodation facilities. When the same questions were asked in a national survey of more than 2,000 polytechnic students the same pattern emerged.

The second test is of the process itself: do the polytechnics and colleges offer a distinctively vocational balance of subjects, modes of study, and methods of teaching to such a degree that it could be claimed that this second objective of the binary policy had been fulfilled? The evidence is not decisive. One test is simply to take a static snapshot of the subject balance in the two sectors. If all subjects are allocated rather arbitrarily to three clusters, 'science', 'social studies' and 'arts', the picture in 1978 was that proportionately more university students were studying science and technology subjects than were polytechnic and college students, and conversely that proportionately more advanced further education students were studying in the 'social studies' cluster.[17]

To try to discover the trends in subject balance in both university and non-university sectors, I have taken the period 1973-8 and examined enrolment statistics in various groups of disciplines. In advanced further education all course enrolments increased by 38 per cent over these five years, from 205,000 to 282,800. In universities during the same period the number of full-time undergraduates, a slightly different category, increased by 20.8 per cent from 203,601 to 245,933. Within these general growth rates subject groups shared a common fate on both sides of the binary line. The 'science' group of subjects, which in the case of advanced further education covered medical, health and welfare; engineering and technology; agriculture; and science, increased its enrolments from 90,800 to 112,600, a rise of 24 per cent over the half-decade. In the universities' 'science' group of subjects (medicine, dentistry and health; engineering and technology; agriculture, forestry and veterinary science; and science) the increase was from 107,000 full-time undergraduates to 123,600, a gain of 15.5 per cent. In the 'social studies' group of subjects (in advanced further education, social, administrative and business studies, and professional and vocational subjects; in universities, social, administrative and business studies, architecture and other professional and vocational subjects) the increases were from 95,400 to 133,800 student enrolments in the polytechnics and colleges (40.2 per cent), and from 48,600 to 62,700 in the universities (29 per cent). Finally, in the 'arts' group (language and literature, arts other than languages, and music, drama, art and design in the case of the non-university sector; and languages, literature, area studies, and arts other than languages for the universities) increased from 16,600 student enrolments in 1973 to 34,900 in 1978, a rise of 110 per cent, in advanced further education, and from 46,800 to 55,600 in the universities, a growth of 18.8 per cent.

In fact this comparison proves much less than it suggests. The measures are inevitably crude because they take no account of the great differences in vocational relevance between courses which bear the same name. It would also be misleading to equate vocational relevance with science and technology or vocational irrelevance with the arts. In the case of advanced further education this latter category includes art and design. On both sides of the binary line the 'social studies' group includes a hotch potch of subjects, some highly specific in their vocational application, others highly 'irrelevant'. What this analysis does perhaps show is first, that although the charge that the polytechnics have become 'polyartnics' popular in some universities cannot be sustained, their most rapid growth has taken place in subjects which are not those in which further education has traditionally been considered to be strong. Secondly, it show that the ebb and flow of subjects seems to be a common phenomenon across the whole of higher education that does not respect the binary line. This has been demonstrated by what has happened since 1978: in both universities and non-university institutions enrolments in social science have stagnated, while those in engineering and technology, and to a lesser extent science and arts, have increased sharply. Certainly, if one were to look at subject balance alone, it would be difficult to conclude that the two halves of higher education were moved by different intellectual, social or market forces.

If the mode of study is taken into account a sharper contrast emerges between the two sectors. It is, of course, hazardous to rely too much on measures of interdisciplinarity, and there are in any case few courses that spread across the boundaries of broad subject groups. However the impression is that polytechnics and colleges have been more adventurous in experiments with the traditional structure of the honours degree. The idea of modular degrees which allow students real although guided choice is more common in the non-university sector, although a survey of polytechnic staff attitudes has shown that it is not always easily accepted.[18]

Many of these degrees, however, are in the broad area of social and professional studies which have been affected by the resurgence of engineering. What impact this has had on the movement towards interdisciplinarity in the polytechnics has not been examined. But there is one measure of the difference between universities and polytechnics which is fairly unambiguous; that is the relative fortunes of sandwich courses. Sandwich courses were seen in the mid-1960s when the binary policy was first forcefully articulated as an important element in the distinctiveness of the non-university sector. This is supported by what has happened since. In the university sector the sandwich course has remained imprisoned within the ghetto of the technological universities and has not commended itself to the traditional universities. The result has been that between 1973 and 1978 the number of students in sandwich courses in universities rose only gradually from 12,923 to 14,741, an increase of 14 per cent and well below the 21 per cent growth rate for all full-time and sandwich students.[19] In advanced further education in contrast the number of sandwich students rose from 33,574 in 1973 to 55,999 in 1978, an increase of 66 per cent and well above the 38 per cent growth rate for all advanced-course enrolments.[20] It appears from these figures that the sandwich-course student is a dwindling species in universities and a thriving one in polytechnics and colleges. In 1973 there were less than two sandwich students in the non-university sector for every one in the universities; today it is almost four to one. As the cuts in universities have been particularly directed towards the technological universities, the relative advantage of the polytechnics and colleges in this respect is certain to increase.

The third test of 'relevance' is the output of the two sectors: do non-university students seem to go into more obviously vocational jobs? On the face of it there is little difference in their pattern of employment. In 1979 51.1 per cent of university graduates went into permanent employment in the United Kingdom compared with 54.5 per cent of polytechnic graduates.[21] More university graduates went into further academic study and teacher training (20.7 per cent compared with 13.5 per cent), while polytechnic graduates were marginally more likely to be unemployed (7.3 per cent compared with 4.9 per cent). However, on closer examination differences emerge. In biological sciences, for example, 40.9 per cent of polytechnic graduates went into permanent UK employment, compared with 35.4 per cent of university graduates. A substantial proportion of the latter continued in further academic study, 26.6 per cent compared with only 15.2 per cent from polytechnics. If the kinds of jobs which the two sets of biology graduates obtained are then examined another difference emerges; the most common area of employment among university graduates was research and development (R and D), while among polytechnic graduates it was quality control and analysis. A similarly revealing contrast can be seen in the patterns of employment among management and business studies graduates. For university graduates the most common area was financial work while among polytechnic graduates it was marketing and selling. In mechanical engineering a much higher proportion of polytechnic graduates ended up in jobs in production, 34.6 per cent compared with only 21 per cent of university graduates. Since 1979, because of the recession, a smaller proportion of polytechnic graduates has gone into permanent employment; there has been a precipitate fall in the number going into further academic study, and a significant rise in those undertaking further vocational training.

The general impression created by these figures is of a greater willingness (if not always success) among polytechnic graduates to enter permanent employment and for that employment to be at the 'sharp' end of industry and commerce, in production rather than R and D, in marketing rather than in financial control. So to sum up the issue of greater 'relevance', students entering polytechnics and other non-university colleges do have a strong perception that their courses will be more relevant than those in universities (although they do not show great confidence that this will be carried through into better career prospects); the balance of subjects within both sectors of higher education is broadly similar, with both universities and polytechnics apparently subject to the same ebbs and flows; and the employment patterns of non-university graduates do suggest that either they seek more 'relevant' jobs or else that employers see them as more suitable for such jobs. In other words the inputs and the outcomes of non-university higher education support the idea that it is of greater vocational 'relevance', while the process in between provides much less sure support for such a claim.

The success of the third objective of the binary policy, the encouragement of sub-degree and part-time courses, is much more easy to assess. It is also perhaps a crucial test of the success of the policy. Critics of the polytechnic pattern of development have concentrated in particular on this aspect of the binary policy. In 1974 John Pratt and Tyrrell Burgess wrote:

> The 'tens of thousands' of part-timers that the early speeches and the White Paper thought equally important as full-time and sandwich students are clearly already beginning to have to fight for their continued existence in the polytechnics, let alone their growth.[22]

After claiming that during the 1960s the number of part-time students in universities had increased at a faster rate than in polytechnics, they concluded:

> Virtually all the changes we have seen in this chapter represent a reversal of the intentions of the Woolwich and Lancaster speeches and the 1966 White Paper. They mean in fact, even in 1968–69, the policy for polytechnics was both failing and could be seen to be failing.

In fact the record is rather more ambiguous. The policy for polytechnics can only be condemned if it can be properly demonstrated that the pattern of courses in the polytechnics has radically diverged from the pattern in further education as a whole. The polytechnics, after all, can hardly be expected to buck the wider trends that have affected all further education. Yet taking all course enrolments in further education, non-advanced as well as advanced, it is clear that there has been a rapid increase in the number of full-time and sandwich courses, and virtual stagnation in the number of part-time students whether studying during the day or in the evening. The relevant figures are: in 1968 there were 347,000 student enrolments on all full-time and sandwich courses; ten years later this total has risen to 499,000, an increase of 44 per cent; the number of part-time day students rose only marginally over the decade from 750,000 to 760,000, a percentage gain of 1.3 per cent; and the number of evening students fell from 757,000 to 722,000 between 1969 and 1978, a decline of 4.6 per cent.[23] It is against this background that the performance of the polytechnics and other non-university colleges must be judged. Clearly, all further education was subject to broad secular trends, the bias towards full-time study embodied in the mandatory grant system, the growing unwillingness of employers to release their employees, the encroachment of degrees on professional qualifications and so on, which affected advanced courses as much or more than non-advanced courses.

It is within this generally hostile environment for sub-degree and part-time courses that the record of the non-university sector must be assessed. First, sub-degree courses. Between 1968 and 1978 the number of student enrolments on Higher National Diplomas and Certificates, Technician and Business Education Council higher awards, and the Diploma of Higher Education rose from 58,504 to 68,297, an increase of 17 per cent. This was much less than the 236 per cent increase in the number of students enrolled on full-time degrees in advanced further education from 25,540 to 85,911.[24] However, it is probably best to be cautious in any interpretation of this disparity. First, the number of students on full-time sub-degree courses rose by 63 per cent. The overall percentage rise was dragged down by only a 7 per cent increase in the number of students on part-time day sub-degree courses and by a 40 per cent decline in evening only sub-degree courses. Secondly, during the first decade of the polytechnics there was naturally a substantial process of up-grading the level at which less orthodox subjects could be studied. So the role of the CNAA cannot be overlooked as a powerful agent in expanding the scale and the scope of degree level work in the non-university sector. Nor can this process sensibly be condemned. Mr Crosland himself had pointed out that under the former regime of university-only validation certain important vocational subjects could not be studied at degree level, and urged that this should be remedied. Clearly, this could not happen without to some extent depressing sub-degree course enrolments. It is therefore reasonable to regard the explosive growth of degree students in polytechnics and colleges during the 1970s as an exceptional phenomenon. Perhaps a fairer comparison is between the growth rates of university degree students and sub-degree students in polytechnics and colleges. Sub-degree courses come well out of such a comparison growing at almost twice the rate (63 per cent compared with 36 per cent).

The second part of this third objective, the encouragement of part-time students both at degree and sub-degree level, is also easier to assess than to interpret. In 1968 76 per cent of all student enrolments for degrees were on full-time or sandwich courses (27,927 compared with 8,558 part-timers), and ten years later the proportion had risen to 83 per cent (91,276 compared with 18,414 part-timers). This is perhaps less of a shift in favour of full-time degrees than one would expect from some of the more categorical criticisms made of the polytechnics' and colleges' record in sustaining part-time work. If all advanced courses, except teacher training, are included, the shift becomes even more moderate. In 1973 the polytechnics had 71,586 student enrolments on full-time and sandwich courses and 44,910 on part-time courses, producing a ratio in favour of full-time work of 62:38. Five years later they had 113,935 and 62,681 respectively, producing a split of 64:36. These figures hardly support the charge that the non-university has abandoned part-time courses wholesale. Indeed, they suggest a substantial and stubbornly maintained commitment to part-time higher education in the face of national policies on student awards and institutional grants that overwhelmingly favoured full-time courses.

The fourth objective of the binary policy was first, to keep a substantial part of the expanding higher education system subject to greater 'social control' than the universities, and secondly, to maintain a substantial local authority stake in higher education. The first of these has been sustained almost without qualification. Polytechnics and other higher education colleges have remained subject to the prevailing system of course approvals, although in the years of expansion that system was applied with considerable liberalism. In the case of teacher training the DES has used its regulatory powers to fix not only the output but also the balance of the output of student teachers and to determine their institutional origins. Independent colleges of education have been closed, amalgamated with further education colleges to form diversified colleges of higher education, or swallowed up as the education faculties of polytechnics. Whether this detailed and continuous exercise of administrative powers actually produced the well-balanced and efficient system which was its object can of course be disputed. The system of course approvals has remained a reactive rather than a stimulatory mechanism. It disposes but does not propose, a weakness that assumed greater importance when because of the cuts in public expenditure from 1979 onwards development in higher education could no longer be simply additive. This weakness has been compounded by the crude and inflexible inputs into this system of control, most particularly the attempt to regulate courses by means of minimum student numbers. It has become clear that these essentially administrative tools of control are no longer able to regulate in any acceptable way a system in the process of enforced contraction, however they may have coped with the gentler challenges of expansion, and that they must be supplemented by more sophisticated political and academic tools. The newly established National Advisory Body (NAB) for local authority higher education seems to be about to move away from a system of course-by-course approval as a means of steering the system and towards approval on the basis of whole programmes of work or even ultimately whole institutions. The NAB is also in the process of bringing financial and course-planning together at a national level for the first time.

The second part of this objective, the maintenance of a strong local authority stake in higher education, has to some extent been a prisoner of these developments in the course regime and in the financial mechanism of the pool. In fact there has been remarkably little serious and sustained debate about the role of local authorities in non-university higher education. Links with the local community, local schools, and between advanced and non-advanced courses have been used as secondary arguments in a primary debate about financial and course planning. The value of democratic accountability in a substantial part of higher education has received even less consideration. The publicity given to some spectacular disputes between polytechnics (usually their directors) and their maintaining local authorities, fuelled by a stream of often patronising anecdotes about prejudiced councillors and unimaginative bureaucrats, has presented the local authorities' role in a negative and even (black) comical light. This is both unfortunate and unfair. Throughout the 1970s and into the 80s many local authorities have been generous supporters of the polytechnics and other maintained colleges both through the advanced further education pool and directly from their rate income.

Certainly, the maintained colleges appear to have been better resourced than the voluntary colleges, even after allowances have been made for their different subject mixes. As a result of the investment made by both local authorities and central government since the adoption of the explicit binary policy in the mid-1960s, unit costs in universities and in the non-university sector has tended to converge. In 1979/80 although universities still had an £800 advantage over the polytechnics in laboratory and workshop-based subjects (£3,814 per student compared with £2,997), in class-room based subjects the two types of institution enjoyed almost identical unit costs (£2,145 per university student, and £2,141 in polytechnics).[25] The extent to which local authorities have continued to cherish their polytechnics and colleges can also be valued precisely by the extra money they spend on these institutions over and above those sums allocated through the pool, which represents the assessment of their needs by central government. In any case, whatever view is taken of the need for a local authority stake in higher education, there is no doubt that the present government, and any likely future government, intend to maintain it. In January 1981 civil servants in the DES proposed, and ministers half-heartedly approved, a proposal to remove the polytechnics and other major colleges entirely from the control of local authorities and to establish a quango on the approximate pattern of the UGC. This plan met with widespread opposition and was abandoned. Later in the summer a consultative paper was issued which offered two contrasting models — model A, which would have reproduced in broad terms the January proposal and model B, which amounted to continued local authority control although with significant modifications.[26] Although this paper was never formally withdrawn, the government effectively pre-empted the outcome of such consultation when it established the NAB, a result which was much closer to model A than to model B.

However, it is important to keep the question of local authority control in proper perspective, although it sometimes grabs more than its fair share of attention. The issue of the local authorities' stake in higher education was as much a sideshow in 1981 as it had been in 1965 when the binary policy was first articulated. The primary issue was, and is, 'social control' in the form of administrative regulation; it was freedom from such regulation which Mr Crosland was unwilling to grant the non-university colleges in the 1960s.

Today the issue has broadened out into the larger question of the proper co-ordination of financial and academic planning, in the context inevitably of dwindling public expenditure on polytechnics and colleges. The true significance of the NAB lies in its role as the effective possessor of the powers that formally belong to RACs, RSIs, and the DES itself, rather than a potential supplanter of local authority control.

There is one final dimension of this fourth objective of the binary policy that remains to be discussed; that is the development of the internal government of the polytechnics and colleges. As a *quid pro quo* for acquiescing in continued local authority control, the non-university institutions were promised a more liberal regime. The DES insisted that they should be allowed much greater autonomy than had previously been the tradition in further education. The actual outcome has been mixed. It is probably fair to say that on academic questions there has been little inclination on the part of local authorities to interfere. Indeed, there have been complaints that local authorities provide too little purely educational input into the institutions they maintain, and that as a result the arguments for the close association of advanced and non-advanced further education and for intimate links with the schools have been considerably weakened. On the other hand, because polytechnics and colleges have no corporate autonomy and do not employ their own staff, it has been impossible to disentangle the financial affairs of institution and of maintaining local authority. How to reconcile the demands of good housekeeping with the rights of institutions to reasonable autonomy has proved in practice to be difficult. The result has been a series of, mainly petty, incidents in which polytechnic managers have been called to account on very detailed, and sometimes very trivial, financial issues. However, these incidents have generated an ill-will out of all proportion to their real significance. Nor have they been balanced by the contrary incidents in which local authorities have provided substantial financial help to institutions in difficulty, which necessarily have been handled more discreetly.

There are in any case two larger issues. The first is the real as opposed to the constitutional balance of power that the confused and even contradictory arrangements for internal government have produced within polytechnics and colleges. On the whole it is the management of such institutions that has won, and the local authority and the academic staff that have lost. Local authorities may be able to make the director account for the consumption of alcohol in the hotel and catering department, but it is the director who in practice has the largest say in determining the overall direction of the institution. Yet the management exercises this power, to borrow Bagehot's terms, in an efficient rather than dignified sense. Because its influence is informal, its decisions are more difficult to challenge. The formal power of decision often remains with the local authority or the governing body, although neither has the effective power to exercise it without the advice and assistance of the institution's management (except in times of crisis when normal relations have broken down). In an important sense the incomplete liberalism of college and polytechnic government has acted as a far more effective brake on the growth of academic democracy than on the power of institutional management. Indeed, it can be plausibly argued that the confusion of college government has encouraged the development of a strong managerial interest in non-university institutions.

The second issue is closely related. If the Robbins Report had been followed, all fully mature institutions of higher education would have enjoyed university-style government: vice-chancellors who were chairmen of senate rather than managers of their institutions, minimalist central administrations, and powerful oligarchical organs of academic self-government. Although without particular emphasis, the binary policy suggested that an institution could be regarded as fully mature without necessarily enjoying such a form of internal self-government. So it can be argued that from the start the intention was to foster strong management within the polytechnics and colleges. Certainly, there is a case for saying that strong management is necessary in institutions which are asked to undertake as wide a variety of tasks as the polytechnics. In a traditional university it was safe to assume that the overwhelming majority of those within the institution shared common intellectual values, which were expressed in a broad consensus about the objectives and balance of the institution and about the teaching and research priorities necessary to achieve these objectives, and to maintain this balance. Whether this assumption can be as safely made today in the universities, of course, can be doubted. But perhaps polytechnics were necessarily more fissiparous institutions, embracing within a common administrative and resource framework a very wide variety of objectives which could not be traced back to common intellectual values. Indeed, some would argue that this diversity of means reflecting an intellectual heterodoxy is a defining characteristic of the binary policy itself. Whether this is accepted or not, there remains a strong case for arguing that because of their past history, their present constitution, and their future mission the polytechnics and other non-university colleges required strong and purposeful management.

The fifth objective of the binary policy was to open paths into higher education to 'new students' who could not or would not aspire to enrol in a university. As has been pointed out, it is doubtful whether this should really be counted among the original objectives of the policy. Partly it was simply a natural consequence of the second (more relevant courses) and the third (more sub-degree and part-time students) objectives; partly it was an objective attributed to the policy by enthusiasts afterwards. Nevertheless, it is worth trying to assess the extent to which this fifth objective has been achieved.

First, in most subjects in which there is a common student market across the binary line degree students in polytechnics and colleges have less impressive scores in terms of grades at A-level than those in universities. Yet the standard of CNAA degrees is carefully monitored to ensure comparability with university standards, and the proportion of students in each degree classification is broadly similar. This would tend to support the claim that polytechnics are efficient teaching institutions which produce the same output standards although the standard of students at input is often inferior. However, this must be seen in the context of the widespread evidence that A-level scores are a bad predictor of degree success, and of the suggestion that in the non-university sector students are sometimes over-taught.

Secondly, more degree students in polytechnics and colleges enter with qualifications other than traditional A-levels. At the beginning of the 1970s only 2.1 per cent of university students had 'other qualifications' for entry, while the percentage for polytechnic and college degree students was 26 per cent. Again, this is not especially surprising. One would expect the polytechnics, growing as they have from further education, to have more students with FE-type entry qualifications while the pressure for places in universities has given them little, too little, incentive to deviate far from the traditional A-level route. Thirdly, many more polytechnic and college students come to higher education after a gap from school. In 1978 56,350 of the 175,574 advanced-course students in polytechnics were aged 25 and over, or 32 per cent. Among part-time advanced students it was 53 per cent, but even among full-time and sandwich students the proportion was 20.5 per cent. In universities in the same year only 16,150, or 7 per cent, of the 245,933 undergraduate students were aged 25 or over. Contrary to some findings, there seemed to be no difference in this respect between part-time advanced and non-advanced courses; their proportions of mature students were almost identical. Nor had any decline in the proportion of mature students taken place since 1973. Five years earlier there had actually been a lower proportion of mature students on full-time and sandwich courses in the non-university sector, 18 instead of 20.5 per cent (17,979 out of 100,065).[27]

Fourthly and finally, there is evidence that polytechnics and colleges draw their students from a wider social constituency than universities. In the first half of the 1970s 27 per cent of undergraduates in universities came from working-class families, while the proportion of working-class students studying for degrees in the polytechnics was 36 per cent.[28] It also appears that there is a class gradient, with the working-class student better represented on other full-time courses than on degree courses, and on part-time than full-time courses. This fits in with other recent findings that there are remarkably few differences of rates of access between social classes to part-time further education, and that 'educational opportunity would be much more unequal if it did not exist'.[29] However, although mildly encouraging in terms of social justice it is probably unwise to place too much emphasis on this fourth objective of the binary policy, which was almost certainly a secondary consequence rather than primary aim of the policy. It can be supposed but never proved that the 'binary' expansion of higher education opportunities in the 1960s and 70s, by protecting with some success part-time and sub-degree courses and the more populist traditions of further education, did more for social justice than the Robbins expansion, which was its only feasible alternative, might have done. But it would be wrong to make too much of what is perhaps an increasingly marginal distinction.

The binary policy has had few outspoken supporters and many critics, some of whom have regarded it as insufficiently radical and others as a barrier to their achieving full 'higher education' status. Yet it has survived for almost 20 years as the most appropriate structure for a much expanded system of higher education. It has done so perhaps because it has not been unsuccessful in meeting some of the most important objectives outlined in the mid-and late 1960s. This analysis has shown that in setting outcomes against objectives three of the main aims of the binary policy have been achieved or at any rate maintained, while the evidence on the other two which anyway were more difficult to define is ambiguous. To sum up this position under the same headings used previously in this chapter:

1) *Pluralism*
The binary policy has meant that the 1962/3 balance between university and non-university sectors in terms of student numbers has been maintained, so avoiding the prospect raised in the Robbins Report of a much expanded system of higher education dominated to an increasing extent by the universities.

2) *Relevance*
Although a difficult term to define, most non-university students believe that their higher education will be more relevant than the education they would have received at university, and the pattern of employment of polytechnic and college graduates supports this belief. However, there is little in the subject balance in the two sectors to support the idea of a distinctive polytechnic higher education, although the non-university sector has protected sandwich courses and experimented more with new structures for degrees.

3) *Comprehensiveness*
Sub-degree courses have not suffered as much as would have been supposed in a decade of rapid up-grading of courses under the influence of the CNAA. Part-time courses have followed a similarly stable pattern. Both types of course have been protected to an extent unlikely in a Robbins-style, university-dominated system of higher education.

4) *Social Control*
Administrative regulation of the non-university sector has been upheld, and now modernised by the creation of the NAB. Local authority involvement in polytechnics and colleges has also been maintained. A strong managerial interest has been fostered in college government in contrast to the pattern of academic oligarchy common in universities.

5) *Social Justice/Mobility*
The polytechnics and colleges have more working-class students, more mature students, and more students with other than traditional higher education entry qualifications.

Notes

1. Speech by Mr Anthony Crosland, Secretary of State for Education and Science, at Lancaster University, 20 January 1967.

2. Eric E. Robinson, *The New Polytechnics: A Radical Policy for Higher Education*, London, 1968.

3. *A Plan for Polytechnics and Other Colleges* (White Paper), HMSO, 1966.

4. *Higher Education*, (Robbins Report), HMSO, 1963, p. 147.

5. Ibid, p. 9.

6. Speech by Mr Anthony Crosland at Woolwich Polytechnic, 27 April 1965.

7. Maurice Kogan, *The Politics of Education*, Harmondworth, 1971, pp. 193–4.

8. *Education: A Framework for Expansion* (White Paper), HMSO, 1972, pp. 30–1.

9. Woolwich speech, 27 April 1965.

10. *A Plan for Polytechnics and Other Colleges*.

11. Kogan, *Politics of Education*, p. 194.

12. 'Government and Academic Organization of Polytechnics', 'Notes for Guidance', Appendix A in DES Administrative Memorandum 8/67.

13. For 1962/3 total, Robbins Report p. 160; for 1980/1 total, Universities Statistics 1980, volume 1 (Universities Statistical Record, 1982).

14. Robbins Report, Table 44, p. 160.

15. Lex Donaldson, *Policy and the Polytechnics*, London, 1975, Table 4.1, p. 55.

16. Ibid, Table 4.6, p. 63.

17. Calculated from *Statistics of Education*, 1978, volume 3 (Further Education) and volume 6 (Universities), 1981.

18. C. Cox, M. Mealing, S. Robinson and J. Whitburn, *Report on the Polytechnic Survey*, London, 1975.

19. *Statistics of Education*, 1978, volume 6 (Universities) HMSO, Table 12.

20. *Statistics of Education*, 1978, volume 3 (Further Education) Table 14.

21. *What do Graduates do?* 1981 edition. Careers and Occupational Information Centre/Association of Graduate Careers Advisory Services, 1981.

22. John Pratt, and Tyrrell Burgess, *Polytechnics: A Report*, London, 1974, pp. 72 and 88.

23. *Statistics of Education*, 1978, volume 3 (Further Education), HMSO, Historical Table, p. 2.

24. Ibid. Table 16, p. 28.

25. Background paper by the Department of Education and Science for Leverhulme/SRHE seminar on resource allocation, 1982, p. 12.

26. *Higher Education in England outside the Universities: Policy, Funding and Management*, a consultative document issued by the Department of Education and Science, July 1981.

27. *Statistics of Education*, volume 3 (Further Education), Table 5, p. 7.

28. Guy Neave, *Patterns of Equality*, Slough, 1976, Table 7.5, p. 85.

29. A.H. Halsey, A.F. Heath, and J.M. Ridge, *Origins and Destinations: Family, Class, and Education in Modern Britain*, Oxford, 1980, p. 192.

Chapter Seven

A POST-BINARY FUTURE

Although the success of the binary policy should be acknowledged, so too should the force of the criticisms that are made of it. Perhaps a useful distinction can be drawn between the binary *policy*, the objectives laid down in the 1960s which were described in Chapter 6, and the binary *structure* which provides the administrative framework for higher education at the beginning of the 1980s. It is also important to keep in mind the duality of the binary policy as both a description of the *status quo* and as a normative metaphor. If both these qualifications are kept in mind, the conclusion may be reached that the present binary *structure* no longer provides the most hopeful administrative and financial environment in which to continue to pursue the original goals of the binary *policy*. In this chapter five flaws, or blockages, in the present operation of the binary policy will be described which tend to support this view.

The Missing University Dimension

The first is that although the binary policy could be said to be as much about the universities as about the non-university institutions, all the emphasis and all the attention have been placed on the latter. For a long time we had only half a higher education policy. Despite tentative suggestions for reform like Mrs Shirley Williams's '13 points' in 1969, the universities were left alone until recently. They were, of course, subject to macro-expenditure policies like all services dependent on public support, and they were also regulated in the broadest possible sense by the government's shifting decisions on how the total number of students in higher education should be split between the two sectors. Apart from these two blunt instruments of policy successive governments have had little practical ability to steer the university system in desired directions (teacher education and medical schools are partial exceptions to this). What dirigisme there was was provided by the UGC, in theory quite independently from the DES. In a sense this was why a binary policy was needed in the first place, to maintain a substantial sector of higher education subject to more detailed 'social control'. Also until the mid-1970s the impermeability of the university system did not seem to matter very much. The expectation was still for substantial expansion, although the projection for more than 800,000 students in 1981 contained in the DES's *Planning Paper Number 2*[1] had been scaled down to 750,000 in the 1972 White Paper. Moreover, the rather less explicit expectation was that much of this expansion should take place in the polytechnics and the colleges. As a broad generalisation the 1960s were the decade of university expansion, the 1970s and presumably 1980s were expected to be the decades of polytechnic and college expansion. Between 1958 and 1968 the number of full-time students in universities increased by more than 110 per cent; between 1968 and 1978 by only 35 per cent;[2] with the non-university sector the pattern was reversed, although the rise and fall of the colleges of education has tended to obscure the picture. In the mid-1970s it had almost become unofficial DES policy that the universities should represent a static or slow-growth sector of higher education, with the polytechnics and colleges acting as the main instrument of sustained growth. Seen in this context, it did not appear to matter that the universities were left alone.

Today, of course, it matters a great deal. Not only is there no real prospect of further significant growth, at any rate of the conventional variety, which means that at the end of the century the universities will still be the largest sector of higher education, but also a central policy for universities has emerged. The fact that this policy is an uneasy combination of the random effects of the overall cut in the universities' grant of 15 per cent by the government and of the selectivity strategy adopted by the UGC to meet this emergency, is less important than the simple fact that for the first time it is sensible to talk in terms of a policy for universities. These two developments have produced a double anomaly. First, the ostensibly 'elite' sector of British higher education will continue for the foreseeable future to be the majority sector also, while the presumably more populist sector under much more detailed 'social control' will enrol only a minority of students (of course, a simple head count would show that the polytechnics and colleges had almost twice as many students as universities, but many are part-timers, so the balance of the commitment of public resources for higher education will continue to reflect the universities' majority status). This position is inherently unstable. Secondly, instead of having only half a higher education policy, the Hamlet-without-the-prince position of the years from 1968 to 1978, we now have two separate halves of a higher education policy which are not co-ordinated in any satisfactory way except at the macro-expenditure (and so student-split) level, and which as a result do not add up to a coherent whole. Although this unfortunate result is not an intended consequence of the binary policy, the present binary structure does make it difficult to resolve. The first flaw therefore is this missing university dimension.

Letting Universities off the Reform Hook

The second flaw is closely linked with the first. It is the way in which the binary policy let the universities off the reform hook in the mid-1960s. For the existence of 'alternative' institutions cast university development in an entirely new, and possibly more conservative, light. To some degree it took the further democratisation of the universities off the political agenda by reducing the educational demands that could be made of them. Universities were no longer the only mature institutions of higher education so they were no longer expected to do everything. Other institutions were available to meet some of the newer, and more destabilising, demands generated by and within a rapidly expanding system of higher education.[3] This was apparent at a rhetorical level. In the early 1960s there seemed to be in the universities a crescendo of interest in reform, of which both the establishment of the new universities and the Robbins Report itself were important ingredients. There was grandiose talk of redrawing the map of learning in exciting and radical ways.

In the mid-1960s such talk died away. Instead, the new universities settled for what has been called 'the pedagogy of cultivation',[4] while the technological universities have remained incompletely absorbed into a university system with still traditional aspirations. Perhaps this retrenchment would have happened in any case. But it is possible to argue that if the Robbins pattern had been followed, the very pace and scale of expansion would have overridden the cautious instincts of the universities, and a significant breakthrough to a mass system of higher education would have taken place on a broad front. Instead, the cautious conservatism of the universities was indirectly encouraged by the binary policy and the creation of the polytechnics. Now that the end of expansion has left the universities as the majority sector of higher education, these habits of academic and social conservatism have been entrenched as the hegemonic values of the whole system. Even if this exaggerated interpretation is rejected and the soundness of the original binary decision reaffirmed, an important issue is left. If the objectives of the binary policy: diversity, comprehensiveness, relevance, social control/accountability and social justice/mobility remain valid, perhaps it will no longer be sufficient in the 1980s to confine the attempt to achieve these objectives to the polytechnic and college sector. Perhaps some or all of the universities should also be expected to make a more serious contribution to achieving these 'binary' objectives than they have made since 1965. In short, perhaps the reform of the universities needs to be put back on the policy agenda.

Concentration v. Accessibility

The third flaw of the binary structure is that the original policy was implemented by trying to concentrate advanced courses in a limited number of large and comprehensive institutions, the new polytechnics. Some critics have suggested that this amounted to a pseudo-university solution to a problem which had been defined as the danger of university domination of the entire higher education system. They argue that the binary policy logically tended to abolition, or at any rate blurring, of the sharp distinction between higher and further education by insisting that the values and practices of further education should have more status (and resources?) within the post-secondary system as a whole, but that the means by which it was implemented made it likely that all that would be achieved was a mild extension and diversification of higher education at the expense of further education. This debate can become an almost metaphysical one in which faith is pitched against faith, but it is not irrelevant to the continued validity of the binary policy as a normative metaphor. The binary policy has to continue not only to work well as an administrative and financial framework, but also to send out the right kind of message about the future direction of the system. Perhaps such fundamentalist critics have something to say on this second aspect of the policy.

However, in a more limited and down-to-earth sense the concentration of advanced courses in the polytechnics has created difficulty, especially over part-time courses. The obscurity of the 1966 White Paper on the proper relationship between full-time and part-time courses has not been much reduced by the practice of the polytechnics and colleges. On the one hand it is argued that part-time courses must necessarily be distributed more widely than full-time courses because part-time students are not portable; on the other that part-time courses need the academic and resource support that only full-time courses can provide. This issue has not only remained unresolved, but is likely to create more difficulty in the future as the demand for short courses and other forms of continuing education increases. How can accessibility to such courses be reconciled with their credibility? The 1966 White Paper seemed to suggest that some arrangement whereby colleges could offer part-time courses under the aegis of, or with the support of, polytechnics, could provide the basis for a solution. Although a system of consortia with their 'cores' made up of polytechnics or other large colleges and smaller college 'satellites' makes good sense in broad theory, both the details and the politics of such schemes would present considerable difficulty. The growth of a strong and sometimes exclusivist polytechnic interest within the non-university sector has not made such desirable co-operation easy to achieve. One disadvantage of the binary structure certainly is that it attracts all attention to the distinction between (and the interdependence of) university and polytechnic forms of higher education; it distracts attention from the equally important relationships between large and small higher education institutions within the non-university sector and between higher and further education. Yet in terms of the objectives of the binary policy, such relationships are of great importance to the future of non-degree (whether sub-degree or continuing education) and part-time courses.

A 'Third Sector'

The fourth flaw in the binary structure is the other side of the coin to the policy of concentrating advanced courses in large polytechnics. It is that, largely because of the vicissitudes of teacher education, this policy of concentration has not been successful. Of the 342,503 advanced-course enrolments in the non-university sector in 1978 only 52 per cent (176,716) were in polytechnics.[5] If only full-time and sandwich courses are taken into account the proportion only rises to 58 per cent (114,035 out of 194,034). Substantial numbers of students remain in other maintained major establishments (54,108) and in direct-grant, mainly voluntary, colleges (25,891). It is not possible to regard these last two totals as a residual element which in the fullness of time will vanish. The non-university sector far from becoming more homogeneous is becoming more heterogeneous. The forced diversification of the colleges of higher education has created not simply an important 'third sector' in higher education, but also a highly diverse sector; some of the colleges of higher education tend towards a liberal arts college model, some towards a proto-polytechnic model, some towards a community college model. Nor by any means do all these institutions place the same value on the traditions and practices of 'relevance' which the polytechnics inherited from technical education. Many are happier with the idea of general liberal higher education along the lines proposed in the Robbins Report. The solidarity of the non-university sector is beginning to break up, to such an extent in fact that it is becoming difficult to accept that a simple binary structure is any longer appropriate. Again, there may be a growing tension between the objectives of the binary policy and the rigidity of the binary structure. Just as it may be necessary to extend these 'binary' objectives to the university sector, so it may be necessary for the binary structure itself to be reformed to reflect the developing diversity within the non-university sector. 'Academic' universities contrasted with 'relevant' polytechnics was never an accurate description of the balance of higher education; today it is damagingly misleading. It vastly understates the diversity of traditions, values, and practices that exist within both sectors, and so underrates the need for such diversity to be encouraged not only between but within these sectors.

The Visible and the Invisible Colleges

The fifth flaw in the binary structure is that it has remained unclear whether its centrifugal administrative intention has been powerful enough to overcome the centripetal forces generated by disciplines.

Do teachers in polytechnics and colleges see their role in different terms from university teachers? Or do they see themselves essentially as university teachers do, primarily as members of the 'invisible college' of their discipline or profession and only secondarily as members of the 'visible college' of their institutions? The evidence is ambiguous. Polytechnic and college teachers do appear to have different backgrounds from university teachers. Only 18.9 per cent of polytechnic teachers have first-class degrees compared with 42.9 per cent of university teachers, and this disparity has not been reduced among recent recruits. University teachers spend 40 per cent of their time on research and 37 per cent on teaching, while polytechnic teachers spend only 18 per cent of their time on research and 43 per cent on teaching. Polytechnic lecturers teach for longer hours (16.7 hours a week on average compared with 15.3 hours in universities). Nor do polytechnic teachers want to do research as much as university teachers: ideally they would like to spend 29 per cent of their time on research, while university teachers would like to spend 50 per cent of their time. Fifty per cent of polytechnic lecturers have never published an article, and only 2 per cent have published more than 20. Among university teachers the equivalent proportions are 12 and 26 per cent. On the other hand almost a quarter of polytechnic lecturers said that their interests lay 'very heavily with teaching', while only 6 per cent of university teachers agreed.

However, when both sets of teachers were asked which post they would regard as the highest achievement in their profession, the ranking of posts was very similar. Top job for both university and polytechnic teachers was a university chair, followed in the case of university teachers by an Oxbridge chair and for polytechnic teachers by head of department in a polytechnic.[6] Such information is necessarily limited. It does not, for instance, tell us whether the greater involvement of polytechnic teachers in teaching rather than research is a reflection of the fact that they do not aspire to research in the same way as university teachers or of an active rejection of the research-oriented values of universities. Nevertheless, rather against the run of anecdotal and 'common-sense' evidence, the empirical evidence does suggest that significant differences remain between polytechnic and university teachers. However, it is not clear what conclusion this evidence tends to support about the success or failure of the binary structure. One interpretation is that 'the reality of the binary system is a blurred division of equality and not a

horizontal division of educational function'.[7] But other interpretations less dismissive of the claims of the polytechnics and colleges are possible.

We can now summarise the five main flaws of the present binary
structure, blockages to the further pursuit of the objectives of the
binary policy as follows:

1) The practice of the binary policy has been an attempt to plan half
a higher education system, and more recently two halves quite independently.

2) The binary structure may have the effect of inhibiting the rather
limited radical instincts of the universities. If the binary objectives
of diversity, relevance, comprehensiveness, social accountability,
and so on are worth pursuing, perhaps the universities should be
expected to make a greater contribution.

3) The concentration of advanced courses in a small number of
large institutions has left unresolved the important question of
access to part-time (and continuing education) courses. It has also
tended to split up higher and further education.

4) There are many advanced course students outside polytechnics
so compromising the policy of concentration. The colleges of higher
education represent a distinctive approach to higher education
which should be properly recognised. Because of the binary structure not enough attention has been paid to the growing diversity
within the non-university sector.

5) Although there are clear differences in background and outlook
between university and non-university teachers, some suspect this
reflects a vertical division of quality rather than a horizontal division of function.

A Post-binary Structure?

A post-binary structure for higher education must be able to fulfil
three conditions. First, it must make it easier to pursue the five basic
objectives of the original binary policy. Secondly, it must be
designed to eliminate at least some of the five flaws in the present
binary structure which were identified in the first part of this
chapter. Thirdly, it must serve as a moralising metaphor which will
help to set a direction and a goal for higher education as successfully
as the original binary policy has done. And it must do these three

things against a background of no or at the best slow expansion and of declining or at the best static public expenditure on higher education. For there is almost no prospect of a renewal of Robbins, or Crosland-style, expansion in the 1980s and 90s, partly because of the inevitable shortage of resources and partly because the quality of any new development is likely to be very different from the replication of existing forms of higher education which accounted for so much of the expansion of the 1960s and 70s. Declining resources, uncertain student demand, the growing demand for more entrepreneurial conduct — all will place the present structure of higher education and the practices and values of its institutions under considerable strain. For this reason it is important to try to identify those organising principles for a post-binary structure around which higher education can retrench and regroup.

The first and most important of these principles is diversity. This, of course, is common ground; even Robbins believed that diversity among universities was essential. One of the reasons for the committee's rejection of the proposal for other-than-university institutions was precisely their belief that such institutions would be too static, trapped in a particular role with no room to manoeuvre and develop. On the other side Crosland argued that diversity was essential because to create a unitary system would imply an omniscience we did not possess. Yet they were not talking about the same thing. The Robbins Committee was supporting the right of individual institutions to make their destiny without artificial restriction; in this way they hoped to create a measure of pluralism within the broad framework of the university as an institution. Mr Crosland, on the other hand, was insistent that diversity must be maintained across the system by allocating different roles to different sets of institutions, precisely because he feared that diversity in the Robbins sense would lead to a gravitation, or even regression, towards the traditional university pattern.

So it is important to be clear which version of 'diversity' it is intended to encourage. In fact there can be little room for doubt that it must be the latter, system-wide, diversity rather than the autonomous, institution-based variety. Although 'academic drift' has not been as baleful or clear-cut as some binary Jeremiahs have alleged, there is still little in the experience of the polytechnics and colleges which suggests that the *cordon sanitaire* of the binary policy has not helped them to keep to the path of virtue. As the diversity of the needs that higher education must meet and the demands that will be placed upon it is bound to increase still further during the 1980s and 90s, the need for a more diverse system will also increase to match this heterogeneity.

It is unrealistic to expect that from an undifferentiated mass of higher education institutions each one can hope to match its own ambitions to external needs in a way which makes sense across the system. So the need for planned diversity seems clear. However, it is only possible to plan to create the conditions for diversity, not diversity itself. National higher education policy should confine itself to constructing broad sectoral boundaries as the minimum preconditions of system-wide diversity, but within them it should pursue policies of course control and resource allocation which stimulate rather than stifle the initiative of individual institutions. The task in the 1980s will be bring together Robbins-style and Crosland-style diversity. No simple binary, or even tripartite, division of higher education can hope to match the diversity of higher education that will actually be required. Such crude system-wide diversity will need to be supplemented by much finer diversity between and even within institutions. Any post-binary structure must not only be able to accommodate and to encourage this growing diversity and to establish barriers to creeping conformism, but also send out a clear message that higher education in the last decades of the twentieth century can encompass much more than simply the higher education that developed out of the Robbins expansion, with Crosland amendment, in the 1960s.

The second principle must be efficiency. In the future higher education will not only be more diverse but also much leaner. This is not simply an unfortunate and hopefully temporary side-effect of the present reductions in public expenditure, but perhaps a necessary condition for adapting to a new and wider role. Ideas about the organic relationship between undergraduate teaching and research may be much less valid if more and more of the teaching in higher education is of vocationally directed, post-experience courses (or even of much more general first degrees). The belief in the domesticity of the college as an important element, which has been very much eroded during the past 20 years but still remains an important ingredient of the subterranean value-system of much of British higher education, and in the intense and interdependent quality of degree study, which has survived in much better shape, will increasingly be questioned in a system with more part-time, 'distance', or other 'casual' students by today's still austere standards. The integrity of the institution itself as something more than a clearing house for client exchanges or a holding company for the resources to be independently exploited by academic experts in specialised branches of knowledge, may also come under challenge. All of these will have a fundamental effect on higher education's present view of appropriate staff student ratios, the balance between teaching and research, and of the relationships of departments and other units with the institution, and so will have a radical impact on the present configuration of resources which is designed to reflect these older preoccupations. In the long run such developments may have a more significant effect on the economy of higher education than the present cuts.

A third organising principle must be accountability. Occasionally this issue is discussed in unreal terms as if there were a choice between being unaccountable and accountable, when the effective choice is really between different degrees and levels of accountability. So long as higher education receives the bulk of its income from public expenditure in direct and indirect forms, it cannot escape being accountable. The present cuts which the system is trying to absorb are clear proof of that. It can be argued, of course, that for many years after the creation of the UGC in 1919 the universities were barely accountable. Regular grants from the state saved them from their earlier chronic dependence on fees and on support from industry and local government, but so long as the total of such grants remained small in terms of public expenditure, and so long as the conventions of respect for the independence of the UGC were upheld, this earlier accountability to students, industry, and town hall was not replaced by an equally rigorous accountability to the state. This allowed a period of what A.H. Halsey has called 'donnish dominion' in which higher education was very much directed by the preoccupations of the academic profession. This period has come to an effective end, partly because of the expansion of the system, partly because of the more recent restriction on the growth of the social state. Yet while the process of accountability has become much more cruel — because there is not enough money to go round — the constitution of accountability in British higher education remains confused. 'Accountable to whom and for what?' is a question that the system itself, its paymasters and its clients have not been able to answer in a satisfactory way.

As a result the age of donnish dominion has drawn to a close to be replaced by a confused interregnum. Three main forms of accountability will perhaps eventually emerge — professional accountability, sometimes slipping into a syndicalist mode, which will be the heir to the old donnish dominion; democratic accountability, no longer perhaps simply in terms of resources but also of the quality of higher education itself; and 'market' accountability to students, employers, government and industry (for research and development). In the 1980s and 90s a whole range of questions concerning accountability — the role of local democracy, the strengthening of democratic accountability at a national level, the opening up of private bodies like the UGC, the rights of the student-consumers, the influence of customers for skilled manpower or research knowledge, even the mass consumption of intellectual culture — will have to be faced. From them flow a large number of more detailed financial and administrative issues which will be discussed in the final section of this chapter. Although the answers to few of these questions are at all clear, it is probably fair to conclude that the theme of accountability will have growing importance in the future organisation of higher education. A post-binary structure must somehow find a proper balance of interests to fill the vacuum left by the decline of donnish dominion.

The fourth principle is one that may well get forgotten in the rush to promote diversity, efficiency and accountability. It is the need to maintain our present traditions of academic and pedagogical freedom. This may at times become difficult. There is a danger that in the enthusiasm for the new utilitarianism the conditions of free enquiry and of free teaching will be undermined. As the customer — contractor principle spreads from research into teaching, it may be difficult to insist upon reasonable autonomy for the individual teacher, department or institution. Yet it will remain important to do so, not simply for the traditional reasons associated with academic freedom such as the right of critical investigation and the duty of balanced teaching, but because if higher education is forced into too subservient a relationship with its diverse clients it will become less efficient as a source of effective teaching and important research. It is not simply that the fiduciary role of higher education must be protected, but that higher education must be guaranteed the conditions for academic pluralism as it makes up much the most important part of the intellectual system. However, it will probably be important to disentangle these conditions for free teaching and research from the decaying fragments of donnish dominion. If this does not happen the intellectual integrity of the higher education system may be compromised by a rearguard action to defend the institutional autonomy of the old order.

The task for the rest of the 1980s and for the 90s must be to try to express these organising principles in a new, post-binary, structure for higher education. As has already been emphasised, a new structure must make it possible to continue to pursue the original objectives of the binary policy, if possible with even greater vigour and on a broader front (i.e. including the universities), but also to avoid the blockages that have built up in the present binary structure. Any new structure must reflect the ends of the original binary policy rather than the particular means which were adopted in the later 1960s to implement them. Equally, it must place more emphasis on the binary policy as a normative metaphor than as an existing administrative and financial framework. One difficulty with the present binary structure is that its success in meeting the original objectives of the policy has not been sufficiently recognised, with the result that the messages it sends to the polytechnics and colleges themselves, to the university sector, and to the world outside higher education (schools, employers, government and so on) have often seemed negative. Their burden has sometimes been the restriction of personal and institutional ambitions rather than the encouragement of new opportunities in higher education. A post-binary structure must take account of this reality, because the values embedded in the system are immensely strong and not always as conservative as fundamentalist critics suggest. To put it in basic terms, a new structure must find ways of promoting the democratic objectives of the original binary policy without at the same time labelling them as second-class in some vague but immensely influential sense.

For this reason above all, it seems sensible to move away from the present over-rigid dichotomy between universities and 'other' institutions and to move towards a situation in which all senior institutions of higher education are regarded as belonging to a common, but heterogeneous, group. Not only is this shift in emphasis necessary for the straightforward reason that it is a more accurate description of what is already a more diverse system than many people suppose (and the binary division is only one aspect of that diversity and not always the most significant one), but also because it is only in this way that the universities can be brought to share in at least some of the objectives of the binary policy (which can be interpreted as the objectives to be pursued in any semi-mass system of higher education). It is only by breaking down the binary structure a little that the universities can be nudged in this more democratic direction.

In Britain we have a particularly narrow and restrictive view of the university, partly because of the weight of tradition, partly because of the failure to achieve a breakthrough to a more mass system, and partly because of the binary structure which encourages universities to take a limited view of themselves. The best way forward therefore would seem to be to combine the necessary shift towards seeing higher education as a comprehensive collection of heterogeneous institutions rather than as divided into two binary camps, with a move towards a much more liberal view of the activities in which it is appropriate for universities to engage. The result might be a much extended 'university' sector which included the present universities, the polytechnics and Scottish central institutions, and some of the larger colleges and institutes of higher education (perhaps after another round of amalgamations with other colleges of higher education (CHEs) or major further education colleges, perhaps by forming federal institutions with nearby universities or polytechnics). About a hundred major institutions would be established which could be called 'universities', although some might prefer to retain a qualifying adjective such as 'polytechnical', just as some technological universities have kept the qualifying phrase 'of technology' while others dropped this description from their new titles. However, it must be emphasised that this would not be a policy of 'back to Robbins'. It would be inconsistent with the objectives of a post-binary system, and also probably impossible in practice, to transfer all these institutions to the UGC list and grant them charters to award their own degrees and generally to accord them all the characteristics of a traditional university. The intention would be the opposite; to move away from such uniformity of treatment, and to absorb the binary structure within a much more liberally defined university sector.

An expanded university sector of this kind would be different from today's university sector in three main ways. First, not all 'universities' would necessarily be autonomous chartered bodies. Many would remain institutions maintained by local authorities. After all, only in Britain is it regarded as anomalous to have universities controlled by local government. Many states within the United States with smaller populations than the larger local authorities in Britain are responsible for a full range of higher education including universities. However, this is not intended to be a proposal to maintain the *status quo* unchanged except for a cosmetic change of title. It would have two important subsidiary effects: first, the new 'university' status of the polytechnics and colleges would lead eventually to a better relationship between institution and authority, which might be reflected in some new administrative status that was a compromise between corporate autonomy and total dependence; secondly, this change would tend to loosen up the system. After all, simply because the Inner London Education Authority or Sheffield City Council have shown themselves more than capable of running their own higher education, it does not follow that Kirklees or Cleveland have the same capacity or wish. So while local authority control could be maintained in areas where it had proved its worth, in other areas where it had been less successful some new arrangements might be devised. Equally possible would be the 'lease-back' of a university to a large local authority if that seemed a better solution than precarious independence constantly threatened by a hostile UGC. In short, the best solution could be sought for any individual 'university' without the danger of its being ruled out of order by some rigid macro-policy.

Within the general mix of autonomous and maintained 'universities' there would be room for direct-grant institutions either of the traditional voluntary college variety or the Cranfield/Royal College of Art-type. Indeed, there might be a case for arguing that a larger direct-grant sector should be created, to give central government its own sector to play with. It is probably through a direct-grant sector that Britain could build up its own system of grandes écoles. The eventual result could be a much expanded 'university' sector in which there was a good balance between autonomous universities, and institutions controlled by local democracy and others directed by the central government. Such a diversity of methods of control and government would be a guarantee of educational diversity, but on more flexible terms than today's categorical binary structure.

The second difference would be that each 'university' would not receive its income from a single source, such as the UGC grant or the advanced further education pool. Indeed, it would work against the spirit of diversity if institutions in the autonomous, local authority, and direct-grant segments of an expanded 'university' system received their funds by quite separate and mutually exclusive routes. Instead, a regime of 'mixed funding' should be allowed, with a maintained 'university' able to receive money from the UGC for a specific purpose, or an autonomous 'university' to be supported on certain conditions by a subsidy from a local authority. The DES (or other Ministry), the UGC and the NAB or any successor body could be encouraged to make greater use of specific grants. Mixed funding would have two advantages; it would allow readier and more effective intervention to produce the results desired by a funding agency, and it would blur the distinctions between the three segments of the 'university' sector, so making institutional mobility easier to achieve. Mixed funding would also encourage institutions to be genuinely comprehensive; dependence on a single source of income tends to force an institution into a homogeneous mould.

The third difference would be that not all 'universities' would award their own degrees or other qualifications, not at any rate in all subjects. Within a highly differentiated system of institutions the issue of quality assumes greater importance and can probably no longer be left to the informal and gentlemanly practices of the past. Even in the universities some more formal system of accreditation may become essential simply to retain some academic order in an increasingly heterodox environment. Within 'universities' which enjoyed traditionally close relationships with clients, whether professions or industry, the exclusive right to award qualifications on the part of the institution might not be appropriate. Finally, among the new 'universities' institutions would be at different stages of academic development. For all these reasons a spectrum of options on degrees and other qualifications would be essential, ranging from the loosest form of accreditation (from which even the most established universities might benefit) to external validation and externally set examinations.

It is not especially easy to imagine how such an extended 'university' sector might work. However, the drift towards institutional diversity of which it would be the culmination is already plain. In Northern Ireland the first steps have been taken towards the creation of a trans-binary institution by amalgamating the New University of Ulster and the Ulster Polytechnic. What would be created there would have many of the characteristics of a new 'university' described here. The automatic assumption that university status leads to material advantage will be increasingly questioned as the UGC's selectivity strategy remorselessly proceeds. Within the universities the solidity of the UGC grant has been shaken not simply because it has been reduced, but because it forms a shrinking proportion of an institution's income as overseas students' fees introduce a directly 'market' element and the research councils introduce an even more *dirigiste* element. The attractions of specific direct grants are growing both within the UGC and within government. The validation position has become more complex, with the CNAA looking towards liberal reforms of its practices, universities validating college degrees, the merger of the Technician and Business Education Councils, and changes in professional examinations and qualifications. So it is already possible to detect the first stirrings of many of the changes which could lead eventually to the development of an extended 'university' system with much more diverse patterns of external control, internal government, income sources and validation practices.

However, the gradual development of an expanded 'university' sector cannot be seen in isolation from the important changes taking or about to take place in adult (or better, continuing), further, and even upper secondary education. A likely development is the growth of tertiary colleges in many areas, which would take over the work of school sixth forms, provide Manpower Services Commission (MSC) courses for early school leavers and the young unemployed, and also offer more traditional lower-level further education. If this happens on a significant scale it will force a corresponding reorganisation of further and adult education for 18-year-olds and above. It is then possible to foresee the gradual development of proto-community colleges which would complement the parallel development of an extended 'university' sector. These colleges would have four broad functions: as what the Americans would call 'transfer' institutions offering the first two years of conventional higher education possibly in the form of Diplomas of Higher Education; as the powerhouses of technician education, a crucial area of skill formation which cannot be ignored (of course, a lot of technician education would continue to be provided in 'universities', but it would be unrealistic to allow the highest levels of post-secondary education a monopoly of such courses); as centres of continuing education in vocational and in non-vocational subjects (some of this work might be done in association with nearby 'universities' as leaders of continuing education consortia and or with the Open University); and finally as out-reach institutions which would search out and try to meet the educational needs of ordinary people. It would be a great mistake to imagine that educational disadvantage stops at the age of 18 or whenever the latest MSC programme runs out; it is then that it is often just beginning.

So beneath the 'university' sector a (community or comprehensive) college sector should be encouraged to coalesce. Again, this development is not as far fetched as it may at first appear. Many a college of higher education, worried about the further decline of teacher training and the continued fragility of liberal arts degrees, will probably dabble in schemes like 'Open Tech' over the next few years. However, two conditions of a successful development are essential. First, such colleges must be readily accessible to part-time and short-courses students; they should be quite literally the local college. This is especially important because under the pressure of youth unemployment and the MSC's activities many further education colleges will be tempted to concentrate on 16- to 19-year-olds at the expense of adult students. Secondly, there must be an effective and binding system of credit transfer so that a student can begin his higher education, perhaps part-time, in a local college and then move onto a 'university' without loss of academic standing.

An extended 'university' sector and a new sector of community or comprehensive colleges would require important changes in the present pattern for the management of post-secondary education. The first essential reform — as essential even if the present exclusively binary structure is retained — is for the creation of an overall commission for higher, or post-secondary, education on the pattern of Australia's Tertiary Education Commission. However, there are two crucial issues. First, what should be the role of such a commission? Should it act as a strategic body that serves as a forum of sophisticated consideration of the issues that face the higher education system, from which it then tries to extract broad principles of development? Or should it be a co-ordinating body that oversees the areas of disputed territory between different sectors and institutions and undertakes the more limited tasks of providing common information and laying down common guidelines? The first of these is probably preferable but more difficult to achieve. Secondly, what should the relationship be between such a commission and existing agencies like the UGC and NAB, and how independent should it be of government? Underneath, but in different degrees of subordination to such a commission, might be a reformed UGC concerned with the detailed allocation of resources to universities; a NAB similarly involved with the maintained 'universities' (today's polytechnics and colleges); a proper continuing education agency, a mix between the Russell Committee's adult education development council and the former Advisory Council for Adult and Continuing Education; a research agency, perhaps a development of the existing Advisory Board for the

Research Councils; and an accreditation and validation agency which would develop from the CNAA but have responsibilities across the system.

In this chapter it has been argued that proper distinctions must be drawn between the binary policy as an administrative framework, an affirmation of the *status quo* of limited pluralism within British higher education in the face of the apparent threat of a university 'take-over' which appeared to be possible in the wake of the Robbins Report; and as a normative metaphor, a semi-political statement about the future direction of higher education. A proper distinction must also be drawn between the ends of the binary policy, those objectives such as diversity of institutions; comprehensiveness in styles, modes and subjects of higher education; social control and democratic accountability; and social justice and egalitarian access enunciated in the 1960s: the means of the binary policy; the creation of a strict and formal binary structure; the attempted concentration of advanced further education in a small number of large and comprehensive institutions, and so on. It is the metaphor and the basic objectives that matter, not the administrative framework and the means of implementation adopted almost 20 years ago. But even in these last two senses the binary policy has been more successful than its critics allow. However, the binary structure in middle age has become in some respects an obstacle to the further pursuit of the original binary objectives which aimed at the creation of a more open and more relevant system of higher education. So it may be necessary to construct a post-binary policy which will try to remove these obstacles so that this pursuit can be continued. But a post-binary policy must not just restore the priority of ends over means (when the opposite is in danger of becoming the case), but also redefine the binary metaphor in ways in which those in higher education can find new meaning and new confidence (the French would call it remoralisation) in the goal of building a more modern system of higher education — a goal that was common ground between Robbins and Crosland 20 years ago, however much their detailed interpretations of the proper route differed, but a goal which seems today to be in doubt.

Notes

1. DES, *Planning Paper Number 2: Student Numbers in Higher Education in England and Wales*, 1970.
2. 'British Universities 1968–78', *Paedagogica Europaea*, Paris, 1978, 2, p. 32.
3. Ibid., p. 31.
4. A.H. Halsey, quoted in Ibid., p. 41.
5. *Statistics of Education, 1978* volume 3 (Further Education), HMSO, Table 14, p. 22.
6. A.H. Halsey, *Survey of University and Polytechnic Teachers*, Oxford, 1976.
7. *The Times Higher Education Supplement*, 16 November 1979, pp. 10–11.

Chapter Eight

Future Issues

Universities, polytechnics and other colleges share both the common experience of retrenchment that seems to be typical of all systems of higher education in the 1980s — and which has been described in Chapter 4 — and also their own particular experiences of retrenchment and disappointment, which have been described in Chapters 5 and 6. However, it is important to emphasise that although in the 1970s, and most especially the 1980s, the modern university seems to have lost its apparently inexorable momentum of the 1960s, this international experience of retrenchment is a complex phenomenon with internal and external causes that are by no means coincident and with political, social, cultural and intellectual dimensions that make it impossible to try to reduce this complexity to any simple message. The message is as much that the future for higher education is ambiguous as that it is bleak. The conclusion is not so much that the 1990s will be worse than the 1960s, but that they will be very different.

Similar lessons can be drawn from the more particular experiences of the universities since the publication of the Robbins Report in 1963 and of the polytechnics and colleges since the deliberate articulation of the binary policy in the mid-1960s. Of course, the more extravagant ambitions stimulated by the Robbins expansion have not all been achieved. The reorganisation of knowledge for undergraduate teaching has taken place only on the most modest of scales. The reorientation of knowledge in terms of intellectual preoccupations and priorities has made more impact, most obviously in the growth of the 'oppositionalism' of the social sciences and the instrumentalism of the applied sciences and other professional subjects. The social base of the universities has been broadened, but not as much as many had hoped. Going to university has become a much more common experience for 18-year-olds in Britain; indeed it has become the almost automatic expectation of many middle-class professional families. Yet the proportion of university students from working-class homes has remained stuck at 25 per cent. In another sense the social base of the universities has shrunk. Since 1945 most have allowed their local roots to wither. They have ceased to make a vital contribution to that civic culture of which so many universities were a product, which has diminished both the universities and that culture. Yet set against this must be the continuing intellectual vitality of the universities. In this more fundamental sense the 20 years since Robbins have been a period of great creativity and high achievement. At a time when so many British institutions seemed to be in at least relative decline, the universities easily maintained their international reputation for academic excellence. So something worked — and probably it was the most important thing of all.

The record of the polytechnics and colleges on the other side of the binary line was equally mixed. Again, no new philosophy of learning has emerged that would allow us to make a sensible distinction between 'doing' and 'thinking' higher education, the former the province of the polytechnics and colleges, the latter of the universities. Nor is it really possible to argue that with the creation of the polytechnics an alternative form of 'people's university' had been created that would lead the final successful assault on the ivory-towerism of the traditional universities. Yet it is possible to argue that the polytechnics have been highly successful in more practical ways: maintaining a strong commitment to part-time and, less certainly, to non-degree higher education; securing a respectable place for paraprofessional subjects that could never have flourished in a purely university environment; keeping closer links with those crucial civic and industrial cultures of their regions, and so establishing a model for a semi-mass system of higher education in Britain which the universities could never have done on their own. Most important of all, their overall success has given firm institutional form to principles for the future organisation of higher education, at a time when the Robbins principle itself seems either too vague or out of date. As with the universities all this must be set against a solid record of considerable achievement in both professional and technological higher education and more flexible forms of basic higher education which in the past has been badly catered for in Britain.

So any attempt to capture the present experience, or to predict the future path, of the post-modern university in a simple formula should be treated with great caution. The two most popular and contrasting views of what is happening to higher education are both flawed. The first view, which is perhaps most popular in the most elite institutions, is that the post-war expansion of higher education was an exceptional event quite out of keeping with the normal pattern and pace of university development that was made possible only by the equally exceptional economic growth of the period from 1945 to 1973. Seen in this light the modern university, at any rate in its most spectacular phase, was a South Sea Bubble. But interestingly, those who hold to this first view do not generally support a return to the values and priorities of the liberal university, but instead call for an intensification of those very qualities most typical of the modern university: its academicism and its instrumentalism. Their critique of the Robbins expansion of the universities is quite distinct from those of the conservative-conservatives of the 'more means worse' brigade who deeply distrusted precisely these qualities, particularly the growing instrumentalism, and of the liberal-conservatives represented by Lord Robbins who equally disapproved of these qualities, especially perhaps the creeping academicism because it threatened to crush the life out of general higher education. Nor does this first view require a repudiation of either the fact or the benefits of the post-war expansion.

The second view is that the modern university is so embedded in the values and processes of modern society that it can survive temporary unpopularity and neglect. Indeed, this view can be extended to the broader suggestion that if the university, so integral a part of society, so much 'an expression of the age' in Flexner's phrase, is in trouble, this is a symptom of a wider crisis in modern culture. This argument will be discussed in the final chapter of this book. The more modest and limited version of this second view, however, merely emphasises that if the modern university is to fail, other distinctive sectors of post-war society will find it difficult to survive in anything like their present form, including large parts of the para-professions that service the social state, and that the progress of high-technology industry will be seriously handicapped. After all, the relationship between the modern university and the 'public sector' of society and the economy, which of course takes in large parts of the private economy through the intermediate institutions of corporatism, is far more intimate and even incestuous than that between the liberal university and the more austerely private society and economy that once prevailed. This may be one reason for the decline in the esteem of the modern university, because it appears much less remote and romantic, but it may also be one reason why it can survive this decline. It has to be remembered that at many points the modern university has played an important part in the bureaucratisation through conceptualisation of many intellectual and not-so-intellectual relationships. There are strong and interesting parallels between the formation through credentialisation of a new professional and intellectual division of labour and the fracturing of the university's knowledge base.

Both these views, as has been said, suffer from serious flaws. The first is ahistorical and ignores the suggestive relationship between the modern university's conception of knowledge, its instrumentalism, and its expansion. The second recognises this relationship more clearly, but refuses to recognise that the trajectory of the modern university is by no means fixed, but can be substantially modified by either the development of internal intellectual values or the pressure of external values. Indeed, it can be argued that the present unease can be traced to both: an instrumental 'overload' and an academic disintegration. Aspects of both were discussed in Chapter 4 and will be discussed again at the end of this chapter. But it is important not to over-simplify by placing too much emphasis on such general, and even global, causes. What is most likely to characterise higher education during the remaining years of this century is not the inexorable working out of some great determinist plan from which significant deviation will be impossible, but the often chaotic interaction of the capacities of universities, polytechnics and colleges and the demands of society and the economy, which could lead to a substantial modification of the values, processes and even structure of higher education. Although it is possible to speculate about the overall pattern of such modification, the key note of the next few years is likely to be one of high uncertainty.

The rest of this chapter, therefore, will not attempt to squeeze the future of higher education into the straitjacket of some general theory. Instead, it will discuss the issues within a pragmatic framework under four semi-independent headings: the input to and the process of higher education, which will cover both the pattern of student demand and whether, and how, that demand can be stimulated, and also undergraduate and postgraduate courses and how they are taught because both input and process are intimately related; the output of higher education, which will cover both the knowledge produced by research and its applications and skills in the context of the graduate labour market; the means of higher education, which will cover the internal processes of change within the system including the all-important 'culture' of the university, its resources, and its structure; finally — and here perhaps a general theory may creep in by the back door — a broader discussion of the socio-economic and intellectual contours of the 1990s that higher education will be both subject to and help to shape, which will cover external demands for lay society, the internal demands generated by the development of academic knowledge, and how these two are related within the common framework of modern culture.

Input and Process

The issue of access is the best starting point for any discussion of the future of higher education because it is a question that dominated, and steered, the post-war expansion of the system through the famous Robbins principle. The principle itself is simple: 'We have assumed as axiom that courses of higher education should be available to all those who are qualified by ability and attainment to pursue them and who wish to do so.'[1] Throughout the 1960s and 70s successive governments largely kept to the generous spirit of this principle, the letter of which in any case was sufficiently vague to permit considerable flexibility in detailed policy. Even today it is difficult to prove that the reduction in public expenditure on higher education since 1979 and the consequent retrenchment of the system has led to a final breach of the Robbins principle. Clearly, its spirit is no longer being respected, but a school leaver with A-level or Scottish Higher grades that would have earned him/her a place in higher education in the early 1960s should still find a place there today, although probably not in the type of institution or subject he/she wants. Higher education remains steered by student demand. Indeed, with the growing competition for places the combination of student preferences and institutional choices may even become a more commanding influence. Similarly, the growing enthusiasm for giving more power to consumers within a more entrepreneurial market will increase the emphasis placed on student demand. So any suggestion that higher education in the 1980s will be less responsive to student demand than higher education in the period of Robbins is almost certainly mistaken.

However, the issue of access is likely to be more confused. The Robbins principle is already out of date for two reasons. First, it will increasingly lose its potency because of the decline in the number of

18-year-olds and the rather more speculative decline in the number of qualified school leavers, both of which have already been described in Chapter 4. For they mean that the principle of access established by the Robbins Committee in 1963 can continue to be respected, even within a contracting system. True to the letter, but not to the spirit. Secondly, the Robbins principle has nothing to say about mature students, part-time students, or students on non-degree courses. Yet it is generally accepted that continuing education in some form will absorb an increasing share of the resources of higher education institutions. The former chairman of the UGC, Sir Edward Parkes, estimated that this share was already 10 per cent and was likely to rise to 20 or even 30 per cent by the end of the century.[2] Within the polytechnics and colleges, with their already much greater commitment to non-degree, part-time, and continuing education, the process will be even more marked. Yet the Robbins principle, with its talk of ability and attainment conventionally defined in terms of examination success, gives no guidance about the criteria on which these less traditional students can claim access.

More recently attempts have been made to stretch the Robbins principle by devising a policy of 'entitlement' under which all adults would be entitled to participate in higher education to some degree.[3] This approach, although hopeful for the future, runs into immediate difficulties. First comes the question of cost. For the foreseeable future the resources to make an honest reality of 'entitlement' are unlikely to be available, and any attempt to find such resources by robbing the mainstream activities of the present system, undergraduate and postgraduate teaching and research, could undermine its present integrity. Yet if 'entitlement' is to be restricted or rationed, the terms on which this is done become crucial from the point of view of equity. Second comes the larger question. Clearly, 'entitlement' cannot mean the right of every citizen to proceed to PhD level. On the other hand it must mean more than simply that every citizen has the right to participate in some form of post-school education. For with only moderate dishonesty it could be argued that such a right exists today if the post-school universe is stretched to include both Oxbridge and the local adult education institute. The principle of 'entitlement' could be made as elastic as the Robbins principle has become. Yet there is a substantial danger that 'entitlement' unless very carefully managed, could become a vehicle for intellectualoid consumerism, which would do very little either to broaden access or to make the criteria for access more relevant to modern conditions.

Third comes the question of planning. Higher education is as much part of production as an object of consumption, in terms of research and as the main producer of the nation's highly skilled manpower. Without necessarily accepting the case for the central planning for student choice as the organising principle for the system, it is possible to argue that genuine 'entitlement' could undermine the minimum conditions for establishing national priorities. Fourth comes the question of relevance. The idea of 'entitlement' has grown out of the worlds of traditional adult education and liberal higher education, and is aimed very much to remedy the social insufficiencies of the Robbins principle under the changed circumstances of the 1980s. Yet the thrust of continuing education is likely to come from a different direction. The most persuasive arguments for the development of such forms of higher education will be concerned with the urgent need for professional and technological up-dating in mid-career and for special-purpose short courses. It is from the desire to remedy the economic insufficiencies of the Robbins principle that the impetus will come. So perhaps before the idea of 'entitlement' can become truly effective it will have to be recast in this more instrumental and even entrepreneurial mould.

Another difficulty in any discussion of access is the inadequacy of the available information. Until recently the conventional interpretation of the pattern of student demand during the 1970s was that it has been stuck on a plateau. According to the discussion document *Higher Education into the 1990s* the age participation rate (APR — the number of students aged under 21 entering higher education as a percentage of the total 18-year-old age cohort) reached a peak of 14.2 per cent in 1972/3 and then stuck at just over or under 14 per cent for the rest of the decade.[4] This interpretation has now been shaken by the DES's recalculation of the APR during the 1970s by excluding those students who did not possess the normal entry qualifications (basically students on certificate of education courses which were phased out during the decade). According to this recalculated APR, participation in higher education continued to increase throughout the 1970s and stood a full two percentage points higher in 1982 than ten years earlier.[5] So the picture has been radically modified. Instead of student demand stagnating it has apparently continued to increase. The experience of individual institutions would suggest that the second interpretation was more accurate than the first, but the fact that such a radical reversal is even possible is a demonstration of the complexity of student demand and the technical difficulty of its accurate measurement.

The illusion that student demand stagnated during the 1970s led to conclusions about the likely future pattern of demand for higher education which now appear more speculative. The first was the widespread assumption that the pool of higher education talent was considerably shallower than had been assumed by the Robbins committee which had confidently stated

> If there is to be talk of the pool of ability, it must be a pool which surpasses the widow's cruse in the Old Testament, in that when more is taken for higher education in one generation more will tend to be available in the next.[6]

During the 1970s the feeling grew that perhaps after all the number of young people able to benefit from higher education was fairly limited. The second was a variant of this first assumption. Also during the 1970s the conviction became more firmly established that what the Robbins expansion, and the parallel development of the polytechnics, had really achieved was to make participation in higher education semi-compulsory for many middle-class families without much affecting the opportunities available to potential students from working-class families. Both conclusions will probably have to be reviewed in the light of the new evidence that student demand for and participation in higher education did not in fact stagnate during the 1970s.

However, there is more to higher education's clear ambivalence about the future pattern of student demand than the confused signals embodied in national policy, which in turn reflected inadequate information. One difficulty is that student demand is becoming increasingly fragmented. The more the potential sources of student lie beyond higher education's traditional recruiting territory, the more universities and polytechnics move away from their heartland of conventional courses, the more difficult it becomes to describe the pattern of participation by measures such as the APR and to capture the changing quality of student demand. Another difficulty is that perceptions of student demand are still very much dominated by the experience of the university half of higher education. During the 1970s it was the experience of the universities that the intense demand of the 1960s did lose some of its strength.[7] For the polytechnics the pattern was the other way round: student demand and consequent expansion were much more intense in the 1970s than during the 1960s, a trend which has continued into the 1980s with the polytechnics and colleges admitting many of the students squeezed out of the universities by their retrenchment since 1981. Yet it is the experience of the universities, not of the polytechnics and colleges, that has dominated the popular view of the pattern of student demand. A third difficulty is that, although for at least five years the message from the DES has been that higher education must prepare for a famine of students and find new and convincing ways of using its spare capacity or else have it taken away, the actual experience of institutions has been quite contrary. They have had to continue to cope with all the pressures of growth, in the case of the universities because they have been asked to educate a few more students with much less money, and in the case of the polytechnics because they have been admitting many more students and been given rather less money to educate them.

The whole picture of student demand and the extent to which it should be satisfied is further complicated by doubt about whether opinion within higher education has shifted significantly towards a more conservative position since the 1960s. The related views that the Robbins expansion was an exceptional episode and that the pool of higher education talent is much shallower than assumed by the Robbins committee have already been mentioned. The widespread acceptance of, or at least acquiescence in, these views does seem to indicate that ambivalence about the benefits of widening access to higher education has grown. To put it perhaps too simply, more and more people in universities and polytechnics seem to be closet converts to the idea that 'more means worse'. They argue with varying degrees of openness that the present character of higher education could be undermined by too rapid or too extensive an absorption of non-traditional students.

This cautious and defensive conservatism may appear to have little in common with the aggressive and ideological justification of higher education for a social and intellectual elite which the 'more means worse' zealots of the early 1960s displayed in opposing the implementation of the Robbins Report root-and-branch. But the substance of the argument has probably changed less than its style. Indeed, as has been pointed out in Chapter 5, it can be argued that the actual behaviour of higher education and especially of the

universities over the past 20 years confirms that the commitment to a
basically elite form of higher education runs very deep in Britain.
The stubborn defence of staff/student ratios that by international
standards are generous (and expensive), the expansion of specialised
honours degrees rather than the proliferation of more general first
degrees desired by the Robbins Committee, the parallel practices of
the CNAA, all confirm this impression. It is interesting to note that
among all the criticisms provoked by the UGC's unequal distribution of the reduced university grant in July 1981 little emphasis was
placed on the committee's quite explicit strategy for contraction,
that the preservation of staff/student ratios was more important
than the maintenance, let alone expansion, of opportunity to enter
higher education. What the UGC was really saying, and there were
few to condemn it for this, was that the intrinsic culture of the
university deserved greater protection in a time of adversity than its
extrinsic purposes. However, it may be wrong to condemn such an
attitude too harshly. Part of higher education's strong commitment
to elite forms can be explained by the entirely worthy ideal that new
and less conventional students should not be offered second best.
Certainly, the much criticised striving of the polytechnics after university status and standards, as much a myth as a fact, it has been
argued in Chapter 6, falls into this category. But even when all the
pleas for mitigation have been made, the worrying suspicion is left
that higher education in a new more conservative and more defensive mood has much less faith in its capacity to absorb new types of
students with less obviously academic or professional ambitions in
the 1980s than in the 1960s, although paradoxically its need to do so
will be much greater.

The present danger is that the issue of access will be seen in
black-and-white, even scaremongering, terms. The temptation may
be to see the choice as one between defending the present semi-elite
system and acquiescing in the creation of some vast disorganised
and even politicised system of mass post-school education. Yet that
is not the effective choice, and no one should be frightened away
from tackling the pragmatic issues of improving and extending
access by such terrible simplicities. One day Britain may have to
decide whether it wants or can afford a genuinely mass system of
higher education. But because of the reductions in public expenditure on higher education in common with all public services, the
adverse pattern of demography, and the comparatively early stage
of development of the British system of higher education, that will

be a decision for the next century not for this. The immediate task is much simpler: it is to decide whether higher education has the necessary nerve to remain true to the limited liberalism of the Robbins Report, which is what the Robbins principle is all about. It is important to be clear about the stage of development that has been reached by British higher education. The decisive rupture between higher education, in practice the universities, and the formation of a ruling elite was made in the 1960s during the early stages of the Robbins expansion and the first elaboration of the binary policy. The decisive break with the idea that students must display reasonable intelligence and moderate commitment before being admitted to higher education is unlikely to come until at least 25 per cent of the age group is enrolled, which would require a doubling of the size of the present system.

The position today is an intermediate one, which is why semi-elite is a reasonably accurate description. Many students, although perfectly intelligent and well educated, may not have the singleminded determination of cadet members of the ruling class. Yet only a small minority of school leavers goes on to any form of higher education. To imagine that this small minority, which represents less than 15 per cent of the secondary school population, cannot be made larger without accepting sub-standard students is wrong. Most secondary schools could send many more of their pupils on to higher education without any significant loss of quality. It is misleading to suppose that British higher education is hovering on the brink of a mass system with credits given for 'life experience' (although a strong case can indeed be made for the development of what has become known as experiential learning[8]) and remedial classes for freshmen. So what should be at the top of the policy agenda is not some rambling shapeless debate about the virtues of 'quality' higher education and the vices of 'mass' higher education (or the other way round), but a limited list of pragmatic reforms that are designed to maintain the Robbins momentum, protect higher education from the pain of declining student numbers, and provide a modest improvement in access for young and not-so-young people. It is not difficult to make such a list which would certainly include:

1) more general sixth-form examinations in a broader range of subjects, the common practice in Scotland;

2) more one year pre-entry courses to help those without formal

qualifications such as that offered by the City and East London College in conjunction with the University of Essex;

3) more schemes that link universities, polytechnics and colleges with selected secondary schools, paticularly those with little experience of entering pupils for higher education, and with whole local authority areas in a determined attempt to nourish local roots;

4) a more satisfactory system of financial assistance to 16- and 17-year-olds who choose to stay on at school;

5) more flexible patterns of study for those at work or bringing up young children (such as shortened days for women with school-age children);

6) more two-year courses on the pattern of the Dip HE, but with more modest entry standards. Seen in this pragmatic context, the whole question of access can be made less alarming and more manageable.

The input to higher education is intimately related to the process itself. There would be little point in developing detailed and sophisticated policies to encourage access to universities, polytechnics and colleges if what they offer in terms both of courses and teaching remains essentially unchanged. Indeed, developing a more liberal curriculum is a precondition of wider access. One immediate difficulty is that the very word 'curriculum' forms a block in the context of higher education, especially in the universities. It seems to imply an organised scheme of safe and secure knowledge, or else the carefully graded development of cognitive and related skills. Both ideas are unhappily received in parts of higher education although they may be perfectly fair descriptions of the aims and practices of undergraduate education, because they seem to fail to capture the tentativeness of knowledge and the anarchy of learning which are seen even at the undergraduate level as important qualities of higher education. This difficulty is not perhaps as trivial as it seems. For the reform of the process of higher education through the establishment of a more liberal curriculum is really dependent on the erosion of the hegemony of the three or four-year honours degree. The honours degree in turn is more than a convenient or conventional form; it is a totem that represents some of higher education's most fundamental values and beliefs, about the nature of knowledge, how it is formed, and how it is transmitted. It embodies those commitments to tentativeness and anarchy. Of course, these commitments are sometimes only a cloak for badly organised degree courses and inadequately prepared teaching, and clearly they apply with much less force to applied sciences and professional subjects (and in the case of natural sciences are largely confined to the postgraduate level with first degrees being seen as laying foundations and establishing a context). Yet the potency of these values should not be ignored. The stubborn persistence of the honours degree would be difficult to explain otherwise.

If this view is accepted, it follows that the greatest opportunity for reform of the process of higher education will arise in those institutions that are on the periphery of the system. Conversely, there will be least possibility for change in the university core where these values are most firmly established. This means that it is most likely that new patterns of undergraduate education will be developed in the non-university half of higher education, particularly in the colleges and institutes of higher education. Not only will their potential students be, relatively, less well prepared in terms of academic qualifications, and so less suitable material for the application of values like the tentativeness of knowledge or the anarchy of learning, but these institutions will be less mesmerised by these traditional values than the universities. It can also be argued that they are more likely to question the present pattern of CNAA degrees than the polytechnics, not simply because such awards clearly embody many of the implicit values expressed through university degrees, but also because of their technological orientation which arises from the practices of the National Council for Technological Awards, the CNAA's predecessor institution.

For this reason above all others these non-polytechnic colleges do have a right to receive a fair trial. What they already offer to students that is distinctive and what they can offer in the future to the diversity of British higher education should at least be properly understood. Their contribution to our local and national senses of community (as much as to a more narrowly defined economy) also deserves to be recognised. Resources may be against them. There may not be enough money to go round under present or foreseeable policies. They may be surrounded by stronger predators. They may have to fight against the apparent imperatives of excellence, in an academic sense, and of concentration in terms of efficiency. They may even to combat the seductions of 'bigness' and 'relevance'. Yet the colleges should still be heard. The game is not as simple as it seemed to be in the 1970s, when monotechnic teacher training institutions saw their entire purpose disappear with the declining demand for teachers. The situation of the colleges that were fortunate enough to survive into diversification and the 1980s is quite different. It is not possible to argue that the new styles of low-intensity, human-scale, liberal arts and (largely non-technical) vocational education which the colleges are beginning to pioneer are things of the past, like certificates of education taught in small and academically isolated colleges of education. These styles of higher education may belong to a mass future which Britain cannot afford, or not yet, or which Britain does not want. But they do belong to some kind of future, not to the past. In this all-important sense the defence of the right of the colleges at least to be heard is a quite different policy exercise from the sad but necessary catalogue of closures in the 1970s.

Many people would argue that the next decade should see a revival of the debate about constructing more popular forms of higher education, outside the large university and polytechnic institutions. This debate was last conducted with any vigour in the immediate aftermath of the James Report a decade ago.[9] Although the debate was still largely imprisoned within teacher education, that report did explore two proposals which have a significance that transcends the immediate concerns of teacher education, and is relevant both to the future of the colleges as distinct from the larger universities and polytechnics and to the theme of this discussion: the role and pattern of undergraduate education. Sadly, these James proposals were interpreted by most people solely in the context of teacher education. As a result the debate was cut short by the institutional crisis that afflicted that sector in the mid-1970s.

The first significant proposal of the James Committee was for a Diploma of Higher Education. Although proposed as part of a particular scheme for the reorganistion of teacher education, this two-year qualification in general higher education clearly could be applied to all parts of higher education. It was, and is, possible to see the DipHE as a parallel qualification to the HND/BTEC Higher. Of course, considerable progress has been made with the DipHE. Yet even its most enthusiastic supporters would not claim that it had yet secured a firm foothold in higher education. It is unknown in the universities, and in the polytechnics and colleges is still seen in most cases as a stage towards a degree, and a teacher education degree in many cases, rather than as a qualification in its own right. Only in a few cases, most notably at the North East London Polytechnic, has the DipHE been able to sustain an independent existence divorced from the BEd. A further restraint is the insistence on the usual two A-levels for entry, in contrast to the one A-level required for entry to a HND course. However impractical such an argument may be under present economic conditions, it is nevertheless important to emphasise that it is only when the DipHE is aimed at students who otherwise would have remained outside higher education entirely, rather than being regarded as a substitute for a degree course, that real progress can be made. Only when the DipHE is seen as a self-sufficient course and as a useful qualification, rather than as a staging post on the way to a degree, that it can begin to make its potential contribution to popularising higher education. Perhaps the colleges with their less intense commitment to conventional degrees may be more fertile ground for such ideas and experiments than the polytechnics, let alone the universities.[10]

The second James proposal was that the higher education of future school teachers should be organised on a consecutive, academic element followed by professional training, rather than a concurrent basis. The immediate intention of the committee was to prise away such education from exclusive employment as a teacher at the end of the course, and as a half-way house to produce a new arrangement that would allow students to delay their commitment to becoming teachers until later in their higher education. Their hope was that this new arrangement could be harmonised with preparation for other analogous professions, like social work. As a symbol of both intention and hope the committee recommended that such a course should lead to a BA (Ed), although the BEd proved to be too strong to be rooted out.

Like the DipHE this new division of a degree into an element of general (liberal?) higher education and a more specifically vocational element holds out great promise. It could become the basis, if sufficiently widely adopted, of a revival of the old ordinary degree which now survives precariously only in the Scottish universities. Indeed, the Robbins Committee had intended that many of the new students coming into higher education as a result of the expansion they recommended should be studying for general degrees. Lord Robbins himself has frequently and publicly deplored the growth and domination of specialised honours degrees. Yet despite this failure in the universities CNAA degrees have followed a broadly similar pattern. There is now little hope that general degrees can be revived in either universities or polytechnics, the first because the cuts will naturally intensify their natural commitment to academicism and to excellence within it, the second because the demands for higher education to be more vocationally relevant will intensify their traditional commitment to instrumentalism. This leaves the colleges, as the only available, and perhaps the most sympathetic in terms of their own traditions, vehicles of any renewed attempt to introduce general degrees into higher education. Perhaps the best way forward will be not to re-invent the ordinary degree, but to build on the James idea for a two-stage degree, general education followed by a vocational element. In turn this might fit in with any development of the DipHE as an independent but complementary qualification, and also resonate with the proposal from Sir Brian Pippard, among others, for a '2 plus 2' arrangement of undergraduate education, with a two-year ordinary degree to be followed for some students by two further years of more advanced (and more specific?) study.

Not all the colleges and institutes of higher education will want to become engaged in such experimentation. Equally, a number of polytechnics, and even in time the occasional university, may wish to participate. Among the colleges there are those which will see their future in terms of orthodox teacher education. They may hope that if they survive the next round of contraction they may be able to establish themselves finally as specialist institutions of teacher education. Certainly, there should be room in a higher education system as large as ours for a few such centres. Other colleges may see themselves as proto-polytechnics, firmly part of the technical college tradition and indistinguishable from the polytechnics in everything but luck and possibly size. Others again may see their future as community colleges catering for the educational (general, vocational, and even recreational) needs of all adults young and old. With school sixth forms being shaken to their foundations and the emergence of a strong tertiary sector marching with an ever more powerful MSC, the relevance of such comprehensive post-18 institutions is bound to grow. But within such institutions the emphasis on higher education, even of the most general variety, is bound to be less. However, the majority of the diversified colleges are likely to be not only suitable but willing vehicles for these two developments, of genuinely free-standing DipHEs that extend the scope of higher education rather than serving as a substitute for degrees, and of a more liberal degree structure, with two years of general higher education being followed by one or two years of vocational or advanced study. It is worth recalling that in the United States it was out of the teachers' colleges that more popular interpretations of higher education emerged most strongly.

Britain in 1982 still has a 'high-intensity' higher education system. In this respect the polytechnics are often little different from the universities. Both are principally concerned with higher education for an elite, in the better sense of that word, and/or of experts. We are still profoundly unfamiliar with the idea of higher education for students who are not going to join a political, social, or economic elite, however loosely defined, or who do not require highly developed conceptual and technological skills. The very idea seems almost a contradiction. It conjures up immediate fears of slipping standards, 'cafeteria' courses, and the other characteristics of American higher education which are regarded with such suspicion on this side of the Atlantic. Yet there is no need for the higher education of the common man to be such a frightening idea. More 'low-intensity' higher education need not lead to a collapse of standards. Indeed, a better-educated population with a more substantial involvement in higher education through local colleges might be far more likely to recognise the need for more advanced, and more expensive, forms of higher education in universities and polytechnics. Nor is it inevitable that Britain's liberal arts or community colleges of tomorrow should mimic those of America today. The job of the colleges in the 1980s and 90s, in which they deserve the support of the rest of higher education, should be to evolve 'low-intensity' styles of higher education in a British mould — higher education for the common man.

Output: Skills and Knowledge

Although input remains the best starting point for, and process a vital ingredient in, any discussion of the future of higher education, more and more emphasis has come to be placed on the output of universities, polytechnics and colleges, in terms both of skilled manpower and knowledge and its technological application. This gradual shift of priority from input to output has taken place over the space of 20 years. When the Robbins Committee began work at the beginning of the 1960s the predominant policy issue was demand — how could the system be expanded fast enough to meet the exploding expectations of young people? This concern held its place at the top of the policy agenda until the early 1970s (and has not yet lost it perhaps in the hearts and hopes of a majority of those practically engaged in higher education). This expansion mentality reached its, probably too distant, apogee with the publication of the DES's *Planning Paper Number 2* in 1969, which predicted that there might need to be as many as 750,000 places in higher education at the beginning of the 1980s, an overestimate as things have turned out of 50 per cent.[11] Today the predominant policy concern is different — how can the system supply enough graduates of the right type to meet the needs of industry and the economy at large? We are all supply-siders now it seems. If there is ever to be an anti-Robbins principle it is probably to be found on the supply rather than the demand side of the higher education debate.

Not that higher education's relationship with the labour market is a particulary new issue. There have always been those who preferred to trust in the apparent solidity of the supply of skills and knowledge rather than the drift of student demand in determining priorities within the system. There is in fact a strong case to be made for the argument that success is always better judged in terms of outputs than inputs, although such an argument necessarily prejudges or telescopes the important debate about the ultimate purposes of higher education. From the time of the Robbins Report, and even earlier, many distrusted the *laissez-faire* approach that was embodied in the austere and altruistic liberalism of the Robbins principle. Indeed, it can be argued that the binary policy and the creation of the polytechnics were a deliberate attempt to be more prescriptive. Certainly, it has been impossible to keep manpower planning down as a policy issue. 'Broad brushes' supported by Lord Crowther Hunt in the Labour Government of 1974-9 were succeeded by 'broad steers' promoted by civil servants in the early days of the new Conservative Government, when higher education appeared to be entering a period of prolonged steady state. Even today it is clear that manpower planning in some form (information technology?) will be the one extrinsic factor that will be allowed to modify significantly the re-ordering or retrenchment of higher education by the UGC and the NAB according to intrinsic academic strengths or educational preoccupations.

The main difficulty with manpower planning is that if higher education is to be regarded as a producer, it has not one but three sets of customers — students, private employers, and the state both as a substantial employer in its own right and as proxy for the broader public interest. Then there are a host of technical problems of definition and implementation which have to be tackled. In the discussion of access it has already been made clear student demand is likely to become increasingly fragmented. It is also clear that it is no longer possible to rely so confidently on the belief that because graduates are in such short supply as a result of the constraints on access to higher education, potential students will either be so well informed about employment opportunities that the demands of the labour market can be safely mediated through their choices, or else such a scarce commodity that employers will have little choice but to accept them. Nor is it necessarily safe for employers to assume that all graduates by the very fact of their selection by a university or polytechnic are likely to be highly intelligent and motivated and so, except in the case of precise professional skills, easily substitutable. Can physicists be so easily trained up (or down?) as engineers? Even if they can, is this a sensible route for the formation of engineers? In any case, this assumption, as well as pandering to a dangerous enthusiasm for adaptable amateurism, neglects the impermeability of the divide between language-based arts and mathematics-based sciences. Finally, the even more cynical argument that in most parts of the economy so few graduates were employed anyway that the labour market was supply rather than demand-led, has not survived the three-fold expansion of higher education since 1960. Whatever strength such arguments once had, it has been very much eroded over the past 20 years. In the United States patterns of student enrolment may respond very quickly and sensitively to fluctuations in the labour market for graduates (although some have argued that the almost instantaneous symmetry of the two is too good to be true).[12] But the same thing does not appear to have happened in Britain to the same extent. Throughout the 1970s universities and polytechnics had spare capacity in science and technology, despite the widespread assumption that demand for graduates in these sub-jects far outstripped supply. The truth seems to be that student choice is a complex cultural phenomenon rather than a simple eco-nomic judgement. If fewer school leavers apply to study sociology it probably has much more to do with the cultural standing of sociologists than their position in the labour market. Only the very optimistic could argue that British students are especially accurate mediators of labour market messages.

Unfortunately, the messages that higher education receives directly from employers are as likely to be flawed or obscure. There seem to be two broad reasons for this. The first is that employers by and large are conservative. They may say that they need more graduates with highly specific skills and detailed up-to-date knowledge, but all too often they go ahead and recruit the 'best' students. These they define in traditional terms of academic achievement, and given the cultural biases of British education that have deep roots in the schools these students are often found in general non-vocational subjects, which helps to explain why physicists end up as engineers and historians as managers. The second is that employers are not necessarily the best judges of their own long-term interests. They simply cannot offer planners the necessary time scale to take proper decisions. Manpower planning in any form is an attempt to construct a market in 'futures', the skills that will be in demand a generation ahead. This is especially difficult in an educational system in which often irrevocable decisions can still be made as early as the age of 14, and in which the period from the conception of a new degree course to its first output of graduates may be as much as ten years. Moreover, it is a market in very long-range futures, because graduates remain in the labour market for up to 40 years. Given the extreme sensitivity of decisions about future demand for skilled manpower, and the foresight required to make them, can employers be trusted with this task? The record of British industry does not necessarily inspire much confidence. An impartial foreign assessment of the quality of British institutions would probably rate industry's performance rather low by international standards and higher education's reputation as rather high. So it is not obvious why the judgements of the former should be allowed to override those of the latter, especially in the area of high technology where those in higher education often have a considerable knowledge lead.

This leaves higher education's third, and potentially most influential, customer, the state. Not only does the state largely support higher education in the first place, it has two vital interests in the output of the system — as a substantial employer through central and local government, nationalised industries and other public services (including, of course, higher education itself), and as the facilitator of technological innovation in the economy in a broader sense and even as the ultimate guardian of intellectual and cultural standards. If students cannot be relied on as the mediators of market messages, and if employers cannot always be relied on to organise the optimal use of highly skilled manpower, can the state do better? The instinctive answer is usually no. But that may be a premature and under-considered response. Manpower planning is impossible without planning. However, for the state to play a more active part in the organisation and supply of highly skilled manpower would require a new attitude. It would no longer be feasible for government to confine its activity to forecasting, however sophisticated. Any form of forecasting itself sends signals to the labour market, which if they are not backed up by prescriptive planning can often confuse rather than guide the pattern of supply and demand. For a start, and as a minimum, the state as a substantial direct and indirect employer has to show greater consistency in its own employment practices and move towards a plan for highly skilled manpower in the public sector. But probably even more can be done. Manpower planning can probably only work at all if it is closely integrated into broader industrial policy, if the supply of graduates is used as an active instrument of prescriptive planning. Perhaps government should be less concerned with reading other people's signals, which are often weak and confused, and more concerned to send out some signals of its own, signals that go beyond rhetoric and form part of a comprehensive planning effort.

The other, and perhaps more important, output of higher education is theoretical knowledge and its practical application through the process of research, scholarship, development and consultancy. The last three aspects are difficult to plan: scholarship is intimately linked with undergraduate and postgraduate teaching, and makes use of common or similar resources within universities and polytechnics, good libraries, staff/student ratios that leave the teacher with adequate time for scholarly work, and so on; development and consultancy are almost by definition entrepreneurial activities in which higher education offers a service for which there is a specific customer demand. Research, however, is different: it is sufficiently distinct from teaching to require different policies and separate organisation, and it uses competing resources. Yet in most cases its priorities are preoccupations which are generated internally through the development of knowledge organised in disciplines rather than externally through the specific demands of customers.

The structure for research established in the 1960s is creaking — some would say, cracking — in the 1980s, despite the clear evidence that successive governments have been determined to protect the science budget even at the expense of the rest of higher education. The dual-support system, under which the UGC is supposed to provide a research 'floor' (often summed up in the phrase 'the well-founded laboratory') while the five research councils make grants for specific programmes, has been substantially undermined, partly because the cuts in the university grant have made it difficult for the UGC to keep its side of the bargain, partly because of the growing disjunction of research and teaching in some disciplines. It is difficult to see how the dual-support system can be restored except on a selective and so divisive basis, by confining the provision of a general research 'floor' to a smaller number of research universities. The equipment grant from the UGC to the universities has been woefully inadequate for several years. Any idea that the dual-support system should be extended, on even the most limited terms, to the polytechnics and colleges has been stubbornly resisted. The research councils since the mid-1970s have been under the spell of Lord Rothschild's 'customer — contractor' principle which tried to organise fundamental research as if it were development or consultancy with obvious and knowledgeable customers and which has had the, no doubt unintentional, effect of under-valuing fundamental research and over-valuing derivative problem-solving research.[13] There is, of course, a case to be made for the charge that Britain produces far too many Nobel Prize winners and far too few good technologists. But that is a rather different, and broader, issue than the one tackled by Rothschild's 'customer — contractor' principle. Finally, the number of postgraduate awards has declined, especially in the beleaguered social sciences, and the career prospects of young researchers, generally on fixed-term contracts, have been blighted by the contraction of the university system. The creaks, or cracks are getting louder year by year.

The causes of this decay in the structure of research lie back in the 1960s when, although the research councils were established, no general organising principle to underpin this new arrangement of higher education's research effort emerged to match the Robbins principle that has steered the development of the system's teaching effort so successfully. The concept, popular in the late 1960s and early 70s, that research should be supported if it showed 'timeliness and promise' was too weak to serve as a framework in which detailed priorities could be established. For this phrase amounted to little more than an unconvincing fudge between the instrumentalist 'timeliness' and the academicist 'promise'. As a result, the two most basic questions of all, 'How much and what kind of research do we need?' remained effectively unanswered. So long as there was a strong dual support system, an equally strong consensus within disciplines about intellectual priorities, and a higher education system with ever increasing financial and physical resources for research as a by-product of the Robbins expansion of students, and with plenty of money and room for a new generation of young research-minded scholars and scientists, a policy of disorganised pluralism may have seemed adequate.

This age of innocence (and independence?) came to an end for two main reasons, both in their different ways symptoms of the so-called British disease of disappointing economic growth. First, the expansion of higher education slowed down to be replaced eventually by a period of deliberate contraction, at any rate for the universities. As unit costs fell and staff/student ratios increased, students still had to be taught so money and time for research were squeezed. At the same time the need to establish much tougher priorities in research made the former policy of benign pluralism inadequate. Secondly, declining faith in the judgements of higher education, and the more urgent need to harness scientific invention to technological change and so to faster economic growth, led to much greater interest by government, industry and the community in the setting of research priorities. The result has been a more and more insistent attempt to subject academic research to the disciplines of the market. So the highly instrumental 'customer-contractor' principle elbowed aside the latitudinarian but essentially liberal principle of 'timeliness and promise'.

There can be little doubt that these two trends, the movement towards concentration whether through the joint government — industry research council directorates established by the Science and Engineering Research Council or the designated research centres of the Economic and Social Research Council, and the growing power of lay customers and of even more powerful surrogate customers, have seriously impoverished the range if not the quality of research in higher education. So long as the 'customer —contractor' principle was complemented or even mitigated by a still vigorous dual-support system, there was some hope that a balance might be kept between fundamental and applied research, between intellectual detachment and utilitarian commitment, between 'promise' and 'timeliness'. It could after all be argued that the former could be protected by the research component in higher education's general revenue, while the latter could be steered by customer demand. But the progressive erosion of the UGC-provided research 'floor' and the failure to extend the dual-support system to the non-university half of higher education have led to a situation in which the scope for independent, uncontracted-for research is very small and the customer has become over-mighty. This imbalance would matter much less if the 'customer — ontractor' principle itself was not subject to flawing ambiguity. The first difficulty is that many of the customers of research are in fact surrogate customers, if needs rather than payment are regarded as the proper criterion. In the case of the private economy this distinction matters much less because market competition is a reasonably effective transmitter of the demands and needs of the ultimate customer, although even here the hidden hand of the state is never far away because of the incestuous corporatism that is so typical of relations between public and private sectors in the area of advanced technology.

But in the case of government, normally the monopoly provider of services that are often 'positional goods' and sometimes ingredients of complex and delicate social and cultural systems, the distinction between real and proxy customer is much more significant. In the endlessly manipulable market of political preferences government may try to modify, divert, or even suppress the demands of the true customers. This difference is important because in its essence the Rothschild principle is that the customer defines the problem and the contractor then tries to solve it. In the natural sciences and in engineering, where the natural customer is 'industry', broadly defined, this may be acceptable because the problems that high-technology companies want to have solved are nearly always interesting scientific problems. But in the case of social sciences, where the natural customer is 'public policy', equally broadly defined, there is likely to be much greater tension between instrumentalism and academicism because the really interesting intellectual questions have as much to do with the definition of problems as with their solution.

The second difficulty with the 'customer — contractor' principle is that it recognises demands but not needs. Although a common and perhaps inevitable flaw, in the context of research it is a particularly damaging one. For the likely result is that any research policy built on the Rothschild principle is likely to be gradualist and perhaps even conservative, rather than creative and adventurist. Who, after all, would have been the customer for the theory of relativity, or the splitting of the atom, or the discovery of DNA? Almost by definition the most interesting scientific problems are likely to be beyond the imagination of today's customers. They may also be uninteresting to today's customers because their extreme novelty makes commercial exploitation difficult. The same problem presents itself in the social sciences but possibly in a more painful form. Today's customers for public-policy research will almost inevitably be those institutions of present power that are naturally suspicious of intellectual novelty. The trouble with the Rothschild principle is that it places too much emphasis on the 'timeliness' of research and pays too little attention to its 'promise'. A secondary trouble is that the 'customer — contractor' principle has done nothing to reduce the sharply contested definitions of 'timeliness', especially in the social sciences. Yet despite these evident shortcomings the organisation of research has become dominated by this over-simple instrumentalism because rival principles and practices like the traditional dual-support system have been eroded.

If it is accepted that the balance must be restored between 'timeliness' and 'promise', there are only two realistic strategies. The first is to try to revive the dual-support system, and is the strategy that still commands majority support within universities. It received authoritative endorsement from the report of the Merrison Committee in 1982.[14] Yet at a time when public expenditure on higher education is being reduced, this strategy could work only if money was taken out of the science budget and given instead to the UGC as part of the normal university recurrent grant. Yet this runs entirely contrary to the policy of successive governments which has been to protect the science budget at the expense of general expenditure on higher education. In any case it is almost impossible to conceive of the UGC being given the extra resources that would be necessary to restore an effective dual-support system across all disciplines and across all institutions (even if it continued to be confined to the universities). One modification might be to allow only 12 or 15 universities an adequate research 'floor' through a much more selective dual-support system, and to abandon the pretence that significant research funding can be provided to most universities as part of their general income. Whether such a policy of creating a research university super league would be feasible against the background of a strong tradition of elitist egalitarianism in British universities is doubtful. It would also require a substantial inroad into the collective autonomy of the university system if it were not to be merely a mild discrimination in the pattern of UGC funding. It would also be a blunt instrument because departmental excellence, let alone individual talent, is by no means aligned with institutional reputations. Nevertheless, ministers have shown interest in the idea of a more explicit division of the universities into research and teaching divisions.

The second strategy is the reverse. This is to abandon the dual-support system with its comfortable confusion of money for teaching and research, and to replace it with a new-style dual-support system under which institutions would receive separate grants for teaching and research, the latter being distinct from the specific research grants made by the research councils. This disengagement of research from teaching might in the long run have radical consequences for the structure of higher education. It might stimulate the growth of research institutes on a more systematic basis because they would no longer have to depend so entirely on vulnerable 'soft' money or else piggy-back on teaching departments. It could also lead, although by a different route, to the creation of research universities, and would almost certainly mean that in many institutions the research commitment would atrophy. However, it would allow the polytechnics and colleges to be given proper research budgets because there would no longer by any requirement to do so on the basis of equal treatment. Its significance for undergraduate education would need to be carefully weighed, especially perhaps in the humanities, where a separate research budget could act as an incitement to give less attention to teaching.

On balance the second strategy is probably to be preferred to the first, and both are to be preferred to a continuation of the present post-Rothschild structure of research in higher education into the 1990s. If this second strategy were implemented carefully it could have two important and beneficial results. First, it might allow the development of more popular and more pedagogical forms of higher education that are not burdened financially or intellectually by some superior research mission. This is particularly important if the reforms of the undergraduate curriculum discussed earlier are ever to become effective. Secondly, it might encourage higher education to address the fundamental questions that were never properly tackled in the 1960s. Then the dual-support system by lumping together teaching and research may have seemed to underpin institutional and academic freedom, because specific grants are clearly an avenue to more detailed control. Today the 'black box' of the dual-support system leaves the field to the Rothschild principle with its over-emphasis on instrumentalism. Yet if the totality of higher education's research effort, the internal element provided in the general UGC grant as well as the external element provided by the research councils and other funding agencies, was made explicitly distinguishable, the inadequacy of the 'customer — contractor' principle would become more obvious. It is important that the future of research in higher education should not be discussed in the limited context of externally funded research. It is also important that higher educations's crucial role as a producer of knowledge should not be seen entirely in terms of research; scholarship on the one hand, and development and consultancy on the other need to be brought into any debate. Only when this total picture is recognised can balanced and co-ordinated policies be devised for these separate segments.

Means: Innovation, Resources, Structure

Clearly, the shifting pattern of student demand and the consequent debate about the terms on which it should be met, the pressure for the reform of undergraduate education which is likely to take the form of a movement away from the traditional honours degree, and the growing emphasis on the output of higher education in terms both of knowledge and of skills, will lead to a substantial modification of the practices, funding and structure of the system. In the 1980s and 90s the means of higher education will be given new emphasis as the ends which the system is expected to meet change. Some would go so far as to argue that the 1960s settlement associated with the name of Robbins for the universities and of Crosland for the polytechnics and colleges may be radically disturbed and even replaced by a new configuration of institutions. Even more important perhaps will be the process of change within institutions to meet these new needs. This is an intractable subject because this process of internal change is little understood. But it is a crucial one because the pressure for change will not slacken but increase. The sources of this pressure are many and obvious — the cuts in public expenditure on higher education; the need for selectivity and specialisation that flows from these cuts; the decline in the number of 18-year-olds after the mid-1980s; the need to attract new students who are either 'less able' in terms of conventional qualifications or less traditional in terms of age, job pattern, social class; the knowledge revolution, particularly in its technological aspect; shifts in the structure of occupations. These external factors, together with the endless changes in the scope, structure and content of academic knowledge, mean that far from slackening, the pressure on universities, polytechnics and colleges to change and adapt will be greater than ever.

Yet the issue of change remains intractable for two main reasons. The first is the difficulty about agreeing an adequate definition of change. Here it is important to remember Martin Trow's distinction between the private and public lives of higher education. In higher education's private life — the advancement of knowledge through research and teaching — there is little evidence of resistance to change. This disciplinary dynamism is most obvious in the natural sciences, but a similarly radical process has been at work in non-science disciplines as well. So a reasonable conclusion might seem to be that higher education's reputation for rigidity and resistance to change, which cannot be denied, is the result of the habits of its public life, its administrative, political and possibly cultural superstructure. In fact this contrast between academic dynamism and political rigidity that the comparison between the private and public lives of higher education may encourage can be misleading. There is the argument that higher education even at the basic level of disciplines and departments is a conservative system, that most scholars spend their time shoring up conventional wisdoms, and that it is only a minority of the most outstanding who actually have the intellectual imagination and courage to advance knowledge in any substantial way. This argument with its perhaps naive belief in some heroic individualistic myth of how knowledge is advanced is certainly overstated. But it is perhaps a necessary corrective to the alternative view of masses of creative and open-minded scholars selflessly and radically questioning the received wisdom of the past. As Kuhn has suggested, the quality of intellectual life in many disciplines is influenced not just by the pioneers on the advancing frontiers, but by the clumps of entrenched and perhaps conservative interest that exist in them all.

Secondly, this rather optimistic contrast between the private and public lives of higher education relies on a clear distinction that in practice it is unsafe to make. The social organisation of higher education is a reflection of its intellectual organisation, not an independent phenomenon. So if the former exhibits symptoms of rigidity, it may be necessary to search for its roots in the latter. At a more mundane level it is obvious that some parts of higher education — those British institutions closest to America's research universities — are much more heavily engaged in the private life of the system than others — the polytechnics and colleges of higher education — which necessarily and willingly operate more at the level of the system's public life in the Trow scheme. Thirdly, this contrast appears to place too much emphasis on research and scholarship. Of course, the advances in knowledge registered by research do feed through postgraduate into undergraduate education, and even finally affect teaching in schools and how intellectual questions are presented to the public. But this is a long and diluting process, which normally guarantees that all the excitement and radicalism will be found at the research frontier where inevitably only a small number of scholars is engaged, and that by the time new theories, facts and preoccupations feed into the rest of higher education they may have ossified into an uninspiring and insipid orthodoxy. So it is probably wrong to place too much emphasis, and so too much hope, on the ability of higher education to change because of its acknowledged intellectual vitality.

However, this does not solve the difficulty of arriving at an adequate definition of change. To be achievable, change needs to be manageable. That means it must have limits. For if change is expected to operate across the whole system, at all levels and in every aspect whether political, social or intellectual, if change as it were is regarded as indivisible, then it will become impossibly difficult to achieve. The only sensible way forward for policy-makers is for the territory of change to be confined essentially to higher education as a political system. Of course, this involves a deliberate simplification because higher education is first and foremost a system of intellectual production, and also a calculated risk because within these deliberately narrowed limits change can be defined in superficial terms. The degree course that has radically changed its content and structure but retained the same title may be labelled an example of conservatism, while the skilfully repackaged modular degree with rather stale and unchanged material may be regarded as an example of dynamic change.

Having disposed of, or at any rate discussed, the first difficulty, the problem of defining change, the second is almost immediately encountered. Is it possible to regard change as a neutral process that is not affected by the desired direction of change, or is the whole

subject simply another aspect of an essentially political programme
for the democratisation (or vocationalisation, or academicisation)
of higher education? There is of course some justification for
believing that those who talk most about change in higher education
are mostly talking about widening access, offering new curricula
and courses, engaging higher education more closely with its enveloping community. In short, enthusiasm for change can be merely a
code for a populist programme for higher education. But it would be
wrong to push this argument too far. While it may be true that the
topic of change still carries with its vaguely liberal presumptions,
higher education is undergoing a constant process of change, a
process that is likely to intensify. The direction of change is a separate question. It is possible for instance to regard the concentration
of resources on embryonic centres of excellence, one possible interpretation of the UGC's 1981 selectivity strategy as a powerful, even
irresistible, form of change. Or to take another example, the next
two decades are likely to see growing pressure for an increasingly
direct linkage between the pattern of higher education and the
demands of the economy. That too would represent a powerful
form of change. So it is not necessarily inappropriate to talk of
change as a neutral, even mechanical, process. Practices like academic tenure, tutorials, or closely interwoven honours degrees are
going to come under growing pressure, whether future change is in
the direction of wider access (the populist route), or concentration
on traditional excellence (the conservative route), or growing
attachment to economic needs (the industrial route). Indeed, the
detailed repercussions of these different forms of change on the
present practices of higher education might be very similar.

Strategies for Change

There are two broad strategies for change in British higher
education, the market and the political (leaving aside the very
important internally generated processes of change which depend
on the advance of knowledge). Which of these strategies is given
greater emphasis may depend on the desired direction of change.
For those who favour the industrial route the temptation to plump
for the market strategy is obvious, just as those who seek a populist
future will tend to favour the political strategy. Yet too sharp a
juxtaposition of market and political strategies as mutually exclu-

sive alternatives is not particularly helpful. There is certainly room for the better reception of market messages by universities and colleges (and polytechnics to a lesser extent). Equally, a political strategy may involve market elements, especially in the area of student support. At a more fundamental level a strategy for change that rested on a strong commitment to encouraging a plurality of political influences would have a great deal in common with a market strategy, particularly within the context of an almost wholly publicly funded system of higher education in which any market would be contrived and controlled by political action. In the end the best way to stimulate change may be to accept a stronger political presence in the making of higher education policy. After all, it is as a political not as an intellectual system that higher education seems to have been slow to change. So it seems logical to attack what seems to be a socio-political problem by socio-political measures. After all, it is only within the context of closer political involvement that issues like the modification of tenure, the reform of student support, changes in the traditional pattern of undergraduate courses, credit transfer, a higher education development fund for innovation, and other policies that are regarded as central to the process of change, can be effectively tackled. Most of the levers of change lie outside higher education or at any rate outside individual institutions. Nor should closer political involvement be seen as a threat to the autonomy and integrity of higher education. There is a strong case for arguing that the state can protect higher education from the more immediate pressures of the market place, very much as the establishment of the UGC in 1919 and the consolidation of a reliable system of government grants to universities in fact insulated universities from the crude pressures of industrial sponsors and fee-paying students.

As with change so with money. The same considerations are almost as relevant to any discussion of the future funding of higher education. The same ambiguities arise and the same strategies present themselves. The determination of the total resources for higher education and their allocation between different sectors, activities and institutions are inevitably contentious matters, particularly in the 1980s when their supply is likely to be much more restricted than it was in the 1960s. For this reason there is a tendency to shy away from the real issues raised by the funding of higher education, either by claiming that all difficulties would disappear if only the state and the nation would recognise the transcendent claims of universities and colleges, or that neutral mechanisms of resource allocation can be designed which depoliticise the clash of priorities. Both views are plainly mistaken. The first, because higher education can never expect to receive all the money it wants or needs, and because even to imagine that this might be possible under extremely favourable political circumstances betrays a limited view of the possibilities of higher education. On the contrary, as the available resources will always be rationed, those who argue that more money is the solution to all the difficulties faced by universities and other colleges are implicitly endorsing the conservative view that the potential of higher education is also limited. In fact the opposite view of the Robbins Committee, in which they invoked the biblical metaphor of the widow's cruse, is more justified: the success of higher education will breed new and more urgent demand, and so sharpen rather than soften the competition of priorities.

The second view, that neutral mechanisms of resource allocation can be developed to take the politics out of higher education funding, has to be taken more seriously. But it too is flawed. The attractions of such a course are obvious. Faced with the need to make difficult and often divisive choices, many in positions of leadership in universities and polytechnics instinctively look first for external scapegoats (the UGC or the NAB) and then for mechanisms that place less emphasis on personal choice. Better some 'hidden hand' of unit-cost norms than 'on my head' must often be their silent prayer. Nor is this desire for depoliticised resource allocation confined to those who suffer most directly and most personally from its absence. There are those who believe in depoliticisation as an act of, well political, faith. They argue that if all students were given vouchers equal to the cost of their higher education which they could spend in institutions of their choice, a 'free' market would be created which would accurately reflect student preferences. So all the difficult choices about who wins and who loses which under present conditions cause so much political anxiety and controversy would be taken by the neutral operation of the market. This view has been most fully developed by those associated with the Institute of Economic Affairs (IEA), although the motives of some IEA authors have been mixed with the aim of reducing the scope of public funding of higher education often taking precedence over the desire to offer more choice to potential students. Nor is this view the exclusive property of the political right. The proposal for 'entitlements', which has already been discussed, comes from the left, yet has a lot in common with the plan for vouchers. Both proposals, although their ultimate goals are very different, arise from a strong sense of frustration provoked by the apparent immobility of present institutions and their capacity to resist radical reform.

Both vouchers and 'entitlements' run into the same difficulties. Their first problem is to define the market; their second to control it. Higher education, unlike primary and secondary education, is a strictly rationed commodity and likely to remain so for the foreseeable future. So before any market can be created, political decisions must be taken about who shall be entitled to have access to this market and on what terms. It is hardly sufficient to say that vouchers, or 'entitlements', are designed to improve the distribution of goods within a predetermined market. In all markets, but especially in markets for tightly rationed positional goods like higher education, the questions of access and distribution are so entwined as to be virtually the same. Nor is it possible to argue with conviction that once the higher education market has been defined, it will be self-policing. Students are not spending their own money in a mass market to which there is universal access. So the overall size of the higher education market would need to be limited by political decision, because the alternative, an open-ended market, is neither possible in terms of public finance nor desirable in terms of academic and professional standards and values. This in turn leads to the clash of competing priorities and how this can be resolved by extra-market means.

The substitution of loans for grants for students would make no substantial difference, unless such loans were to be at fully commercial rates of interest and cover the full cost of higher education (including the appropriate overheads for research and other non-teaching activity). This last consideration raises further objections to the plan to construct a higher education market. Some are technical, like the proper costing of overheads. Others are fundamental, because no method has ever been proposed to incorporate the fiduciary as well as the instrumental roles of higher education in such a market which would be steered almost entirely by a combination of student preferences and specific demands for research and development. To some enthusiasts for so-called privatisation this latter objection may not matter much. Yet even such enthusiasts may find it difficult to avoid the conclusion that the higher education market can never be more than a series of separate markets all equally contrived, for undergraduate education through vouchers or 'entitlements', for research through the customer — contractor principle, and so on. Not only would the definition of such markets be an esentially political act, but also the co-ordination of these separate markets which could be highly complex would be similarly a political task. The only result would be to wrap up what would inevitably remain extra-market choices, either because they involved political or because they involved academic judgements, in superficially neutral mechanisms for the allocation of resources, and so to mystify a debate about priorities and purposes that should be as explicit as possible.

In any case in Britain the present structure for the determination and allocation of resources for higher education is unlikely to be overturned and replaced by an entirely new system designed on radical principles. A much more likely development is the steady accumulation of power at the centre, in the DES and in national agencies like the UGC and the NAB. Within institutions a similar process of concentration of power over the allocation of resources is also likely as institutional leaders are obliged to exercise a tougher political will, and more and more emphasis is placed on the proper management of available resources. This process of concentration need not threaten the integrity of higher education, provided that it is an open rather than a secret process. The realistic alternatives are either an even more thorough concentration of power, outside higher education entirely, or else a collapse of managerial integrity which make it quite impossible to establish sensible priorities. But the allocation of resources cannot be in itself the main instrument of change. The real task is more limited and so more manageable; it is to ensure that the mechanisms for funding higher education are in harmony with the political and academic priorities that have been established for the system by other means. Those means certainly include the structure established for the government and adminis-tration of higher education, which in turn must be in harmony with the fundamental values, intellectual as much as socio-political, that are embodied in the institutions of the system.

The structure of higher education is immensely important, far more important than many working within the system are prepared to concede, because the terms on which a nation chooses to organise its system of higher education are the clearest possible indication of the priorities that it is expected to pursue. Far from being an administrative irrelevance, structure is a powerful metaphor about the public purposes of higher education, and these public purposes are intimately linked with the deeper currents of intellectual life. The importance of structure in Britain today is heightened by the fact that the present structure, in broad terms the Robbins — Crosland settlement of the mid-1960s, is showing clear signs of obsolescence. The main reason is that it was designed in a period of expansion, and requires to be adapted to the rather different circumstances of the 1980s with their messy mixture of contraction, steady state and entrepreneurial growth. This has been intensified by the prospect of demographic decline and its uncertain effect on student demand.

Yet, when discussing an alternative structure for higher education, it seems important not to get too close. For even if the short-term factionalism of special interests is suppressed and the entirely natural ambition of institutions, and sectors, to achieve greater status is regulated, there is still a danger that too short or too narrow a perspective may lead to excessive concentration on administrative and procedural detail. As with the allocation of resources, means may be seen as superior to ends unless great care is taken. What really matters about any structure are the values and practices that it embodies. The first question should always be: 'What balance of preoccupations and priorities is represented in a particular structure of higher education?' The second, still crucial, question is: 'Does it work, in the sense of promoting its primary purposes and being acceptable as sensible administrative practice?' Unfortunately, in recent years the debate about the best structure for British higher education has often been stood on its head. Formal discussion has been largely confined to administrative and procedural questions, whether the composition of the UGC or the methods of the NAB, quickened by an incompletely suppressed expression of factional interest. On too many occasions the honest and important differences of opinion about the priorities of higher education which these imperfectly represent remain implicit.

For this reason it is important to step back a little from day-to-day controversy, not in a spirit of apolitical academic detachment, but to gain the elbow room to ask fundamental questions. Perhaps the most important is: 'What does our present structure of higher education signify?' For, as has been explained in Chapter 6, it is not as simple as it seems. In simple descriptive terms the convenient dichotomy of the binary policy established after 1965 by Anthony Crosland and his successors as Secretary of State for Education and Science tends to obscure a confusing, and growing, diversity. In the non-university sector the polytechnics jostle with the colleges of higher education, themselves sub-dividing into proto-liberal arts and proto-community colleges (to borrow some approximate American models). The important contribution of ordinary further education colleges that offer some advanced (i.e. higher education) courses is no less real because it is often unrecognised. In Scotland a different pattern altogether prevails. Even in the apparently homogeneous university sector there are important and distinct sub-types of which the technological universities at one end of the spectrum and Oxbridge at the other are only the most prominent examples.

Secondly, in terms of interpretation the confusion is even greater. The binary policy has remained highly controversial despite the progress made by the polytechnics in particular under its protective aegis. One reason is that it has never been clearly established what the policy was supposed to signify. Was, and is, its main purpose to establish the polytechnics as a rival, a complementary, or a subordinate sector to the universities? Of course, no sophisticated and long-acting policy can ever be so exclusively simple. But its reputation and so durability do depend on the general view of which of these three aspects has predominated. One view is that the binary policy has provided a cordon sanitaire behind which the polytechnics have been able to flourish in a way that would have been impossible within a unitary system. The record does show that despite the run-down of teacher education, the main thrust of expansion during the 1970s took place in the non-university sector in sharp contrast to the 1960s when university expansion was at it most spectacular. It also needs to be emphasised that the binary policy has never been extended to include any official attempt to restrict the polytechnics and colleges to particular subjects or to lower-level courses — in contrast, for example, to the strict hierarchy that has been applied in California. However, other less favourable views of the binary policy are possible. By and large the polytechnics have been discouraged from undertaking research except on the strictest of customer — contractor bases. Too heavy-handed an emphasis on local as opposed to national responsibilities, and on part-time and sub-degree courses can reawaken fears that the binary policy is an instrument to keep the polytechnics in their place. The recent proposal from the NAB that serious consideration should be given to placing more emphasis on two-year courses[15] has been treated with considerable suspicion precisely because it was seen as an unbalanced proposal; universities being unlikely to respond to such a shift in emphasis away from honours degrees, polytechnics and colleges

would be the almost exclusive providers of new two-year courses.
Lurking behind these different views of the binary policy there are
important differences of opinion about the priorities of a modern
system of higher education. Some would argue that universities and
polytechnics can remain socially relevant, and so intellectually vital,
only if they move further away from the traditional model of a
university and incorporate parts of the more open and relevant
traditions fo further and adult education. Others see an important
distinction between 'academic' and 'problem-solving' knowledge
which could become the basis for institutional differentiation within
the system. Others again see the main blockage as restricted access
to, and consequent elitism, of the university/higher education
club, a category that embraces all existing institutions of higher
education. And that is just the binary policy and the arguments that
swirl around it. But the present structure of British higher education
is far more than just the division between university and non-
university sectors. The distinctions within sectors are at least as
important as those between them. It has become conventional to say
that the Robbins Report was 'rejected' in the sense that its recommendation that the demand for more places should be met almost
entirely by the establishment of new universities was not accepted.
But in fact the Robbins recipe was half or possibly three-quarters
cooked. A very substantial expansion of university education did
take place during the 1960s. New universities with the opportunity
to undertake radical experiments in new forms of higher education
were established. The colleges of advanced technology were trans-
ferred to the university sector so firmly establishing the practice of
sandwich courses there. The result is that not only is a majority of
students still enrolled in universities, a balance that is hardly likely to
be affected in the remaining years of this century, but also the
universities have become much more heterogeneous, a fact imperfectly recognised by the public, the government, the UGC, and
possibly the universities themselves. Similarly, within the non-
university sector its historic heterodoxy has increased and the tidy
but misleading symmetry of the binary policy has broken down, as
has been described in Chapter 6.

The conclusions that can be drawn are perhaps two. The first is
that the structure of higher education is an immensely influential
metaphor. The signals that it sends out about the purposes and
priorities of the system are uniquely powerful, incorporating as they
do not only the material incentives that steer institutions, but also

the less obvious hierarchies of status and esteem that animate those who teach and research within them. Yet it is probably wrong to exaggerate the autonomy of structure; it is as much a symptom as a cause of the values and priorities of higher education. The structure of our system can be understood and so changed only by paying attention to the fundamental values that it reflects, the intellectual values of the 'private life' of the university and the social, economic, political and even cultural values of its 'public life', which will be discussed in the concluding section of this chapter. The second conclusion is that for this very reason the structure of higher education is immensely complex. It must embrace not only the obvious features such as the binary policy and the growing differentiation in both university and non-university sectors, but also the internal practices of institutions and also the semi-autonomous cultures of separate disciplines. This second conclusion therefore concentrates our attention on changes in both the intellectual system of which the modern university is such an important component, and of the socio-economic system that it shapes and serves.

Prospects for the 1990s

It is not entirely clear how justified we are in regarding the intellectual and the socio-economic systems as separate in this way. Ladd and Lipsett have argued that in the United States: 'Almost certainly, the intellectual stratum will provide in a continuing fashion the principal nexus from which pressures for social change will emanate in post-industrial America.[16] Whether the same confident statement could be made about (de-industrial?) Britain can be questioned. But even here the connection between the academic world and the practical world of affairs seems to be increasingly incestuous, with the time lag between the discovery or refashioning of theoretical knowledge and its practical application ever diminishing. As was argued in Chapter 4, nothing really happened in the 1970s to modify Bell's predictions about post-industrial society and the centrality of theoretical knowledge within it. If anything, the experience of the last ten years has tended to place even greater emphasis on high technology as a source of economic growth and social consolidation. Yet higher education and the intellectual system of which it is part have more autonomy than that implied by their obvious capacity to establish the limits of technology in terms of the available theoretical knowledge. The university is a cultural institution with its own powerful traditions, as was argued in Chapters 2 and 3, and those traditions have been shaped as much by private academic as by public socio-economic values. Writing against the background of the destabilising student troubles of the late 1960s and early 70s, Parsons and Platt insisted that 'the cognitive-rationality value-pattern' was the heart of the university.[17] They argued that higher education is a fiduciary system and therefore cannot give primacy to interests external to it. 'The university must define values and goals in terms of the primacy of cognitive educational functions.'

This discussion of the relative autonomy of the intellectual system can be linked to the two views of the future of higher education which were outlined at the beginning of this chapter. The first is that the development of the modern university has proceeded too far, that it is in danger of losing its soul, a view that Parsons and Platt are implicitly endorsing. Those who hold this view are drawn to the conclusion that the relative autonomy of the intellectual system should be emphasised. For they are bound to argue that the disease from which the modern university is suffering is an overload of functions. According to this view the modern university grew out of the liberal university by a process of accretion. New roles, and so new values, were simply added to the old, nearly always without much attempt to secure the stable integration of the new and the old in a common institutional and normative framework, Moreover, much of the pressure to adopt new roles came from outside the university — from student demand, from the demand for highly qualified manpower, and so on. To this extent the development of the modern university was a contingent process. What radicalism it represented in higher education practice was really imported from outside.

So the danger in the future, according to this view, is that the core cognitive values of the university will be submerged under a tide of instrumentalism. Ten years ago the threat may have come from the affective values imperfectly represented in student revolt; today it comes from the instrumental values of those who insist that the duty of the university is to service the needs of the economy or society. The cure, therefore, must come from the reassertion of the core values of the university, which are by implication its private, academic values. This temptation to blame the instrumentalism of the modern university for its present incoherence is understandable enough. But it tends to ignore the important fact that the academicism which is to be reinforced, in the sense of the codification of theoretical knowledge, has by no means an unchallenged claim to be regarded as the core function of the university. An analysis of the main features of the liberal university suggests that the cultivation of a humanist rationality in a specific cultural context has as strong a claim. It also tends to ignore the implication that the academicism and the instrumentalism that are such prominent features of the modern university have common roots, and that the same processes which have stimulated the one have also stimulated the other.

The second view of higher education's future is that it is so embedded in the processes of modern society that its trajectory is determined by socio-economic trends that are external to the system. Naturally, those who are drawn to this view tend to minimise the relative autonomy of the intellectual system. It is difficult not to be impressed by the force of such arguments, while not accepting that the influence of such socio-economic trends is an entirely sufficient guide to the future of higher education. The most powerful trend is likely to be the growing importance of high-technology industry. This will stimulate higher education in two obvious and direct ways. First, higher education is likely to be one of the most prolific sources of the science on which high technology will depend; and secondly, universities and polytechnics will train the new corps of ultra-experts that will work in such industry. But the indirect consequences for higher education are at least as important. The majority of the technological intelligentsia will find its expertise, and so its status, undermined by the accelerating turnover of theoretical knowledge and of its high-technology applications. Two results will flow from this: much greater emphasis will have to be placed on continuing education, partly because it provides a much more rapid means of introducing new knowledge into industry than conventional undergraduate education, partly because the knowledge acquired by graduates will require constant updating and in some cases replacing. In turn this may lead to a new balance in undergraduate and immediate postgraduate education, which could no longer be regarded as self-sufficient, but rather as laying the foundations on which later stages of continuing education could be built. The natural policy, therefore, might be to reform under-graduate education by making it more general in the sense that it placed greater emphasis on method and principles and less on detailed content. This latter element could then be provided in a more intensive form through the medium of continuing education (of which new forms of postgraduate courses could be the first stage).

Broader socio-economic trends that can easily be identified might also push higher education in this generalist direction. The first is that some of the most important blocks to the development of a high-technology economy are human rather than technical. Usually the science is easier to get right than the social and economic conditions that allow it to be exploited. Even at a later stage in the process of innovation, the machines usually work if the workers are prepared to work them. Indeed, the more radical the technology and so the more beneficial in its potential application, the more resistance it is likely to meet because of its disturbing effect on the existing patterns of employment. The scale and character of these difficulties suggest that tomorrow's scientists and managers will require a broad understanding of the human dimension of technical and industrial change as much as a detailed knowledge of high technology. If this is correct, it too would tend to push higher education along a generalist path. Indeed, this argument can be carried one, perhaps speculative, stage further. It could be that the greater emphasis on participation in the workplace, which the introduction of new patterns of employment will demand, will combine with the widespread development of constantly changing high technology to shift the whole balance of professional and technological higher education away from the authority of the expert towards collaborative human skills.

Another trend, already discussed in Chapter 4, may reinforce this movement towards a more generalist higher education. Clearly, a high-technology society will be one that can either enjoy a high degree of leisure or suffer a high level of unemployment, depending on the foresight and liberality of its political leaders. In either case the role of higher education as an object of cultural consumption will be given new emphasis. Its function as a 'positional good', in Hirsch's phrase, will have the same effect. As higher education loses its power as a sieve for employers and as an employment ticket for graduates, it will be seen less in instrumental terms (except perhaps in a purely defensive context) and more in humanist terms, less as a few essential rungs on the ladder of social or occupational advancement, and more as a personal right without which students would feel deprived as individuals. The pattern of demography will push in the same direction. As the number of 18-year-olds declines, more students will come to higher education from different backgrounds.

Some will come in mid-career with severely vocational goals to undergo intensive courses of highly specfic continuing education. But others may come to university or polytechnic without the instrumental ambitions of the adolescent on the brink of a professional career. Similarly, any widening of the present narrow social-class base from which higher education draws so many of its students may have the same effect. Working-class students, after all, may retain some vestigial collectivist and even fraternal values which are in opposition to the highly individualistic and competitive values of the entrepreneurial middle class. All these socio-economic trends may produce the apparently paradoxical result of renewed pressure for a more general higher education at the very time when the economy is moving faster and faster towards high technology.

There is one final factor working in this same direction that perhaps deserves to be mentioned. It involves the morality of knowledge, an issue with which the modern university has always been very uncomfortable. In *Literature and Science* Matthew Arnold wrote:

> Following our instinct for intellect and knowledge we acquire pieces of knowledge; and presently, in the generality of men, there arises the desire to relate these pieces of knowledge to our sense of conduct, to our sense of beauty — and there is weariness and dissatisfaction if the attempt is baulked.

But that was long ago. Pascal's words — 'reason's last step is the recognition that there is an infinite number of things which are beyond it. It is merely feeble if it does not go as far as to realise this'[18] — were even longer ago. Higher education today is uncomfortable with such thoughts. Its sense of a moral order has been undermined by the professionalisation, and segmentation, of academic knowledge. Its pedagogical ambitions have shrunk to the merely technical. Any attempt to resurrect such considerations, when they are not smiled away, are treated as irrational and so potentially subversive. The pessimism of the humanist was well expressed by Steven Marcus when he wrote:

> In this newly emerging context of the university as part of the system of production, the role of liberal or humanistic education becomes increasingly problematic. And we may well ask what is the essential role of such an education in the production system of a technobureaucratic order whose dominant values are charac-

teristically expressed in forms of utilities and commodities.[19]

The ambition to form disciplines of knowledge that integrated intellectual and moral experiences so typical of the liberal university seems today to be in vain.

And yet the pressure for such integration — Arnold's weariness and dissatisfaction — has not disappeared. Indeed, it is possible to argue that in a society that has less confidence in the omnipotence of science and feels more fear about its own future, this question of the morality of knowledge may become increasingly important again. Again, the outcome may be an apparent paradox: at the very time at which high technology seems to be acquiring greater and greater influence in determining the shape of future society, there may be a growing reaction against the moral inadequacy of the technocratic values on which its success depends. In advanced countries the resistance to nuclear power is a clear example, while in the developing world the rise of religious fundamentalism and the rejection of Western values that this implies may be symptoms of the same phenomenon. The first instinctive reaction of the modern university may be to regard such movements as a retreat from reason and a new form of Luddism. Yet within the tradition of the liberal university can be found grounds for taking a more detached, and occasionally more positive, view. Technocratic knowledge claims to provide a complete and adequate description of reality. Yet that claim can only be sustained by the inhibition of the moral imagination. Higher education can hardly ignore this issue, especially as the development of high technology is likely to make it more contested. Any attempt to take account of it may reinforce the movement towards a new generalism which has been produced by other socio-economic trends, some of them, paradoxically, intimately related to the development of high technology itself.

The modern university, however, is first and foremost a part of the intellectual system. Although the view that cognitive rationality must be its core value may be too circumscribed, nevertheless it is difficult to argue that the 'private world' of knowledge has a greater influence over its development than the 'public world' of affairs. On the face of it trends within the organisation of knowledge, which were discussed in Chapters 3 and 4, are towards ever greater specialisation rather than renewed generalisation. Norman Birnbaum has written:

The increasing domination of canons of specialization in the university meant that it was impossible to form individuals by imparting a limited set of cultural pinciples. The intrinsically dynamic force of the specialized science did not compel those exposed to these sciences to think anew about their fundaments — continuously. The dynamic force of the specialized disciplines was turned outward. It was codified in disciplinary procedures for registering and integrating new knowledge (insofar as the disciplines were scientific, and in ways frequently illusory insofar as they were not). Society was influenced, even changed, by the application of new knowledge — persons were not.[20]

Some might disagree with Birnbaum's detailed comments on the impact of specialised sciences on the university. Yet there can be no question that his description of the outcome is essentially correct: the university abandoned any attempt to organise knowledge in terms that would make it possible to educate a general public.

Steven Marcus has carried the line of argument a stage further and argued that the decline of the liberal university and the fragmentation of knowledge which was its most prominent feature was closely linked with 'the beginnings of the decomposition of bourgeois culture', the high culture of the nineteenth and twentieth centuries.[21] Seen in this light the academicism and instrumentalism of the modern university are not only two sides of the same coin, but its development can be suggestively if not casually compared with the debasement of modern mass culture. The explosion (or implosion?) of specialisation has made it impossible to sustain high general standards of cultivation on which all can agree and for which all can accept some responsibility. Even if this extension to the argument is not accepted. It is still difficult to deny the normative disintegration of the modern university. What common intellectual values are shared by the biochemist and the historian, or by the research-minded professor and the extramural tutor? As has already been pointed out in Chapter 4, it can be argued that the modern university has become little more than a shared bureaucratic environment, sustained by sentimental tradition and group self-interest. This process, of course, has gone much further in the United States than here in Britain. But the difference between the growing diversity of British higher education, which is regarded as a positive phenomenon, and the evident disintegration of the modern university as an institutional form, which is generally regarded as a negative phenomenon, can be very slight indeed. Searching for an appropriate image Birnbaum writes:

> The Tower of Babel comes to mind, but there, a common project was impeded by the absence of a common language. Here, there is no common project. We are reduced to a Hobbesian ideological condition, a war of each idea against every other.[22]

There is certainly plenty of evidence of the negative consequences of the constant fracturing and re-fracturing of knowledge. But can there be any reasonable expectation that this apparently inexorable trend will be reversed? The likely demands on higher education from the socio-economic system have already been discussed: despite the rapid movement towards a high-technology economy these pressures are at least as likely to push universities and polytechnics towards more general courses as towards still greater specialisation, although general should not perhaps be confused with liberal. However, the eventual outcome is likely to be governed more by movements within the intellectual system. Here too the trends are confused. Greater specialisation may appear to be inevitable; yet many of the most productive areas of research are not to be found in the core of traditional disciplines, but at their edges where disciplines rub against each other. Of course, it can be argued that this is merely to replace one form of specialised knowledge with another. But it can also be argued that the excessive compartmentalisation of knowledge may inhibit the development of such trans-disciplinary work and so come to be regarded as a block to intellectual progress. Even in the most specialised areas of research the capacity to integrate the formerly unrelated can play an important part in opening out new routes to knowledge. The attempt to produce over-arching integrative disciplines so typical of the liberal university may have been abandoned, but within the modern university a more limited version of integration is a vital element in the formation of new knowledge. The influence of social science methods in history, the partnership of biology and chemistry, the interaction of mathematics and engineering in information technology, all are examples of this more modest form of integration. So even within the context of research-driven disciplines it is not obvious that progress can only be made by greater and greater specialisation.

In a rather broader context this becomes even less sure. The inherent tension between conceptualisation, which in the form of 'theory' could be said to mirror the academicism of the modern university, and specialisation, which in the form of 'technology' could be said to mirror its instrumentalism, has already been touched on in Chapter 4. The rather similar tension between the view of higher education as an essentially pedagogical process and the view of it as a technological product has also been discussed. Without seriously suggesting that there might be a return to the older values of the liberal university, it is possible to speculate that in the future the intellectual system may again place emphasis on meaning as opposed to information, on process as opposed to product, on integration as opposed to accumulation. Those who have committed themselves to the academicism of the modern university in the mistaken belief that this might serve as a defence against the university's invasion by instrumental and occasionally even non-cognitive values, may revise that commitment when it becomes apparent that the professionalisation of scholarship and the constant fracturing of knowledge are not only academically unproductive in crucial instances, but also as much an enemy of the liberal university tradition as these newer values. Then they may come to regret the attenuation of the general intellectual values concerned with the formation of the student. At the other end of the spectrum those who welcomed the new instrumentalism because social and professional relevance seemed to challenge the hegemony of what they regarded as a reactionary academic tradition, may also come to regret their commitment when the society to be served is no longer the comparatively benign social democratic state of the 1960s but the neo-conservative state of the 1980s, and the economy no longer the Welfare State economy of the 1960s but the high-technology high-unemployment economy of the 1980s. They too may find a new enthusiasm for higher education in the context of the autonomous individual.

To reduce a discussion of the future of higher education to the simple question — post-liberal or post-modern? — is clearly naive. Yet this question does have the value of reminding us that it is not inevitable that the most prominent characteristics of the modern university will intensify and continue. It is too easy to fall into the trap of believing that higher education must follow a fixed path, whether elite-mass-universal or liberal-modern-post-modern. In a similar way it is too easy to assume obvious relationships, such as to suppose that the academicism of the traditional university was superseded by the instrumentalism of the modern university, when in fact both were contemporary and even complementary phenomena. Today there is a danger that many will assume that higher education will inevitably become a more intensely academic and/or technological enterprise with ever greater emphasis on intellectual specialisation and professional relevance. The flaws in this view are, first, that the messages from both the intellectual and the socio-economic systems do not necessarily support the prediction that past trends towards greater specialisation will continue into the future without much modification, and secondly, that it is as much a mistake to believe that greater specialisation and improved integration of knowledge are mutually exclusive possibilities as to suggest that academicism and instrumentalism were enemies rather than allies. The keynote of this chapter has been one of uncertainty about the future. It can be as useful to dislodge naive predictions as to substitute more sophisticated ones. At any rate that is all that has been attempted here.

Notes

1. *Higher Education* (Robbins Report), HMSO, 1963, p.8.
2. Interview with Sir Edward Parkes, Chairman of the University Grants Committee, *The Times Higher Education Supplement*, 22 October 1982, p.9.
3. See, for example, *Education after 18: Expansion with Change*, a Labour Party discussion document, London, 1982, pp.13-23.
4. Department of Education and Science and the Scottish Education Department, *Higher Education into the 1990s*, February 1978, Table 5.
5. William Waldegrave, MP, in the House of Commons, November 1982.
6. Robbins Report, p.54.
7. 'European Universities: Ten Years after 1968', *Paedagogica Europaea*, 1978, 2, p.32.
8. Norman Evans, *Learning for Life*, London, 1981.
9. *Teacher Education and Training* (James Report), HMSO, 1972.
10. See G.D.C. Doherty, 'The DipHE — Suffering a Sea Change', and G. Eley, 'The DipHE as a Terminal Qualification'. Papers presented to a seminar on the future pattern and role of the Council for National Academic Awards' undergraduate awards, 1982.
11. *Student Numbers in Higher Education in England and Wales*, Education Planning Paper Number 2, HMSO, 1970.
12. Richard Freeman, 'Responses to Change in the United States', in Richard Lindley (ed.), *Higher Education and the Labour Market*, Society for Research into Higher Education, University of Surrey, 1981.
13. *A Framework for Government Research and Development* (Rothschild Report), HMSO, 1972.
14. Report of a Joint Working Party on the Support of University Scientific Research (Merrison Report), HMSO, 1982.
15. *A Strategy for Local Authority Higher Education in the Late 1980s*, London, 1982.
16. Everett Ladd, and Seymour Martin Lipsett, *The Divided Academy*, Harvard University, 1975, p.313.

17. Talcott Parsons, and Gerald Platt, *The American University*, Harvard University, 1973, p.88.

18. Pascal, *Pensées, Harmondsworth, 1966,* p.170.

19. Steven Marcus, 'Some Questions in General Education Today', in Michael Mooney and Florian Stuber (eds.), *Small Comforts for Hard Times*, New York, 1977, p.292.

20. Norman Birnbaum, 'Students, Professors and Philosopher Kings', in Carl Kaysen (ed.), *Content and Context*, New York, 1973, p.431.

21. Marcus, 'Some Questions', p.295.

22. Birnbaum, 'Students, Professors', p.447.

Chapter Nine

THE REPEAL OF MODERN SOCIETY?

It is now 20 years since the publication of the Robbins Report, almost a generation ago in years and much more in mood. Robbins came out when Britain on the confident authority of its retiring Prime Minister 'had never had it so good', and according to its alternative Prime Minister was about to experience 'the white heat of the technological revolution.' Neither view was quite as brittly complacent as later critics suggested: Britain in 1963 was much richer and certainly more materialistic than it had been in 1945 after six years of war and a decade of depression (and is yet richer and more materialistic in 1982), and the nation was on the brink of a socio-technological revolution that has turned everyday life upside down during the last 20 years. Nor were these two views trivial: a strong belief in the firm likelihood, if not certainty, of continued material growth and an equally strong belief in the progress of technology, perhaps too naively and too mechanistically inter- preted, are assumptions also to be found in Robbins. It was out of these two beliefs that the committee fashioned its own particular version of the larger idea of Progress, in a political and even moral rather than simply a material sense, the idea which in different shapes had informed all former impulses of social reform since the 1830s. The purpose of Robbins was to design a modern system of higher education to fit a modern society the development of which could almost be taken for granted. Anthony Crosland's binary modification had the same goal; the only differences were that it showed less respect for the Newmanesque traditions of a liberal education and that in the middle and later 1960s the building of a modern society seemed both more urgent and more inevitable.

Today the political economy of Britain has undergone a radical shift towards pessimism. First, no one is really confident that the rates of economic growth enjoyed as recently as the early 1970s can be recovered in the foreseeable future. By itself this loss of faith could be compensated for by tougher attention to priorities, in national life, in social policy, and in higher education. It need not prove fatal to the idea of Progress and its sister Reform. But Britain seems to face much more than a mechanical problem of scarce resources. Secondly, faith in the beneficence of science and technology has also declined. No longer is it seen as a broad path to material wealth and so to human well-being; today it is seen more often as a rocky, narrow and difficult path, the only route to economic salvation perhaps, but along which many will be sacrificed. Nuclear danger, 3 million unemployed, Toxteth, have become the sombre motifs of technological change. Even this second change the ideal of Progress might have survived. The enthusiastic and mechanistic view of the benefits of science and technology so common 20 years ago could have been replaced by a more objective and more human approach. Belief in the beneficence of technological progress might have been battered, but it would have stayed intact. However, in more recent years legitimate concern about the pace, style and direction of scientific change has been overlaid by a more general and less legitimate distrust of learning and contempt for reflection, which has produced a damaging decline in national expertise. Our incapacity to accept the inevitable sophistication of the issues and decisions about, say, nuclear power has been mirrored by a similar unwillingness to come to terms with the broader complexity of modern society.

Thirdly and most decisively, that almost Whiggish faith in the religion of Progress has collapsed. No longer is it possible to see the moral improvement of man, or nation, as coterminous with or growing out of their material improvement. Not only has that material improvement become uncertain, but its relationship with a moral order of society has become obscure. The effect on education has been enormous. Of course, another Robbins is impossible. The social and political consensus and the intellectual confidence on which such grand enterprises are built no longer exist. In 1963 it was possible to look forward with both assurance and accuracy across the coming generation because the ground on which one stood seemed solid and the future direction of British society benign and predictable. Higher education marches with the nation, and if the nation has lost its way there is no way in which higher education can find its future path. But it goes deeper than consensus and predictability. The moral mechanism of Progress has broken down. Social responsibility, civic duty, high purpose, and its other cogs and wheels are worn out or no longer engage one another. If progress towards a modern society, in which the British experience material advancement, moral self-improvement, and social and political reform have been so entwined, is no longer inevitable and desirable, how does higher education's own modernisation make sense in this growing vacuum?

Perhaps the shift in the mood of Britain since the 1960s has moved beyond pessimism and even negativism, towards an increasingly fierce rejection of reality. Enthusiasm for things as they once were (maybe) and should be still crowds out more sober acceptance of things as they are. Feeling is more and more regarded as superior to reason in the conduct of public affairs. As a result the hardheaded pragmatism with which the British have traditionally pursued their national, group and individual interests seems close to disappearance. Britain is now exhibiting some of the familiar and alarming signs of a 'blocked' society. We have lost the vocabulary of Progress and Reform and with it the once comfortable capacity to give political expression to social and economic choices. The terrible simplicity of the choices so over-enthusiastically made during the Falklands War demonstrated not that 'Britain can still do it', but how eagerly the nation seized the opportunity to duck the real choices facing it by engaging the ersatz choices of distant glory. So we happily stick our union flags in the back windows of our cars (probably Toyotas or Renaults) to demonstrate our 'Britishness' as we crawl to work (because of the rail strike? the lack of decent roads? the starvation of public transport?). Other nations do not make the same sentimental mistakes about where their true interests lie. They make their pasts work for them, not against them, in the building of a modern society.

The Falklands episode also revealed how degenerate the public conscience of England has become. Hugh Gaitskell, a right-wing Labour leader, produced a crisp, moral response to the challenge of Suez, while Michael Foot, a left-wing successor, managed only an unconvincing fudge of principle and opportunism. Similar phenomena can be observed right across British life. Has there really been such a decline in consensus within industry to justify a climate of confrontation between employers (and the state) and trade unions uneasily reminiscent of the early 1920s? Is greater productivity to be won by coercion and the destruction of the dignity of labour? Is it sensible to regard public and social services as optional consumption? None of these are mistakes that are made by neighbouring nations, most of which have no comfortable tradition of political quietism which Britain has traditionally enjoyed.

Some, of course, attribute this evident degeneration in political life to 'Thatcherism', the outlook and policies of the present government. Although much of the blame for the more terrible simplicities of recent years must rest with the new *poujadiste* Conservative Party, this explanation is much too narrow. It assumes a government's power to direct rather than simply to drift with a national mood, and it ignores the clear evidence of similar addiction to terrible simplicity in other and in no political parties. Others taking advantage of the relaxed gaze of the historian may attribute the present mood in Britain to one of those periods of national 'blockage' when political and even intellectual categories are inadequate to explain emerging social and economic realities, although they may argue about whether it is a serious (Spain in the seventeenth and eighteenth centuries) or mild case (Britain in the years leading up to 1832 or between the two world wars). A third explanation is more alarming. It more directly implicates education, and particularly higher education, and applies more broadly to all advanced industrial societies, although to Britain more than most. It is that we are witnessing the quickening erosion of those values associated with self-improvement, work and duty which have sometimes misleadingly been described in a short-hand way as the puritan work (better, life) ethic. With the decline of formal religion, rationality and its instrument education, became a new form of social morality and so the basis for conduct in public life. In modern secular societies the school or the university filled the place occupied by the Church in traditional societies.

Indeed, it is possible to go further. Ten years ago the late Talcott Parsons warned that the affective and anti-rational values which he identified in student revolt in the United States could lead to what he called 'the repeal of the educational revolution'. The consequence of this, he argued, would be to disarrange that configuration of intellectual (and moral) beliefs, political practices and social attitudes which he held responsible for the development of modern society, first in north-west Europe and then throughout the world. This was a configuration on which the Robbins Committee could firmly rely 20 years ago, a solid sub-structure of individual and collective beliefs and habits which was not much disturbed by the political turbulence of national life. If in 1972 the comparatively mild and even benign phenomenon of student revolt could provoke in more prosperous times such fears, how much greater a threat is

presented to that educational revolution by the political recidivism
of the lean and hungry 1980s. Today the challenge comes from
inside not outside established power. In Britain where the retreat
from civilised and sophisticated reality has gone furthest, and
because of a long tradition of pragmatic adaptability the experience
is most unfamiliar and so most uncontrollable, the prospect is a
frightening one. It is of the unravelling of modern society, not so
much of its material structure but of its political, intellectual, and
possibly even moral, fabric. It may be the commanding ideas, even
metaphors, of modern society which give it meaning and make it
work that are under most immediate threat.

This third explanation implicates education (and especially higher
education because it commands the commanding values of the
system) in both a passive and an active sense. It is implicated as
victim because schools, colleges and universities are likely to suffer
from the priorities of this new political primitivism. Either they will
be ignored as remote and irrelevant in anything but their most utilitarian purposes, so forgetting that it was as active exponents not as
passive instruments that education systems helped in the formation
of modern society. Or they will be actively discriminated against as
centres of rationality-subversion that is a standing reproach-threat
to the new national mood (and so pushes them, as in other 'blocked'
societies, into the unwanted and uncomfortable role of foci of an
oppositional intelligentsia). It is implicated also as accomplice. Any
threat to 'repeal the educational revolution', in Parsons's phrase,
can only be fully explained by the insufficient success of education
in winning solid support for a proper intellectual tradition, and so
for a strong moral order in a secular age, and through a process of
social reform for the kind of modern society that alone can embody
it. Although it may be denied by both Marxist and neo-conservative
determinists, the relationship between education and its enveloping
society is not simply instrumental as the largely passive servant of
socio-economic demands, but also normative as the active creator,
in intellectual forms, of the commanding values which themselves
help to mould these demands. Hence its responsibility for any
failure of conviction is correspondingly greater.

So any comparative lack of success by education, as a source of
the modern impulse in society, has two components. First, there
must have been a social failure in the sense that the values which are
embodied in the system appear incomprehensible and so irrelevant
to the mass of the people. This failure may be most apparent in

higher education (a 12 per cent age participation rate, an absence of public protest about university cuts, and so on), but it has probably been most crucial in the upper secondary school. The revolution in higher education associated with Robbins and Crosland in their different ways 20 years ago could have been consummated only by the completion of the secondary revolution associated with Butler 40 years ago, and radically, but perhaps not decisively, redirected by comprehensive reform in the 1960s. As an instrument of social consolidation education has not commended itself entirely to the British people. Higher education's direct share of the blame may be less than that of schools. But through the values it has promoted and protected and the model it has established, it has encouraged a narrow view of all education, and so perhaps put at risk Parsons's 'educational revolution' by not adapting these values sufficiently to meet the new demands of a mass and liberal society.

The second component is a broader intellectual failure in which higher education is more directly implicated. It is that universities and other institutions have cultivated either an academicist view of knowledge that is inwardly directed and self-justificatory, or a technocratic view that exalts expert technique over human purpose. Higher education is too often seen as no-one's business but that of those immediately engaged in it, scholars, teachers, learners and other consumers of expert knowledge. Its broader social responsibility has been forgotten. The pursuit of knowledge narrowly conceived has overridden the cultivation of rationality within society. Perhaps for this reason Britain has only the most vestigial intelligentsia because the main role of an intelligentsia is to communicate academic learning in a sensible way to society at large, a role that is barely recognised in Britain. Perhaps in traditional societies mediating intelligentsias were less necessary because their overlapping elites were so cohesive, but in open modern societies they play an important role in bringing codifications of knowledge to bear on the conduct of national life. So in Britain we have the clear paradox: a higher education system of considerable academic brilliance, and a society sunk deeper into philistinism, suspicious of new ideas, and scornful of rationality. Both go their own ways. Both lose.

The part that education can play in the reindustrialisation of Britain's political economy, in particular the necessarily incestuous relationship between higher education and high-technology industry, is easy to accept if difficult to implement. But the part that education must play in the remoralisation of British society has barely been glimpsed. Indeed, the very idea appears to some a dangerously waffly and even sentimental distraction from the main thrust of educational change towards the reinforcement of (mainly vocational and technological) expertise. Yet if the analysis so far is accepted, reindustrialisation and remoralisation are parts of the same process of rebuilding modern society. If the present shift towards a kind of atavistic unreality in public life is evidence of a threat 'to repeal the educational revolution' and so to disarrange that configuration of beliefs and practices typical of a modern and liberal society, the role of the education system as a source of authentic and engaging values is as important as its capacity to act as an instrument of socio-economic change. Indeed, it can be argued that education can be effective as such an instrument only if it is equally successful in establishing firmly those intellectual values, and through them convincing metaphors of a moral social order, that make sense and so use of the available instruments of change.

In both the process of reindustrialisation and of remoralisation higher and further education are particularly influential. In the former process they are both the final formers of the division of labour (and so highly important in fixing social structures and distributing life-chances) and the most available instruments for the improvement of skills; in the latter they form the cognitive and cultural mirror in which we remember our past, experience our present, and anticipate our future. If we misremember our past, misrepresent our present, and shrink from the future, if the mirror is cloudy and opaque because higher education generally regards knowledge as a product rather than a process, then the task of remoralisation is arguably more urgent and more basic than that of reindustrialisation.

Indeed, there is a strong case for believing that Britain is as well equipped as many nations for this latter task, but that the former we barely acknowledge and so fail to accomplish. The trouble with secondary schools, for instance, is probably not that they are less good either than schools once were, whatever nostalgia for the grammar schools may suggest, or than schools in rival nations, but that our public culture makes it difficult to organise the effective social and economic use of what the schools have actually achieved with individual pupils (although this post-school failure eventually and inevitably is communicated back into the culture of the schools). Similarly, there is probably much less wrong with Britain's scientists and engineers (and civil servants and bankers?) than there is with the intellectual and social environment in which they must try to realise their talents.

Schools, colleges and universities bear some responsibility for both aspects, the technical/instrumental and the intellectual/ normative. So any strategy for renewal, or reversal, must address the demands of both reindustrialisation and remoralisation. For if the latter is entirely subordinated to the former, the 'technical' problems of Britain's political economy will continue to be solved with fair success while the 'cultural' problems will still be ignored. The unfortunate result will be that these technical solutions will not only not be properly rooted in corresponding social and intellectual advances, but may even be undermined by contrary movements. So any strategy must also be comprehensive. It must be as concerned, or according to the preceding analysis even more concerned, with the remoralisation of the mass as of the elite. It must embrace not just those who pass through higher and further education to later form the administrative and technical cadres of British society; with strong democratic institutions and a persuasive mass culture higher education's graduates must operate in an environment deeply influenced by other 'graduates' from dead-end jobs, Manpower Services Commission make-work programmes and the dole queue. Perhaps the most important single fact about British higher education is that it is effectively inaccessible to more than 17 people out of every 20, and about traditional further education that considerably more than half the population never gain any qualifications after leaving school (if they have even those). It is here that the educational revolution has been most decisively frustrated.

Yet it is precisely in this area of the education, or non-education, of 16 to 19-year-olds that there is today most ferment and so possibility of progress. It is here that the threatened repeal of the educational revolution can be most effectively resisted. By the end of this century two great changes will have taken place in the education of late adolescents: the traditional school sixth form will have disappeared, at any rate in its present institutional form, and a start will have been made towards the creation of a post-secondary (although partly in a sub-secondary form) system for all. The first will be the result of demographic decline which is rapidly making the present organisation of upper secondary schools hopelessly uneconomic. It is an irony that the grammar school sixth form, still in too many ways the commanding totem of our secondary schools, will fall an eventual victim to a failing birth rate rather than to the malevolence of egalitarians, and that the comprehensive school will finally be freed from its oppressive grammar school inheritance by the same inexorable process. For the only way in which 11 to 18 secondary schools, or 13 to 18 high schools, could be maintained would be through a ruthless programme of closures and amalgamations which would almost certainly be frustrated by localist feeling and parental resistance. Sixth form consortia between conventional secondary schools will probably never be much more than a stop-gap solution. Separate sixth form colleges are unlikely to be established on a predominant scale because of the instinctive administrative distrust of single-purpose institutions, because there will still be enough life in the comprehensive spirit to raise powerful objections, and because of the evident diseconomy of running two parallel post-16 systems.

So the future would seem to belong to the tertiary college, a comprehensive institution which combined the present functions of the traditional sixth form and of mainstream craft and (lower) technician education in technical colleges. Measured in terms of administrative convenience and of the best use of scarce resources this will be the best solution in most areas. Yet the implications of such an amalgamation of grammar school-type sixth forms and of technical colleges for a redefinition of educational values are very considerable, exciting to some, threatening to others. Under these conditions the much closer association of the academic tradition represented by O and A-levels and the vocational tradition represented by Business and Technician Education Council, Royal Society of Arts, City and Guilds and so on, would be inevitable. Eventually the 'new sixth' and the 'new FE' might form a common pattern of education, with deep and essentially hopeful consequences for any joint strategy for reindustrialisation and remoralisation.

The second change will reinforce the first and perhaps compel a tertiary college reorganisation. From the summer of 1983 all school-leavers who are not in the minority that continue in full-time education in school or further education, or in the tinier minority that find a job, have been offered a year of combined education and training under the auspices of the MSC. This represents the first hesitant step towards the building of a (minimal) post-secondary system for all. It is the first time in Britain that secondary education has been regarded as no longer sufficient, an idea of almost revolutionary potential in terms of both educational practice and values.

Because the MSC has too often been seen as a body external and even hostile to the traditional education system the influence of its activity has been consistently underrated. Perhaps by relying too much on an over-simple view of what happened to higher education in the United States after 1945, we have trained ourselves to expect that any expansion of post-secondary education in Britain would take a similar form. Our gaze has so exclusively been fixed on the development of universities, polytechnics and colleges that we have largely failed to take account of the possibility that the expansion might take place at a much 'lower' level, and even outside the traditional institutional framework of education. Yet it can be argued that this is what is beginning to happen with the activity of the MSC. Nor should this development be so surprising. The main blockage to the educational revolution in the United States in the generation after the war may have been in higher, or at any rate post-18, education; in Britain there is a strong case for suggesting that it occurs much earlier at 16 (with a backward shadow blighting the freedom of 14 and 15-year-olds) in the sixth form dominated by a highly academic tradition, and in a further education system equally dominated by a skilled craft tradition. Perhaps in Britain the kind of social and economic pressures that supported an expansion of college education in the United States are encouraging an expansion of much lower level further education. In terms of remoralisation too the growth and persistence of youth unemployment makes late adolescence the most obvious and most urgent point of intervention.

New technology, higher productivity, better wages all mean that there will be fewer jobs for young people even after economic recovery takes place. All advanced societies, the successful and the unsuccessful alike, will have less and less need for adolescent labour. In the long term this change, which will not be confined to the young, will require a re-ordering of work itself. But in the short term it means that the education system can no longer assume that those young people who find its essentially cognitive values uncongenial or just mysterious will simply 'drop-out' into a job. Nor can schools, and colleges, assume that their further socialisation, or moralisation, will be completed by the institutions of working life. If they 'drop-out' to the dole, they can hardly be expected to be sympathetic to the values of an educational system that they failed and that failed them, nor to appreciate that their alienation is ultimately subversive of modern and liberal society. If the work of the

MSC, or to a lesser degree the development of comprehensive tertiary colleges, is seen as an attempt to rescue these young people as
much as citizens as workers, then it should be regarded as an
educational initiative rather than as experiment in industrial
training. A new deal for this 'marginal' majority, creatively applied,
could mean a new deal for all education and even a new deal for
British society.

Universities, polytechnics and other colleges are the cutting edge
of the educational revolution — so in any repeal of that revolution
they will be first blunted. For this reason they have a particular
intimate relationship with the formation of modern society and
consequently much to lose from its erosion. In the process of
reindustrialisation higher education plays the most dynamic and
most influential role of any part of the educational system; it not
only 'invents' the future through the advance of science and all
knowledge, but also applies it through a mixture of technology and
(elite) pedagogy.

In the parallel process of remoralisation it is the source of new
idea-values and the arbiter of their best arrangement — to such an
extent, however modestly denied by those in higher education, that
it has the effective power to establish commanding metaphors of
private value, public conduct, professional competence, even of a
moral order of society. The self-consciousness of modern society
and its assessment of the possibilities of change are the invisible but
powerful products of the intellectual values favoured within higher
education. A contrast is sometimes drawn between the 'public' and
the 'private' lives of higher education, between its political arrangement and administrative structure and its intellectual values as
expressed through the preoccupations of disciplines of knowledge.
Yet the two are hopelessly entwined. If remoralisation and reindustrialisation are seen as part of a single process of consolidation of
modern society, the 'private' values of higher education are as relevant as its 'public' structure to this theme.

The structure of higher education should also resonate its values,
accurately in terms of present conditions and eloquently in terms
of future possibilities. In Britain so far as we have any structure
or policy for higher education it is the binary policy, Anthony
Crosland's mid-60s modification of the original Robbins blueprint
for expansion. This policy was both conservative in the sense that it
tried to protect the 'open' tradition of further education from being
overwhelmed by the more hermetic tradition of the universities, and

radical because it acted as an influential metaphor to remind everyone that in modern Britain higher education must be much more than simply the universities, however liberally redefined by Robbins.

It is possible to argue that if the Robbins pattern had been followed, the very pace and scale of expansion, the unavailability of alibis, would have overridden the cautious instincts of the universities and led to a significant breakthrough to a mass system of higher education on a broad front. Instead, the cautious conservatism of the universities was indirectly endorsed, and with the end of expansion has now been entrenched as the dominant view point within higher education as a whole. Even if this interpretation is rejected and the basic rightness of the binary decision is reaffirmed, an important question is left to be answered. If the basic binary objectives — diversity, comprehensiveness, relevance, social control (or better, accountability) and social justice — are good for the polytechnics and colleges, why should they not be applied to the universities also?

Many, particularly perhaps in universities, will instinctively regard these as secondary, administrative values, which because they are designed to improve the articulation between higher education and society may be relevant to the theme of reindustrialisation but should not be confused with the 'private' academic values of scholars. Such a view overlooks several important considerations. First, structure should resonate values; if it does not it will cramp or distort them in ways that are no less influential just because they offend so many people's ideas about the proper hierarchy of values. Secondly, reindustrialisation and remoralisation are part of a common process with, in the context of a threatened repeal of the educational revolution and through it of the undermining of modern society, the latter being perhaps more important than the former. There is and should be no way in which higher education can compartmentalise its 'public' relationship with lay society from its 'private' mission in teaching and research.

Thirdly, this view is based on the probable misconception that within higher education, or even within universities, there is a stable and identifiable core of common intellectual values which all will recognise and respect. In fact within the private world of higher education, if that is a fair description, there are tensions just as great as those which surround the public issues of structure, accountability, access and so on — and not just because the intellectual revolutions within individual disciplines are often more frequent and more intense than those in the scope and structure of the system as a whole. This theme was discussed in Chapters 4 and 8.

Two further points can be made. The first is that if modern society does depend on that configuration of belief and practice which has been produced by the educational revolution, and if that revolution is threatened by repeal, then higher education must do all it can to resist that repeal. It is probably only by wholeheartedly accepting 'binary' objectives that higher education can safeguard the precarious place of rationality in public life, and so protect its own cognitive values. The second is that there is a strong and suggestive parallel between the tensions within higher education and those within modern society. Both are finding it difficult to integrate their exploding experiences. Both are struggling to establish a meta-language with which they can extract not only meaning from these experiences but also moral significance. In a, rather clumsy, word both are engaged in a process of remoralisation, with what success cannot yet be determined.

So two tentative propositions can be made about the future relationship between higher education and modern society. The first is that it is perhaps only by wholeheartedly accepting the 'binary' objectives — pluralism, comprehensiveness, relevance, accountability, and social justice — that higher education, *all* higher education, can safeguard the presently precarious place of rationality in national life and so protect its own cognitive values. For a higher education system that stands on the social margin cannot expect to avoid making its own most intense preoccupations marginal also. If modern society (in its double form as the creator and guarantor of free institutions through social reform and the promoter of material prosperity through effective technology) does depend on that configuration of belief and practice produced by the educational revolution, and if that revolution is now threatened with repeal because contemporary Britain is losing its once secure grip on the vocabulary of Progress and Reform, then higher education has both 'public' and 'private' reasons for resisting that repeal. It has been argued that it can only do so by the double process of reindustrialisation and remoralisation. A proper balance has to be kept between the well-understood instrumental (high technology, skilled manpower) and fiduciary (scholarship, pedagogy) roles of universities and other higher education institutions, and their much broader intellectual, even cultural and moral, responsibilities. These arise from higher education's present position as the commanding institution within the wider intellectual system and its influence over the ideas-values that provide the raw material for the moralising metaphors of modern society.

The second is that there is a strong and suggestive parallel between the tensions within higher education, both 'public' and 'private' and similar tensions within British society, which were hinted at in the first of these articles. Both are finding it difficult to integrate their exploding experiences. As a nation we find it more and more difficult to come to terms with the necessary sophistication of the real choices facing a modern society, while retaining a confident sense of a moral social order. Social, or academic, morality in far too many instances has become contaminated by an anti-modernist spirit (equally among 'Thatcherites' and 'Bennites' in national life, and in higher education among those who argue that the appropriate strategy is a retreat into the *laager* of 'excellence', a recreation of the disappearing donnish dominion). Modernism, which can be stretched to include everything from Keynesian economic management through nuclear power to the Robbins expansion of the universities or the establishment of a polytechnic alternative, is regarded more and more as an anaemic, amoral affair. Both modern society and higher education are struggling in ways that are incestuously linked and with equally indifferent success to establish a meta-language that is more than technical and administrative and which can impose a moral structure on their exploding experiences.

Both propositions are of equal importance. But even if both are broadly accepted, the first is much easier to get to work on than the second. The most obvious and most hopeful strategy is to try to create a post-binary system of higher education in Britain as has been outlined in Chapter 7. Like the original binary policy this must have two aspects; as an administrative framework for the 'public' life of higher education, an affirmation of the *status quo* of limited pluralism which might still be threatened by a carelessly conservative 'back to Robbins' policy of bogus integration; and as an authoritative normative metaphor about the future direction of the system's 'private' life.

The possible influence of such a reform of the 'public life' of higher education on its private values, and so indirectly on the intellectual contours of modern society, can only be glimpsed. Yet it is possible that a more open system of universities and colleges might encourage an intellectual flexibility which not only reduced the oppressive marginality of higher education, but also provided a firmer foundation for the protection, and even the advance, of more rational conduct in public affairs. If the codification of theoretical knowledge, in terms of natural sciences and technology, is regarded as the mainspring of a modern economy, it can be argued that the codification of similar knowledge in the social and human sciences is similarly crucial to the healthy development of modern liberal society. So the pursuit of knowledge, however technical, or detailed, or even esoteric, can never be separated from the social and moral obligations it incurs.

Admittedly the prospects for such a remoralisation of knowledge do not appear good. As was pointed out in Chapter 2, no single discipline today can aspire to be a sufficient framework in which the most important ideas that arise from human experience can be incorporated, an over-arching context for intellectual life — as philosophy may have been in the later eighteenth century, or political economy in the early nineteenth, or history in the Victorian age. The ambition of English to fulfil a similar role between the wars was always a desperate affair, a rearguard defence against the inrush of barbarians. Sociology enjoyed only a brief pretendership in the late 1950s and early 60s. The dismal science of economics, today's contender for hegemony, lacks a proper moral dimension.

Nor does it seem very realistic to hope for a better integration between academic values and the intellectualoid preoccupations of lay society. The experience of the last half century has been the opposite, a growing divorce between 'knowledge' in a professional sense and 'ideas' as ingredients in public culture, although it can be argued, as it was in Chapter 8, that there are as powerful centripetal, integrative forces in intellectual life and modern culture as there are centrifugal ones. Some would argue that the impoverishment of public culture and the professionalisation of academic knowledge are inexorable processes. Yet, under the shadow of a possible repeal of the educational revolution, that cannot be the end of the argument. For to end it there may condemn higher education, and the values it embodies, to marginality and erosion. There is already sufficient evidence in the negative currents in British society to suggest that this may not always be an exaggeration. More is at stake than the institutional self-interest of higher education. Also threatened may be that configuration of belief and practice typical of modern society, and that metaphor of a moral social order that is a guarantee of both freedom and progress.

INDEX